At the Borders of the Wondrous and Magical

"A fascinating, exciting, and original collection of different aspects of the enchanted medieval worldview by a long-established master of the subject."

RONALD HUTTON, PROFESSOR AT THE
UNIVERSITY OF BRISTOL AND AUTHOR OF
QUEENS OF THE WILD

"This book brings together a rich collection of essays by Claude Lecouteux about borders and thresholds—between night and day, land and sea, illusion and reality, the sacred and the profane, the worlds of the living and the dead—and the numerous beings that frequent them, including ghosts, demons, dragons, fairies, totem animals, and nature spirits. This is a book about enchantment that is itself an enchanting read."

CHRISTOPHER MCINTOSH, AUTHOR OF
OCCULT GERMANY AND *OCCULT RUSSIA*

"Claude Lecouteux's work is highly respected for its meticulous scholarship in elucidating connections deeply embedded in ancient literature, folklore, and beliefs. This book delves into many unseen aspects of Eldritch existence hidden in plain sight. It is a splendid addition to his fine corpus of work."

NIGEL PENNICK, AUTHOR OF
FORTUNA AND *CELTIC TREE ALPHABETS*

"This book retraces the quintessential work of Claude Lecouteux, focusing on long-neglected subjects like monsters, fabulous creatures, and mysterious forces that we never know whether they are natural or magical. He has opened up a fertile breach, now being taken up by new generations of researchers, for whom Lecouteux represents not just a pioneer but a model to follow, including from a methodological point of view—starting from words, starting from texts."

KARIN UELTSCHI, PROFESSOR OF MEDIEVAL LANGUAGE AND
LITERATURE, UNIVERSITÉ DE REIMS, FRANCE

"As we've come to expect from Claude Lecouteux, *At the Borders of the Wondrous and Magical* is a meticulously researched and compelling work. The legends and folk beliefs he has gathered together give us a window into the ontology of the medieval mind and its understanding of the human place in the natural world. This standpoint invites us to re-examine our own relationship with the wondrous and haunted world, leading us to the foothills of the imaginal."

DARRAGH MASON, AUTHOR OF *SONG OF THE DARK MAN*

At the Borders of the Wondrous and Magical

NATURE SPIRITS, SHAPESHIFTERS, AND THE UNDEAD IN THE NEVER-ENDING MIDDLE AGES

CLAUDE LECOUTEUX

Edited and Introduced by
FLORENCE BAYARD and ASTRID GUILLAUME
Translated by Jon E. Graham

Inner Traditions
Rochester, Vermont

Inner Traditions
One Park Street
Rochester, Vermont 05767
www.InnerTraditions.com

ISBN 978-1-64411-993-8 (print)
ISBN 978-1-64411-994-5 (ebook)

Printed and bound in China by Reliance Printing Co., Ltd.

10 9 8 7 6 5 4 3 2 1

Text design and layout by Debbie Glogover
This book was typeset in Garamond Premier Pro, Gill Sans MT Pro, Moret, and Mrs Eaves OT used as display typefaces

To send correspondence to the author of this book, mail a first-class letter to the author c/o Inner Traditions • Bear & Company, One Park Street, Rochester, VT 05767, and we will forward the communication.

Scan the QR code and save 25% at InnerTraditions.com. Browse over 2,000 titles on spirituality, the occult, ancient mysteries, new science, holistic health, and natural medicine.

Contents

PART IV

BORDERS AT THE MARGINS
OF THE KNOWN WORLD

Claude Lecouteux, A Ferryman Who Smuggles History through Stories

Florence Bayard and Astrid Guillaume

If Claude Lecouteux has always shown an interest in borders, it is to demonstrate that they are in no way inviolable and each holds a promise of enrichment—and not only because treasures are sometimes hidden in mountain valleys and hollow trees, or at the bottom of seas and lakes . . .

To a curious spirit like him, such borders cannot help but be attractive. And for a humanist like him—so rare in today's world—they provide a guarantee of contact with the Other, a means not only for knowing "others," but also oneself.

For him, this search has always entailed going *beyond*: by examining every detail and secret to be found in old texts, one therefore goes beyond that which might be obvious. He looks past appearances *toward* those places that remain poorly known. This means accepting the incongruous and striving to understand how it manifests in a variety of languages, cultures, thoughts, and writings.

Striving to understand—this has been his constant motivation over many years of research. His interest in borders—both as thresholds and limits, and all those liminal spaces that surround us—has made his work a *passageway*, and everyone who knows him well will say: "Claude Lecouteux is a smuggler in the noblest sense of the word: a smuggler of history and of stories."

And he is not merely satisfied to set sail with us or lead us to places we never would have seen without his guidance. He provides us the keys we need to travel without him, and the courage to cross over into the borderlands of foreign realms. Thanks to him, the Unknown no longer frightens us so much, if at all. Instead, it stimulates our curiosity and desire to accompany him into the beyond.

With him, even monsters are no longer frightening—no matter if they are witches, ogres, or vampires, or cynocephalic beings, or Hydras of the abyssal and hadal zones of the ocean's depths. Even the strangest and most mysterious phenomena, even hybrid creatures, even ghosts and revenants no longer have the power to scare us, whether it is a question of encountering a dead man without a head—or one cleaved in half by an ax—crossing the path of a three-legged horse with eyes of fire, or being overtaken by a distraught wild woman running away from who knows what, or even meeting and domesticating household spirits.

These others, this otherness, no longer has the power to frighten because Lecouteux explains to us what they are, where they come from, how they are made, and especially why they are there and why they fade in and out of sight, only to pop up again later, and how to earn their favor and good graces. With Lecouteux, we understand them better and learn how to know them, sometimes even tame them, ensuring that a "marvelous" encounter takes place.

As a gifted diachronic linguist, Lecouteux also explains (again something extremely rare in our time) the origins of the words that describe the wondrous beings, events, elements, and stories he studies. He examines the dialects of ancient languages as well as their developments and linguistic and cultural interactions. When you read Lecouteux, everything he presents and explains seems so simple, but that doesn't take into account the vast number of hours of research that his works conceal, and the extensive knowledge one must have of countless ancient languages, some practically forgotten today, in order to decode, understand, analyze, compare, classify, summarize, structure, and present all the data that he gives us in its simplest possible form. His many disciples, enthralled by his courses at the Sorbonne and still faithfully present at his side, are the best testament to this. Lecouteux's works may be accessible to any and all, but they could not have been put together by just anyone: very few researchers today possess his encyclopedic knowledge of ancient languages and diachronic linguistics, as well as that of civilization, history, and literature. His is a rare learning—commensurate with that of the great scholars of the past centuries that he studies.

He forges a connection for us beyond the borders of linguistics, civilizations, and history, and one that lies even further beyond the limits and thresholds that he invites us to cross. This is true whether we have crossed over to the other side, or the "others" have come to meet us, or if we have simply lingered at the portals to this other world. With his help, we are able to cross over this border—which is also that of our own limitations—sometimes by means of a bridge, a ford, or even a hollow tree, all backed by solid historical documentation.

With the work of Lecouteux, we are still in the natural world, the same one that surrounds us today. Urban spaces appear only rarely in the texts he studies because he is more interested in the daily life of simple folk than in the deeds and doings of the "high and mighty" who inhabit the cities. Folk culture is his core concern: the culture of the people, the peasants, the culture of our countryside. This culture is one that is ancient, visceral, deep, and vital, and forms our very being. And it is truly his role as a ferryman that allows us to meet these ancestral beings that dwell in our homes, forests, and mountains—but especially in our imaginations, fantasies, and fears as well.

Nature is omnipresent in Lecouteux's research. It is an inhabited and haunted nature. As he puts it so well: "Man has always been aware that he is not the world's first inhabitant" ("The Backdrop of the Adventure Sites in Medieval Romances"). Similarly, in "Borderlands of the Otherworld," he writes: "We need to acknowledge that man is not the earth's sole inhabitant but that he has neighbors, his world is haunted, and their presence forces him to take certain precautions and compels him to respect taboos—in short, it shapes his life similarly to how it is structured by territorial boundaries and domains, bailiwicks, advocateships (*avoueries*; Swiss *Vogteien*), and so forth." Writing in a style that is both simple and rich, Lecouteux transports us into seemingly inaccessible worlds that are yet so close. There he introduces us to a small population of mythological and historical supernatural beings who are still a constant presence in contemporary literature, films, and games.

The human being is not the first inhabitant of the earth, something he is aware of, nor is he the sole inhabitant; he shares this land with other living beings. It is easy to grasp why biodiversity needs to be respected in its whole, for we are part of this nature that is as fragile as it is all-powerful. This is why the dominant position humans have appropriated is also an obligation. A moral and ethical bond connects them to their environment whether it is visible or invisible, domestic, wild, or liminal. Forgetting all these beings that inhabited the world of our ancestors is tantamount to forgetting this bond. Discovering and understanding this liminality opens an individual to unforgettable encounters.

Don't be led astray—Claude Lecouteux has never advocated a return to sometimes burdensome beliefs. Instead, he has highlighted the value of knowing, understanding, recontextualizing, and respecting them so that we might better discover our history in age-old stories. In his thoughtful, humble, and reserved way, attentive to the sensibility of his fellow man, he invites us implicitly and discreetly to cross this border from time to time, this liminal line from which one never returns exactly the same, and to open the doors of the otherworld to allow in the "little" people, this fabled populace of widely disparate beings, in order to frighten or re-enchant the world a bit.

And this is something our world clearly seems to need: receptiveness to any kind of Other with the re-enchantment, reappropriation, and rediscovery of past beliefs and customs. Perhaps this would be the first step toward a reconciliation with the nature we mistreat so badly, and toward a reconciliation with ourselves, a reconstruction that will be most welcome after so many deconstructions, for we have become somewhat lost for so hastily and categorically turning our back on the imaginal realm, the magic of the world and its manifold beauty.

So, let us follow this ferryman and walk confidently in his footsteps. There are numerous exciting adventures and amazing encounters that undoubtedly await us. And, as he is celebrating his eightieth birthday today, let us thank him for his many years of fascinating scholarship and research that he shares so simply and unassumingly with anyone and everyone—not least of all his loyal readers, who are now found throughout the world.

Introduction

Florence Bayard and Astrid Guillaume

At the Borders of the Wondrous and Magical is a journey into the world of Claude Lecouteux. The articles collected here are an invitation to cross over the various borders that Lecouteux has examined throughout his long life as a researcher.

But there are not only *borders* waiting to be crossed in the work of Lecouteux—there are also *thresholds* that we must decide to step over or not, and *boundaries* best left inviolate for fear of losing one's life or suffer their aftereffects or vestiges for several generations.

French readers are likely familiar with the little "test" you need to pass before entering enclosed spaces in Brittany: the stile. Of course, there is also a main entranceway, sometimes closed with an iron gate, but this is (was) reserved for specific events that call for processions: weddings, burials, baptisms, or other rites of passage requiring this kind of space. But to enter ordinarily, you had to cross over the stile, which meant going up a small ladder and then straddling a piece of shale. The main benefit of this obstacle was certainly to prevent animals from entering the sacred space, but it also gave a clear signal to the human being entering that he or she was stepping into another kind of space.

When we say "frontier," we are also indicating *transition*. The notion of transition is essential throughout this book, as are the notions of "open" versus "closed," and thus "the other side" as well—the unknown other space where entities dwell that are more or less human. They are sometimes hybrid in form, as they exist between two worlds: dwarfs, elves, fairies, witches, giants, dragons, genies, evil dead, revenants, and so forth—all of them creatures that Lecouteux has tried to identify as definitively as possible through his quasi-archaeological work, adeptly sifting through and utilizing all manner of documents in various ancient languages with the conscientious rigor he is known for.

So it is with a stone—the illustrated Ramsund runestone—that we will begin our exploration of a small part of this peerless researcher's work, as if to indicate that we are now entering an extraordinary domain where scientific precision knows how to listen to the imaginal realm accompanied by faery, while remaining accessible to everyone.

Part I of this collection brings together five articles that illustrate an essential aspect of Claude Lecouteux's scientific methodology. He works by "scrutinizing the old texts and cross-referencing their information"; he then picks out the *ethnological observations* and unveils the *wealth of information* in these writings,* whatever they are written on (parchment, stone, bell, amulet, or other talisman) and whatever their genre (sagas, legends, or carved inscriptions). All bear traces that preserve a sometimes-unconscious collective memory, whose secrets he is able to reveal by resorting—cautiously—to a form of "mental archaeology."

Lecouteux "starts with texts, always texts, or in a pinch, archaeological findings, but he never develops things gratuitously. He definitely knows how to wonderfully extract the essence from the documents he analyzes—indeed, this is one of his strengths."[1] His research attests to the importance of the Middle Ages for understanding tales and legends, beliefs, medieval poetry, and rituals—not only those of the past but also in our own time. They enable an analysis and a better understanding of human beings across time.

A stable substratum emerges from this—hence the need for transcendence and a bond with the Other—along with evidence of the

---

*The italicized phrases that appear here are direct quotations from the articles in this collection.

ceaseless evolution, perpetual transformation, and *remarkable vitality* of these elements. It explains why these tales still speak to us today and continue to astound us; why these beliefs—and the beings and objects, gestures, and rituals associated with them—continue to thrive, though they are revised, reworked, and recast in sometimes extreme ways, for example, in fantasy literature. Nevertheless, they remain recognizable for whoever holds the keys to understanding them—keys that Lecouteux provides. Indeed, he still "tries to demystify the subject by showing that it is not as difficult as one might think, provided one has adequate analytical tools."[2]

With Claude Lecouteux, everything becomes clear. With his historical and anthropological knowledge, we may better understand today's *resurgence of magic, witchcraft, and shamanism*, as well as the longevity of the feeling that we are living in a haunted world that is not restricted to the visible and the "rational." As an illustration of this remark, one need only pause and consider the omnipresence of vampires, living dead, werewolves, and other creatures of this type in the popular media (comic books, TV series, films, literature): *a closer look at the most recent accounts will reveal that mindsets have scarcely evolved on this plane.* The article we have chosen to open Part II of the collection allows us to define more profoundly one of these figures that has never left our imaginations and still triggers our deepest fears: the evil dead.

The subject of the second article, the "grimoire," is a word still steeped in deep mystery even today. We need only cast a glance at online sellers to see that such books remain highly coveted objects, especially if their seller (or author) knows how to exploit their legend and invent a fascinating origin story for them. For example, *one grimoire was found chained up in the cellar of a monastery; another is written in blood or phosphorescent ink, sealed with the imprint of a skull; while yet another is presented in the form of a pocket bible with a black cover and red pages.* Lecouteux helps the reader to better grasp the history and enduring qualities of this particular object. As a philologist, he traces not only an etymology but its contextual and cultural development.

But we need not only turn to these legendary books to explore our imaginal realms. Lecouteux possesses the particular skill of an archaeologist to pay attention to even the most minute traces and supporting materials, no matter how insignificant they may appear. To demonstrate how closely magic is entwined in everyday life, he discusses the door or roof of the house, whose "little" mythology[3] he explores, and bells, big and small—all evidence of how everyday beliefs and magic intimately overlap in the Middle Ages.

It appears that he finds no subject insignificant, especially if it has a connection with what seems to interest him the most: our humanity. "He is ceaselessly questing for whatever can really set our hearts racing and our desire soaring by way of so many 'monsters' and 'marvels.'"[4]

Grimoires and bells can come to life and travel about on their own: no object seems to be limited to a single function. And while the magic book is often connected with a desire for power, between white magic and black magic, and for protection when called for, the same is just as true for bells that summon the spirits, in their dark aspect, and also offer protection from storms, in their good aspect ("Big Bells and Little Bells: Beliefs and Magic"). A similar ambiguity is found among legendary figures such as the blacksmith, which we have chosen for our anthology as the preeminent marginal figure ("Weyland the Smith"). Both are equally ambiguous: one evolves between the evil woman and the good lady, the other dwells on the threshold of two worlds and can assume animal shape, has an almost organic connection with nature, and perhaps reflects the human being's contentious relationship with it—a relationship that fluctuates between respectful fear and a desire to dominate.

This illustrates Lecouteux's fondness for unearthing the origin of these figures as well as the lexicon that describes them. Rather than accept assumptions, he digs through the evidence and deciphers the encoded mysteries. He studies the genesis of words, beliefs, tales, and legends, and strives to grasp the how and why. By so doing, he carves "a path for approaching the connections between history and ethnology that validates everything we might call 'interdisciplinary.'"[5] The path he opens is a crosslinguistic one that demonstrates the circulation of ideas and languages.

The four texts that comprise Part III carry us into other domains and "untamed spaces": the wild sea; the dark, tangled forest; the steep, high mountain; and clouds that are opaque or luminescent. The "Magnetic Mountain" of the opening essay in this section is closely connected to the sea and sailing, and here Lecouteux contributes to the study of travel narratives inspired by a taste for the wondrous. "The Raft of the Winds" invites us to set sail on clouds connected to the otherworld, but also to magic and enchantments, similar to a maritime expanse that forms a frontier behind which mysteries are hidden. *The otherworld, in all its forms, is frequently separated from our own world by clouds, but it is also bathed in a singular light.* Clouds are home to spirits personifying atmospheric phenomena that are also ambiguous, just like the objects and beings we met earlier. Clouds bring both beneficial rain and destructive hailstorms; they filter a marvelous light and darken the sky with disturbing shadows. Tempest or gentle spring rain, deluge or rainbow, they are situated between wonderment and terror, and as means to tame the weather they create, one may have recourse to the "weather masters" themselves who stand at the border of the beneficial and the harmful as they have the power to summon the helpful rain necessary for the crops to grow, but also know how to create devastating storms. In his article "The Masters of Weather," Lecouteux reveals the relationship between place spirits and bad weather. He sheds light on the human desire to master the elements, as well as on the awareness of how small humans are—and how dependent they are on the very same elements that elude them despite their rites and rituals.

The mountain, as omnipresent as the sea, closes this section dedicated to nature and the elements ("Mythical Aspects of the Mountain in the Middle Ages"). This is the site deemed to best represent the world of the spirits and the land of the dead. By its vertical axis, it is the meeting point between our world and the sacred in its positive and negative aspects. It gives shelter to giants and dwarfs as well as the gods and the dead. It can be seen in place names and obviously denotes a natural and mythical frontier whose guardians are "monsters." Sharing in two worlds, it also reveals its dual, ambiguous nature. It is a place of achievement and refuge as well as perdition: *it is both heaven and hell for pagan and Christian alike.*

The fourth and final part of this collection pursues more extensively this notion of threshold and border. This is why we find lands previously explored there. But now man is more in evidence; he is situated at the heart of nature and "wilderness," for *whether the stories are the work of clerics or spread through the countryside, the fundamental information remains the same: man lives in a haunted world.* What's involved here is an examination of the relationship between man and this world and its inhabitants, and what the conditions or consequences are of his incursions into these closed but accessible domains.

In "The Sea and Its Isles during the Middle Ages," we find travel narratives and their imaginary geographies[6] that gave birth to legends and clearly express the fear inspired by *unknown spaces and dangerous waters,* but they also fed a proclivity for the marvelous and dreams in which all things are possibile. When confronting nature, subjectivity seems to be all-powerful: it embellishes the world and transforms it into fantasy.

This explains how various places that went on to become the hazardous sites of the medieval romances are *also those around which beliefs revolve and live.* In fact, *man has always been aware that he is not the world's first inhabitant, and every civilization has crafted its cosmogony accordingly,* based in this profound feeling. Thus, we learn that when seeking to domesticate a location upon which to build a house, it is necessary to "tame" the place and especially the beings that spend time there: the land has to be tamed, and the threshold respected. It can be transgressed in all sorts of ways, of course, but this will have consequences.

We also understand that the world is bipartite, divided between a *locus amoenus* and a *locus terribilis.* The division of the two spaces is not as clear-cut as some would have us believe, and passageway from one to the other is possible, notably in the marches of these domains ("Borderlands of the Otherworld"). A careful reading of the documents from the medieval North and West reveals that the earth is inhabited by spirits of all sorts who coexist with men—peacefully, neutrally, or hostilely. *Man is not the earth's sole inhabitant . . . he has neighbors, his world is haunted, and their presence forces him to take certain precautions and compels him to respect taboos—in short, it shapes his life.* While the first temptation is to draw a borderline between them and him, he must submit to the obvious: never will this contact be completely sundered, never will nature and the beings symbolizing it cede their primal right ("The Spirits of Nature and of Humans in the Middle Ages"). The earth does not belong exclusively to humans, and the latter have everything to gain by respecting what some see as their nonhuman, plant, or animal neighbors and others see as spirits or the dead. It is probably not insignificant to note that the hero's adventure, in the heart of the "wilderness," often ends with the revelation of his own identity. Looking at this through our modern eyes while remaining prudent, couldn't we also imagine that this nature, all too often overlooked today, brings the individual back to himself, restoring his true dimensions and his proper place in a shared world? Recent studies on the liminal animals we brush against when crossing over a *threshold*, a *borderline*, are one example,[7] which shows that the notion of an invisible but clearly present *frontier* is fully present in our daily relations with other living things.

The texts gathered here show that *making the texts speak* also allows us to understand human beings and their beliefs, putting them back within a world in which the human is just one element among many others. This underscores the profound respect Claude Lecouteux has for what he has always refused to call "superstitions"—for does a hierarchy of values really exist? Here again, between religion and beliefs, between superstitions and Christian reformulations, we realize that the boundary is often quite thin. The importance of nature and of all that dwells within it takes man back to his *homo* roots—a species that for a time knew how to live *with* rather than *against*, when it had not yet invented religions nor tried to take control over its environment.

This is how Claude Lecouteux, as a fabulous storyteller, makes it possible for us to grasp some of our history, the history of our imaginal realm, which forms an important part of our humanity. He is, in fact, not only an eminent researcher, but also a "storyteller, novelist, poet, and pedagogue"[8] who has mastered the rare art of conveying the most difficult things in a way the public at large can understand them, as these texts will yet again demonstrate.

FLORENCE BAYARD, PH.D., has been a lecturer in the Department of Germanic Studies at the University of Caen Normandy since 2002 and is a member of the Research Team on Literature, Imagination, and Society (Équipe de Recherche sur les Littératures, les Imaginaires et les Société). She is the author of *L'Art du bien mourir au XVe siècle* (The Art of Dying Well in the Fifteenth Century; 1999) and has published a French translation with commentary of the fourteenth-century text *Der Ackermann aus Böhmen* (The Plowman from Bohemia) by Johannes von Tepl (2013) and an edition of the fourteenth-century *Petit livre sur la surabondance des grâces* (Little Book on the Abundance of the Graces) by Christine Ebner (2020).

ASTRID GUILLAUME, PH.D., is a specialist in the semiotics of human and animal cultures, the diachronic linguistics of French and German, and translation studies. She is a senior lecturer at the Sorbonne, where she supervises dissertations in semiotics and zoosemiotics. She has published editions and translations of early texts, and is the editor of the volumes *Idéologie et Traductologie* (2016), *Traductions et implicites idéologiques* (2017), and *Making Sense, Making Science* (with Lia Kurts-Wöste, 2021). She is the founder of the journal *Cahiers de Sémiotiques des cultures* and two academic societies: the European Observatory for Pluralism and the French Society of Zoosemiotics.

PART I

FROM DOCUMENT TO IDEA
Making Texts Speak

1

The Ramsund Stone

The Mindset behind the Runic Inscription

The illustrated stone of Ramsund, dated to around 1030 and situated near Eskilstuna in Södermanland (Sweden), includes a carving depicting scenes from the legend of Sigurd/Siegfried: Regin beheaded near the tools of his forge; the hero sticking his thumb in his mouth, his steed with a chest (Fafnir's treasure) on its back; and the birds perched in a tree. All these drawings are inside a band in the shape of a dragon that the valiant hero is piercing with his sword. Inside this band there is a runic inscription that says: "Si(g)rid, mother of Alfrik, daughter of Orm, made this bridge for the soul of Holmgeir, her husband, Si(g)rod's father."[1]

On its own, the inscription does not pose any problems to decipher and we know that the bridge alluded to is, in fact, a dike that makes it possible to cross through the swampy environment. On the other hand, no study has been made, to the best of my knowledge, about what links this dike called a "bridge" and its destination—Holmgeir's soul. While we might immediately think of establishing a connection with the bridge to the beyond,[2] there is one fundamental difference we should not overlook. Whether it is found in medieval visions or in Germanic-Scandinavian mythology (Gjallarbrú), the bridge is not connected to the sublunary world but located entirely outside it. As we saw, however,

The inscription on the illustrated stone of Ramsund,
carved around 1030 near Eskilstuna in what is now Sweden

Sigrid expressly states that this bridge, this dike, has to serve her husband's soul; it is therefore an offering, a kind of petition for a specific purpose.

Light can be shed on the mindset behind this inscription if we refer to folk beliefs and traditions collected by ethnologists in Romania.[3] After death, the soul of the deceased has to travel a long road before reaching its destination safe and sound.[4] This road is strewn with ambushes and obstacles, and all measures taken at the time of death aim at facilitating this final journey of the deceased. Like in Christian literature of revelations and visions, the geography of the otherworld is characterized by difficult, hilly country.[5] Steep mountains loom up out of plunging valleys; the soul has to follow bramble-choked paths across thorn-covered moors, precipices, ravines, rivers, and so forth. Darkness rules, which is why we give the dead candles and tapers. These specific objects, given to help the soul on its journey, are found almost everywhere. Eventually, the soul arrives at a large gulf (a torrent or river) that it is unable to cross without a bridge. This is fundamentally different from the standard bridge of the beyond that all souls have to take, and which causes those of evil men to tumble into hell. It so happens, and this is where Romanian beliefs are particularly interesting: Each soul can only cross this obstacle with his or her own bridge. There is only one per individual, and each one is guarded by an angel (or a demon) who forbids any but its intended owner from crossing it. So, the individual has to have built such a bridge while still alive. It doesn't matter how rudimentary it is, even two planks laid over a ditch will permit this crossing. If the individual neglected to build such a bridge, this duty is incumbent on those near and dear to the deceased. They must build it immediately after death, for the soul does not leave the body right away—an idea we find held by many Indo-European peoples.[6]

By having this dike constructed over the swamp, Sigrid therefore gave her husband the material means he needed to reach the beyond. This construction is an offering intended to prevent the deceased from becoming stuck between this world and the otherworld, and thus potentially transforming into a *draugr* (revenant). It might appear that what we are seeing here is the collusion of two different religious assumptions—one pagan and the other Christian. In fact, no ancient Germanic texts mention the kind of obligation preserved in Romanian beliefs, although we do find some parallels. While there is no notion of building a bridge, the idea of facilitating the deceased's passage into the otherworld can be seen in funeral rites like placing the dead individual in a boat or burying him with a horse. Sigrid's act reflects a Christian idea widely spread by means of the literature of revelations, which should come as no surprise as the evangelization of Sweden began around 830 on the initiative of Archbishop Ebbo of Rheims. Olof Skötkonung was baptized near Husaby (Västergötland) in 1008, and the English monks David and Eskil, as well as the Swede Botvid, were spreading the faith in Södermanland in the eleventh century. The inscription on the Ramsund stone could very well be evidence of Sigrid's Christian faith.

2

Eyrbyggja Saga

The Saga of Snorri Goði

Written around 1230, this Icelandic saga of sixty-five chapters, whose plot primarily takes place in Eyri, Þórsnes, and Álptafjörðr ("Swan Fjord") on the Snæfellsnes Peninsula, offers a realistic account of the life of Snorri Goði. A *goði* was a local leader who had a kind of pact of vassalage with the freemen of his district. They gave him their obedience and support and accompanied him to the assembly or Thing (*þing*), which they attended as his liegemen (*þingmenn*).

Disputes were settled at the Althing (*Alþing*), the assembly of free men held at Þingvellir (the Plains of Parliament) during the summer solstice, next to the Law Rock (*lögberg*) where the lawspeaker (*lögsögumaðr*) recited the law. Local things (*várþing*) were also held in the spring.

The author describes how Snorri settled in Helgafell in 979; his quarrels with Thorarin the Black; his marriage to the daughter of Styr, with whom he had nine daughters and eight sons, all of whom married well; his battle against Arnkel, whom he slew in 993; and his efforts to achieve—by any means necessary, even the most devious—supremacy over the region. Relations had developed between Iceland and Greenland since the discovery of the latter, and Snorri visited it with Thorfin Karlsefni, who headed one of the expeditions to Vinland, "Land of Wine," most likely Labrador. There they had clashes with the natives they called *skrælingar*, whose description matches that of Eskimos.

What makes this saga such a treasure trove are its ethnological observations concerning paganism, law, and funeral rites. We learn about the games with clods of turf (*torfleikr*) or balls—soccer, *avant la lettre*—which often degenerated into brawls. Place names preserve the memory of certain events: for example, Ófeigsfoss, "Ofeig's Falls," carries the memory of a slave who committed suicide by hurling himself into this cataract. "Twist-Foot's Knoll" (Bægifótshöfði) is a reminder that Thorolf Twist-Foot is buried there.

The *Tale of the Greenlanders* (*Grœnlendinga þáttr*) and the *Saga of Erik the Red* (*Eiríks saga rauða*) describe Vinland as a land where wheat and grapes grew wild, and where the climate was so mild that snow did not fall there in the winter. Many have questioned the nature of these resources without managing to specifically identify them.

These texts also mention Helluland, the "Land of the Flat Stones," and Markland, the "Land of Forests," discovered by Thorfin Karlsefni.

Beliefs hold a significant place in the *Eyrbyggja saga*. Unusual events are scattered throughout, such as the severed head Egill found on the ground that spoke a verse of sinister omen to him, for fragments of skaldic poetry pepper the text. Later there is a blood-charged cloud of sad foreboding; and when an eagle carries off a dog, it is regarded as a portent of mighty events.

The characters here are worth noting; among them we meet revenants; sorcerers; berserkers (*berserkir*); seers such as Spá-Gils; brigands like Ospak and his gang; fools; and a man who has more than one shape (*eigi einhamr*), meaning someone who can change his nature—an individual resembling our notion of a werewolf.

I will examine, in order, the elements that make this such an instructive and attractive saga, for its realism and its roots in the life of a small community—with quarrels that often have murderous consequences—all form a gripping testimony.

THE REVENANTS (DRAUGAR)

Before dying at Frodwater, Thorgunna, a native of the Hebrides (the chosen land for witches), asked that her bed curtains and bed be burned once she was no more. When she was being transported to her final resting place through terrible weather, the funeral party was obliged to stay over at a farm, and they placed her corpse in a shed. Noises were heard that night and they found the deceased naked and cooking food to eat; she then brought the meal to her coffin bearers. Her last wish was not carried out, because her bedding was very beautiful, and the consequences were disastrous.

A Moon of ill-omen (*urðarmáni*), revolving counter to the Sun, became visible in the common room at Frodwater. A shepherd died, revenants were seen, and six people died, all at the beginning of Advent. Then a noise was heard in the storeroom where the dried fish was kept, as if someone was tearing it to pieces (*heyrt var í klefann, at rifin var skreiðinn*). Thorodd and five men perished at sea while going to get fish and returned, dripping wet, to their funeral banquet. From this it was deduced they had been given a warm welcome by Rán, the Sea Goddess. Next, a seal's head appeared—this was the animal double of the deceased—which burst out of the floor and stared at Thorgunna's bed canopy. During this time noise was heard coming constantly from the storeroom, day and night. One day, when it was time to take out the dried fish to eat it, a man opened the closet and saw a tail sticking out that looked like a singed oxtail but thick with fur like a seal's tail. People grabbed hold of it, but the tail disappeared and was not seen again. All that remained of the fish were the skins. Right after this Þórgrima the witch (*galdrakinn*) died and joined the band of revenants led by Thorir Wooden-Leg (*viðleggr*) and Thorodd and his men. The decision was made to burn Torgunna's bedding and summon all the revenants to justice. A "door-court" (*duradómr*) was set up, a trial was held, and they were condemned to vanish—which they reluctantly did, each uttering a sentence before leaving.

A strange death was a guarantee that the deceased would come back. Enraged and discontent, Thorolf Twist-Foot (*bægifótr*) died sitting in his high seat. His son Arnkel went up to him from behind, ordering that no one come forward until he had closed the dead man's eyes—a precaution against the evil eye—mouth and nostrils. Despite everything, Thorolf's burial caused disturbing phenomena: the oxen that had pulled his sled were bewitched; the dead man's shepherd was found dead not far from his grave, black as coal, with every bone in his body broken. The birds that landed on his burial mound dropped dead. Dreadful noises could be heard at night. Þórólfr returned home and lashed out at his widow, who succumbed to his attacks. The corpse of the deceased was dug up and carried off to a remote location. But he was tenacious and would leave his grave and kill people and animals. He was dug up again and his body was burned, but a cow licked the stones on which the ashes had been strewn and gave birth to an evil bull that—here is a significant detail—had a broken hoof, thus reproducing Thorolf's handicap. This sequence in the story reflects the idea of reincarnation.

THE WITCHES

Three witches are featured in the saga: Geirrid, nicknamed *tröllið* ("the witch"); Thorgrima; and Katla.

Snorri started a lawsuit against Geirrid because Gunnlaug, who had been learning magic from her, was found beaten and covered with blood, with the very flesh torn from his bones, and it was rumored that she must have "ridden" him (*hafa riðit honum*), which means a black magic spell that is also called *gandreið*, the "ride on the magic wand." But Snorri lost the lawsuit.

Because her son Odd had cut off a woman's hand, Katla used a technique for creating optical illusions (*sjónhverfingar*) to conceal him from his pursuers. To kill her, they first put a sealskin bag over her head to avoid the evil eye, then stoned her. Her son Odd, who had also been discovered, was hung.

Meanwhile, Thorgrima galdrakinn ("expert in magic") was able to summon a storm.

It was customary to name the places where witches had been executed so that they could be avoided. The texts mention a "sorcerers' skerry" (Skrattasker) where they were drowned, and a "sorcerers' cairn" (Skrattavarði) where a sorcerer was buried.

The sagas mention different practices ranging from curses to the crafting of objects with supernatural properties, such as a shirt that makes its wearer invulnerable. Sorcerers and witches practice magic illusions (*sjónhverfingar*), charms (*galdr*), binding (*seiðr*), and sending one's double (*sendingr*). The adjective used to describe them is "greatly learned [in magic]" (*fjölkunnigr*).

LAW AND TRIALS

The saga depicts a series of trials, as Snorri and the Icelanders spend their time quarreling. Snorri and Arnkel dispute over a forest, and the goði tries to have him murdered by a hired killer. Another trial against Arnkel for the murder of slaves features the principle of monetary compensation for achieving reconciliation of the warring parties, something this society sought above all else.

Erik the Red (Eirík hinn rauða), who discovered Greenland, was accused of murdering Thorgest's sons, but he managed to escape. In another trial, Snorri was charged with the murder of Vigfus. Law is omnipresent in this saga and shows that the Icelanders of this time were extremely litigious. One revelatory detail: following charges that were deemed too lenient for a homicide, a law was passed stating that a young woman or man less than eleven winters old could never serve as the principle plaintiff for a murder.

When they returned in an inopportune way, the dead were held on trial: a "door-court" (*duradómr*) would be convoked to which members would be assigned, an accusation lodged, and witnesses produced. Verdicts were handed down against a troop of revenants to stop them from interfering in the lives of the living.

PAGANISM

The saga gives us a good glimpse of pagan rituals and worship, information that is often corroborated by other texts. Making his way to Iceland by boat, upon sighting land Thorolf Mostrarskegg threw the pillars of his high seat (*hásæti*, *öndvegi*) overboard, in order to settle at the place where they floated ashore. The image of the god Thor (Þórr) was carved on one of them and he would decide where they would land. Once he recovered them, Thorolf built a temple in which he set up his high-seat pillars, which had "god-nails" (*reginnaglar*) driven into them.

By throwing the high-seat pillars into the sea, the colonists were leaving the choice of their settlement place in the hands of the gods. We should note that the help of the gods was necessary since the settlers would be stealing the land from the local spirits (*landvættir*), which could be dispersed in several ways. We should also realize that the figureheads on the prows of boats were detachable and bore images intended to drive away the local land spirits in the place they were landing. Later, when returning home from being at sea, the figureheads were removed.

There was a raised platform like an altar in the center of the building. On it there was a ring upon which people swore their oaths. The vessel used to hold the blood of animals sacrificed to the gods was also there. All men had to pay a tax to this temple, and the priest was responsible for its upkeep and for organizing sacrificial feasts there at his own expense. Thorolf Mostrarskegg held a mountain he named Helgafell ("Holy Mountain") in special veneration and believed he would enter it when he died. This belief is confirmed by another passage in the saga: "Thorstein Codbiter (Þorsteinn þorskabítur), died at sea and one of the local shepherds saw the north side open, revealing large fires inside, and he heard joyous shouts and the sounds of drinking horns being clinked together" (*Hann sá inn í fjallið elda stóra og heyrði þangað mikinn glaum og hornaskvöl*).

The adoption of Christianity at the Althing of 999—which is recounted in the *Kristni saga* (Saga of Christianity)—changed very little, and Icelanders continued to worship the gods of their ancestors. They were described as being of "mixed faith" (*blandinn í trúnni*). They believed in Christ but appealed to Thor if danger threatened. Moreover, it was not forbidden to practice the old religion as long as one did so in private.

An exceptional document because of its wealth of information and its depiction of people and places, the *Eyrbyggja saga* resurrects a half-pagan, half-Christian past at a time when the Church held power and the Norwegian king, Hákon Hákonarson (b. 1204, reigned 1217–1263), was seeking to take possession of Iceland by any means necessary.

3

The Hidden Face of Tales
and Legends

The tale is not a simple amusement or teaching tool; it transports elements, themes, and motifs possessing a very long history. It came to be within a society that provided a framework of references whose components are history, folk beliefs, law, and real life. For her part, Bernadette Bricout speaks of a "world woven of history and memory."

During the Middle Ages, the boundary between tales and legends was vague and porous. The two genres were composite, and constantly exchanging their elements. The modern criteria of definition are barely applicable: that the tale is characterized by its happy ending, contrary to the legend; or that the legend exists outside time and space, whereas the tale is deeply rooted in reality, and so forth. There are exceptions to these rules. In the medieval era, tales were concealed in collections of *exempla** and in compilations like the *Gesta Romanorum* (Deeds of the Romans), the oldest manuscript of which dates to 1342. They are also hidden in historiography, homilies, farces, fables, and lays. The old texts—the vast majority of which were written in Latin—collected oral story traditions, but then transposed these tales into the courtly, chivalrous world. The wondrous is everywhere present: fairies like Melusine

---

*[An *exemplum* (pl. *exempla*) is a short tale used to illustrate a moral point, for example in the context of a sermon or didactic text. —*Ed.*]

and Morgana; swan maidens; and women with the shapes of eagles who carry those they fall in love with back to their kingdom. Dwarfs and demons, water nymphs and wild women haunt this world; giants play the role of antagonists; magicians are generally ill-intentioned, except for Merlin the Enchanter, and often change their victims into a dragon or a hind, who are rescued in the nick of time, with only a few exceptions. What the folklorist Vladímir Propp calls "magical means" can be found at every twist in the plot: elixirs of life, healing salves, magic rings, and stones with healing or protective virtues that even allow their bearers to live underwater or—if placed under the tongue—to understand foreign languages. Or they may simply have a revitalizing effect. There are flowers with rejuvenating fragrances, shields that heal amputations but replace the missing limb with a gold artifact, and generative objects like the horn owned by Auberon, the king of the fairies, or the Grail. We find magical capes that make the wearer invisible, a wondrous staircase on which every step corresponds to a sin or a failure with respect to the code of courtly values, automatons that point the finger at the loss of virginity, and a variety of spells and curses. The imagination seems to know no boundaries here. The Middle Ages—which are, alas, so poorly known to anyone but the specialists—represent an important landmark in the history of stories.

The value that medieval tales hold for this study is threefold. First, they provide us with testimony about their antiquity; next, we learn what their dominant themes were and the motifs of which they were constructed; and finally, they supply us with valuable information on the mentalities of yore because they are bristling with elements borrowed from beliefs—for example, leprosy can be cured by the blood of a virgin—as well as being rich with borrowings from the civilization in which they were immersed.

There are well-known motifs like the deserted castle; the castle that vanishes; blindness healed by magic; the animal guide; the stepmother; taboos on seeing or revealing; talismanic rings offering protection from fire, drowning, or poison; the hollow mountain; the fountain of youth; and the magical plant that opens locked doors. We find here the themes of the werewolf; the quest for the vanished wife or husband;

the journey in the otherworld; as well as singular variations of the tale of Cupid and Psyche. Marie de France retold the story of the Matron of Ephesus, and Hartmann von Aue's *Gregorius*, written around 1190, is one of the medieval forms of the Oedipus myth. The *Story of the Seven Sages*, which tells the story of King Rhampsinit's treasure, was already presented by Herodotus. The Middle Ages passed this down to us along with many other things. Around 1325, we find the story of Orpheus in England with a happy ending, and five hundred years later, a Shetland ballad directly inspired by the medieval text; only the names of the characters have changed.

Let us consider a few examples of what medieval literature gives us by way of magic. In one tale we have a cleric who is an inveterate gambler and unlucky: he comes to a crossroads, traces a circle around himself, and invokes the devil, who makes a contract with him.* In another legend, Charlemagne, the victim of a spell, sleeps with his deceased wife; when a prelate removes a stone from the dead woman's mouth, she crumbles into dust.

The magician par excellence is the sorcerer Virgil, the creator of numerous wonders, such as a statue that daily informs the emperor Titus of all infractions of the law; a talking head; talismans; and automatons that protect cities. He acquired his knowledge of magic by discovering a vial holding seventy-two devils that he agreed to free on condition they teach him the Notary Art. Using necromantic magic, he hid an egg in the foundations of a castle in Naples over the depths of the sea. Whoever touches this egg would cause the city to shake, and whoever breaks it would cause it to be swallowed by the sea. On the Magnetic Mountain, Virgil also discovers a fly in a glass vial. The fly asks to be freed in exchange for the grimoire of Zabulon that has a statue of this mage—a magic statue that gets its power from a letter placed in its head. Virgil frees the demon in the shape of a fly, obtains the grimoire, and then tricks the devil.

The dead are omnipresent in the Middle Ages and while ghosts

---

*For the full tales, see "The Diabolical Pope" and "Love Spell" in Claude and Corinne Lecouteux, *Tales of Witchcraft and Wonder: The Venomous Maiden and Other Stories of the Supernatural*, trans. Jon E. Graham (Rochester, VT: Inner Traditions, 2021), 43–44 and 50.

are quite scarce, there are many, many tales of revenants—the latter are often souls in torment in the more Christian lands. They come directly out of folk beliefs. In the much more pagan lands of the North, they return for revenge and to kill, advise, scold, or punish those who fail to respect the traditions. They can only be confronted in a battle to the death. One tale informs us about a deceased man who forbade his wife to remarry. She did not heed him and he smashed her skull with a mortar. In the mindsets of earlier eras, the deceased were never dead; they led a new life in another world that took the shape of a hollow mountain or a burial mound. They have their own religious services at night and woe to anyone who intrudes into that church. They own an inn where they spend the money that the living placed in their graves. An Icelandic saga features a beheaded revenant who strolls about with his head in his hand, which cannot help but remind us of the Headless Horseman in *The Legend of Sleepy Hollow*. Several texts refer to the deceased having sexual relations with their spouses and engendering children. A Danish ballad, "Aage og Else," presents a dead man who returns to ask that his fiancée no longer weep for him:

> *Every time you weep,*
> *Every time your heart is sad*
> *My coffin fills to the brim*
> *with clotted blood.*
> . . .
> *Every time you are glad,*
> *Every time your heart is gay,*
> *My grave is full of red roses.*

Many will recognize here a variant of the well-known motif of "The Pitcher of Tears": a child is painfully pursuing the procession carrying a pitcher of water and asks the living to tell his parent they should no longer mourn him because their tears fall into his pitcher and he can no longer support its weight. In the thirteenth century we see a dead person complaining that her shirt is soaked by the tears of the living mourning her.

Let us now take a look at one of the oldest strata of tales: shamanism. Stories reveal numerous traces of it—of course no longer as an ecstatic technique, to use Mircea Eliade's description, but as themes and motifs that are scattered throughout the texts, and which make it easier to grasp what is concealed beneath stories that seem so simple on the surface. Shamanism represents the world as divided into three levels connected by an axis. Travel between these levels is possible via trance, which creates a spirit double. Let us recall the most striking themes:

- The outer soul: shamanism is marked by the belief in several souls, which are located in different parts of the body, mainly in the bones.
- The ladder made of bones.
- The journey into the beyond in order to retrieve someone.
- Rebirth from one's bones after dismemberment.
- The tree or plant that rises into the heavens; the cosmic tree.
- Becoming a bird or being accompanied by a bird in order to make an initiatory journey into the heavens and beyond.

Let us consider each of these themes in detail:

The outer soul is found in the tale type "The Ogre's (Devil's) Heart in the Egg" (ATU 302), "The Youth Sent to the Land of Ogres" (ATU 302A), "The Man on a Quest for His Lost Wife" (ATU 400), and "The Princess on the Sky-Tree" (ATU 468).* It is not a question of the soul but of a life force that is found outside the body, in an egg, or in a series of containers. This theme is also present in "The Singing Bone" (ATU 780), where a flute made from a bone reveals the identity of the murderer of the person to whom it belonged.

The ladder made of bones appears in the tale types of "The Magic Flight: The Girl as Helper in the Hero's Flight" (ATU 313A) and

---

*["ATU" refers to the Aarne-Thompson-Uther Index, a comprehensive numbered catalog of folktale motifs used by folklore scholars. —*Ed.*]

"The Nurse Looking for Her Brothers" (ATU 451). In "The Green Mountain," a maiden has to be cut into pieces, boiled in a stewpot, her bones extracted from her flesh, and used as a ladder. The boy gathers the dead maiden's bones together in a cloth and boils them in the pot to restore her to life in full health. Theodor Vernaleken (1812–1907), Austria's answer to Jacob Grimm, tells how the Master of the Winds eats a chicken and gives its bones to a young girl seeking her seven brothers. She makes her way to a glass castle that has no doors or windows. She sticks the bones in its smooth surface and, using them like a ladder, she succeeds in freeing her brothers.

Going to find someone in the otherworld is one of the shaman's specialties. This consists of bringing back the spirit or soul of a person who has been carried off by a demon or an illness. To do this, the shaman enters an ecstatic trance to take a journey with the support of his spirit helpers. We find this in "The Quest for a Lost Wife" (ATU 400) and "The Search for the Lost Husband" (ATU 425). In these, the hero goes into the otherworld and, after a variety of ordeals, returns with the object of his or her quest. The archetype here is the story of Orpheus.

Nicole Belmont has shown evidence for the kinship of the French fairy tale "The Devil's Daughter" (ATU type 313) with the myth of Orpheus, noting the convergences and inversions of the two stories. In addition to the journey to the otherworld, "The Devil's Daughter" has preserved a fundamental element of shamanic beliefs: the cutting of the body into pieces. In the myth, Orpheus is dismembered by the Bacchantes, who scatter the pieces of his body. In the tale, the woman is dismembered by a man who gathers the pieces of her body together and restores her to life.

Let us go to Greenland. The great polar explorer Knut Rasmussen collected a number of Inuit tales that feature as their hero a shaman named Avggo who visits the beyond.

After visiting all the places frequented by the great shamans, he decides to visit the "celestial land of the dead." He summons his spirit guides and plays his drum before finishing his incantations. Once the spirits have gathered, he begins his trance journey and flies toward the horizon where heaven and earth meet. There he finds a staircase that he struggles to climb and makes his way to the large celestial meadow. A crowd presses upon him and his spirits. Among them is his father, who provides him much information about this land of the dead. Seeing that the night is ending, his father tells him: "Now, you must make haste to return before day breaks; otherwise you will have to remain here for eternity."

On another occasion, Avggo decides to visit the land of the dead beneath the earth. His soul departs with his spirit guides into the depths of the sea. They come to a kind of path that takes them even deeper until they finally reach the border between the earth and the sea. This border is formed by a river of foam that can only be crossed by jumping on the stones that are interspersed there. They cross and then scale a very slippery cliff "where the dead have the habit of wandering during their journey between the earth and the underworld." Here, he is welcomed by a crowd of people. Avggo discovers all the marvels of the abysses before returning.

The gradual transition from shamanism to the fairy tale occurs can be discerned in "The Ancestor Who Visited the Land of the Dead." In a state of despair, a woman whose two sons had died lost consciousness. After two days, everyone thought she was dead. She then saw that she was on the way to the land of the dead, where she saw a large hole in the celestial vault. She made her way there by crawling and came to a revolving stone where a voice asked her: "Is this a dead person who has just arrived?" She then saw her grandmother, who shouted at her: "You must answer: 'I am not a dead person, I am a living person who has just arrived.'" The question is repeated a little further along, and she gives the same answer. She then enters a house where she finds her sons trapped in ice because she was grieving their deaths too greatly. "It is your tears transformed into ice that is covering our feet," they tell her. The grandmother suggests she return home, and she reluctantly heeds her. She passes by the stone, which is now motionless, and reaches the hole that led into the sky, where she encounters a young man of her land crawling up toward heaven. She pushes him in before her and despite his resistance she brings him back home. Through the window she sees the body of a young man laid on the ground and whom everyone thinks is dead. But because she has brought back his soul, his body resumes life. The young woman's soul reintegrates with her body and she comes back to life as well.

Without the text stating so explicitly, the woman behaves like a shaman and retrieves a soul from the beyond. The primitive belief is masked, and a folktale motif is introduced into the text, "The Pitcher of Tears" (an ATU type 769 tale).

Rebirth from one's bones is a theme that was already in use at the beginning of the thirteenth century in the *Gylfaginning* (The Deluding of Gylfi), which forms the second part of Snorri Sturluson's *Prose Edda* and where the following episode from the life of the god Thor can be read. In this tale Thor is traveling with Loki in his chariot drawn by goats. "As night was falling, they came to a farmer's home and arranged to get lodging there for the night. That evening, Thor took his goats and killed them both. They were then skinned and placed in a cauldron." Everyone ate. "Thor laid the goatskins down between the fire and the door and told the farmer and his household to toss the bones onto the skins. Thjalfi, the farmer's son, kept the thighbone of one of the goats and split it with his knife to get the marrow." In the morning, Thor lifted his hammer and recited "incantations over the bones of the goats. They came back to life, but one of them was limping on its hind leg."

Josef Haltrich (1822–1886) recounts a story collected in Transylvania that is similar to this one. A shepherd slaughters his lamb to feed Jesus and Saint Peter. Once they have ended their meal, Jesus advises him to gather up all the bones and place them on the animal's hide. The next day, the animal was full of life.

Humans can be given the same treatment. In "My Mother Slew Me; My Father Ate Me" (ATU 720), the hero comes back to life once his bones have been collected and reassembled correctly.

A tale from Lower Saxony is worth mentioning as it depicts an incredible process: an enchanted princess could only be freed by a prince that had gotten lost in a forest while hunting, was twenty years old, and agreed to being dismembered three nights in a row by spirits. "The next day, a stag will appear holding a vial of oil in its mouth, the princess tells him. It will gather together all the bones of your body, put them back together as they should be, and anoint them. They will then fall back into place and become covered in flesh. Once this is done, you will come back to life." The spirits, twelve in number, cut off his head, dismember him, and devour his flesh, leaving nothing but bones. The stag does its job and the prince comes back to life. He successfully passes this test but fails at another. The princess vanishes and he sets off to find her.

Finally, we have an account from the Brothers Grimm that shows us how a torture like this can be described euphemistically. A young man finds an enchanted maiden in the form of a snake in a castle. She asks him to free her:

> "How can I do that?" asks the boy.
>
> "Tonight, twelve black men bearing chains will arrive. They will ask you what you are doing here, but don't say a word, don't reply, and let them do what they wish. They will torture, beat, and stab you, but let them do this and say nothing. At midnight they will have to leave. Twelve more will come on the second night; and on the third night, twenty-four will come and cut off your head. But at midnight they will lose their power and if you have been firm and not spoken a single word, I shall be freed. I will come find you with a flask of the water of life. I will cover you with it and you will be restored to life as good as you were before."

Through the examples I've just described, which are all representatives of an ATU type 400 tale sequence, we can see evidence of the slow process of degradation of a belief that is as old as the world. Cut off from its roots within a civilization, it withers, leaving only rare vestiges that are now incomprehensible and have fallen to the level of simple fantasy motifs in fairy tales. Historical evolution, religion, and time have all done their work, but the collection of flotsam and jetsam still allows us to glimpse what is hidden behind these motifs.

The tree or plant that rises into the heavens theme is especially familiar because of the story of "Jack and the Beanstalk," but it is also confirmed by "The Fisher and His Wife" (a French version of tale type 555), "The Healing Vixen" (Afanasyev nr. 11),* and "The Princess on the Sky-Tree" (ATU 468). This is a variant of the cosmic mountain that provides access to the otherworld when climbed or tunneled into. Among the Native Americans (Arapahos, Chilcotins), the sky can be reached by climbing up a tree that keeps growing taller as you ascend it.

Flying: Becoming a bird or being accompanied by a bird appears, for example, in "The Three Kidnapped Princesses" (ATU 301) and in "The Marvelous Eagle Gives the Hero a Box (ATU 537). Here, and in other tales where assistants are involved, we find the last traces of the shaman's spirit helpers. The hero of the story receives help and/or advice from animals (often out of gratitude), and it is thanks to their assistance that he succeeds in his quest. The eagle and the horse are featured most frequently and represent a psychopompic function. As an example, let us look at the tale of "Three Deserters" collected by Zingerle brothers. After freeing three princesses held captive in the underworld, the hero is betrayed by his companions and remains trapped underground. He asks a dwarf to help him. The latter replies:

> "I am going to help you if you follow me. I can transform myself however I please. I am going to change into an eagle and carry you, but this flight will tire me a lot. So, you must quickly slaughter a lamb and cut it into three pieces. You will have to give me a piece every time I scream, otherwise we will fall and you will die."
>
> The dwarf immediately put his promise into action and carried the young man holding the meat in his claws. The bird had already screamed three times for meat and he had not yet finished soaring upward when he screamed for a fourth time. The lamb had been devoured, what could he do? The soldier quickly sliced off a piece of his calf and gave it to the eagle. Several minutes later, they flew into the open air.

---

*[This refers to the Russian folktale collection of the nineteenth-century ethnographer Alexander Afanasyev. —*Ed.*]

The return to this world involves a sacrifice; implicit here is the concept that no one can return from the beyond without paying compensation.

The tales must be decoded as the shamanism is never overt but beneath the surface. "The Three Brothers and the Three Sisters," an Albanian folktale (ATU type 304), offers a wonderful illustration of how it is concealed within a story. A prince sets off in pursuit of his wife's abductor, and a falcon carries him to a high mountain whose name is "the other world." The meat carried by the hero to feed the raptor is insufficient and he has to cut off a slice of each of his thighs. When they reach the top of the mountain, the bird regurgitates the swallowed pieces, the prince puts them back in place, and he is healed. He finds his wife, who hides him, but her abductor finds him, kills him, and drinks his blood; "As for the skin and bones, he threw them behind his house." The falcon sees them, flies to the two mountains that open and close, gets through, fills his beak with swallow's milk, and restores the prince to life. The prince persuades his wife to pretend to be ill so her abductor will tell her where the seat of his power is hidden. She eventually finds out. "My strength is in such-and-such mountain where lives a boar," he tells her; "He has a silver tusk. In this tusk there is a hare. There are three pigeons in the belly of this hare. That's where my strength resides." Once the prince kills the pigeons, the abductor dies and the falcon returns the couple home.

We must turn to countries quite far from Europe to find folktales where shamanism is more obvious. Recorded in Mexico in the 1950s, the following one offers two fine examples:

1. A prince, with the aid of the devil, abducts the king's daughter with whom he is smitten. The demon leads him into a jungle cave and tells him to enter the otherworld through it. But how to kidnap the one he loves? The devil tells him: "Take this box, drum, and flute. Go to the cave, rub the balm on yourself, beat the drum with your right hand and play the flute with your right. When you have done this long enough, you will turn into a jaguar. Go to where the royal park touches the jungle

and pretend that your hind legs are paralyzed. Let yourself be captured; they will imprison you in a courtyard. Pretend to be asleep. People will want to show the sleeping jaguar to the princess. Grab her, cross through the park into the jungle, then make your way into the otherworld through the cave. Following these instructions, the prince abducted the princess.

2. Another man who is in love with the princess is thrown into despair by her abduction. One day he gives alms to a female pauper and tells her of his woes. She offers to help him and brings him into the jungle to an ancient chapel that is half in ruins. They go inside. The beggar lights candles and incense. "Stand in the middle," she commands him, "breathe the smoke in deep and when you hear me singing, sing with me."

   Several hours later, an angel appears and the man feels wings sprouting out of his back. The angel carries him to a mountain; they enter a cave there and go into the otherworld. Taking advantage of the jaguar prince's slumber, they kidnap his captive and return to the royal palace, whereupon the angel disappears.

If we set aside the Christian elements of this story (the devil and angel), what we are seeing is a trance-inducing session of the shamanic type with the help of a drum (the essential attribute of every shaman), a flute, and a salve, which likely contains a hallucinogen. The transformation into an animal, which is to say a splitting of the individual's personality, is based on the function of the desired objective here: abduction. The second session, which is more Christianized—it takes place in a chapel of "ancient times"—rests essentially on the song and the smoke the love-struck man has to inhale. In each of these cases the journey into the otherworld requires a "specialist": the devil and the pauper, both of whom are the result of an acculturation process. They have replaced the shaman of the original stories, which are likely far more ancient than the year when they were collected.

Among the Tlingit, a native people of North America, "The Chain in Arrows" recounts a journey into the beyond in order to bring back a boy who vanished after offending the Moon. The son of a village chieftain fired arrows at a star, and they eventually transformed into a ladder that he scaled for two days in order to reach the sky. He meets his grandmother, who tells him how to find the house of the Moon where the boy for whom he searches is being held. She gives him a pinecone, some sweet briar, a piece of aromatic wood, and a fragment of a whetstone. He makes his way to the Moon's house, hears his comrade howling in pain and helps him to get away by leaving the pinecone in his place, which he has bid to imitate the boy's howls. They both flee and come to the grandmother's house, who orders her grandson: "Go and rest at the place where you first came. Think of nothing but the playground that you had." They obey and find themselves at the foot of the ladder. They hear a drum in the village chief's house where a funeral feast has been organized for them, then they rejoin their respective families.

Folktales are the conduits of beliefs and traditions, and fragments of myths. They give us a glimpse of the mentalities of earlier times, plunge us into a world where anything is possible, where animals talk, where metamorphoses are considered to be natural accidents, where the devil has replaced the spirits that the Church has demonized. It is therefore a good idea to reread these stories, which still retain all their mysterious charm and evocative power.

4

Fantasy and the Middle Ages

Fantasy is available in a wide variety of forms from novels to film, from graphic novels to role-playing games (*World of Warcraft*). It is based on what could be called the "medieval fantastic," crafted from faery and magic and features of stereotyped characters—beautiful, willowy, and evanescent elves; portly bearded dwarfs; and so forth—and a bestiary dominated by dragons and griffins à la Tolkien's *Lord of the Rings*. Fantastical beings from the mythologies and folk traditions of the Middle Ages are omnipresent. Modern Fantasy re-creates a world where the marvelous reigns supreme, a world where everything is possible and the irrational has its rightful place. It is a realm into which the readers, viewers, or "role-players" voluntarily enter and immerse themselves with shivers of delight, temporarily accepting the existence of parallel and coherent worlds that are accessible thanks to supernatural means.

Fantasy is the nucleus of an incredible alchemy, a crucible in which coalesce the desires, fears, dreams, and big questions of humanity (Can one communicate with the otherworld?). Fantasy is the new shape of epic legends such as *Beowulf* or the *Nibelungenlied* (for example, in Alex Alice's graphic novel *Siegfried*) in which Good confronts Evil through a hero in quest of some sort of Grail. With its strange mix of traditional narrative forms and powerful quality of syncretism, Fantasy blends reminiscences from various mythologies. This includes Celtic mythology, from which some legendary names (Lugh, Arianrhod) are drawn, and Germanic mythology, from which come elements that were employed by Tolkien such as the trolls, elves, Gandalf, and magical words like "sagas" and "runes," as well as ancient scripts like runic and Ogham that inspired the inscription on the One Ring of Frodo's quest.

But what Fantasy essentially exploits is the world of medieval Europe. It is enchanted by the magic of names (King Arthur, Morgana, Merlin, the Lady of the Lake, and Ragnarök[1]—the name of the eschatological battle that became "Raghnarok," the little dragon of a French graphic novel series) and words (succubus, incubus, wizard, magician), and when we go back further in time we find Conan the Cimmerian. The worlds of Fantasy (Narnia) are situated in a remote past and an "elsewhere" that is almost dreamlike, if we judge it by its depiction in certain graphic novels (cf. André Houet's *Chroniques de la nuit des temps* [Chronicles of the Night of Time]). These are worlds that appeal to the anthropological structures of the imagination and resemble those described in the medieval visionary literature of revelations, in which men project a double and undertake a journey into the beyond, as in works like the twelfth-century *Visio Godeschalci* (Vision of Gottschalk) or Saxo Grammaticus's early thirteenth-century *Gesta Danorum* (Deeds of the Danes), which in Book 8 describes the two journeys of Thorkillus to the home of Utgarthilocus, the giant king of a deadly world.[2] Old beliefs long buried—beliefs in divination, omens, and destiny (incarnated by the Norns)—come to the surface in a world haunted by visible and invisible beings, spirits, demons, ghosts, revenants, and were-creatures, all ferocious and often dangerous.* A medievalist has no difficulty retracing the prehistory of the figures featured here and often discovers that his or her own work has been pillaged in the crafting of these beings for a contemporary audience.

The elements of ancient forms of nature worship and the veneration of the gods of a resurgent paganism are also visible in Fantasy, but what is most striking is the resurgence of magic, witchcraft (cf. the French graphic novel series *Magus* by Debois, Cyrus, and Annabel), and shamanism. The magical "panoply" comes entirely from the

---

*I have discussed these figures in my other books, many of which are now available in English.

Middle Ages: incantations, spells—*Avada Kedavra** and *Rennervate* used in Harry Potter[3]—talismans,[4] various charms, potions, divinatory trances, glamors, and transformations. As for the magical objects found in Fantasy, their origin is crystal clear: the wondrous swords (Excalibur), magic stones (carbuncles: the family of red gemstones), bows that never miss their target, helmets of terror, are all drawn from the medieval legacy! Behind Gandalf we can see the profile of Merlin, and Morgana is reconstituted in the world of Fantasy wearing other features. But aren't the modern authors the distant descendants of Shakespeare with his revenant in *Hamlet*, his witches in *Macbeth*, his elves and fairies in *A Midsummer's Night Dream*—and of Spenser with his *Faerie Queene*?

In graphic novels, where the text is often reduced to the bare minimum, myth, legend, and the marvelous are expressed by drawings that are sometimes reminiscent of Victor Hugo's watercolors. These modern illustrators can be seen as direct descendants of the Pre-Raphaelites who painted scenes of the faery world, and of Gustave Doré, Edmund Dulac, or Yan' Dargent, many of whose paintings, for example, *The Washerwomen of the Night*, are inspired by folk beliefs. This art is distinguished by scenery that resolutely departs from the real to produce oneiric visions, subjective and particularly suggestive images, which the viewer then decodes through a personal cultural prism. Here again, the Middle Ages are a goldmine: this is the source for the dark tangled forests, wild mountains, fetid marshes and desolate moors, the mist-enshrouded castles, disreputable crossroads, ruins, and grottos. All the landscape clichés of the adventure tales of medieval legend (see chap. 14) are present in modern Fantasy. And this same source also provides the journeys into other worlds, the quests for everlasting life, the fountain of youth, the lost talisman, and the bird fairy taking flight.

"Fantasy," a word whose meaning is more than just "the imaginary," overlies a polysemous and syncretic ensemble created from elements of both the faery world and science fiction (SF), albeit without the projections into the future and technology. Nevertheless SF replaces the swords with light sabers, the armor with space suits, the knights with

---

*Here we will recognize "Abracadabra!"

Jedis, and Yoda takes the place of the old elf sage.[5] There are many points in common between Fantasy and SF and at times it can be difficult to distinguish one genre from the other (as is the case, for example, with *The Mercenary* series of comic books by Vincent Segrelles).

The growing success of Fantasy, especially in the form of role-playing games, can probably be attributed to the fact that it offers us a temporary respite from the tribulations of contemporary life with its procession of fears and disasters. By re-enchanting the world, it removes the leaden veil that hangs over people and draws the Middle Ages forth into the present, offering dreams and a change of scenery—in sum, an escape. By reinvigorating archetypes, Fantasy appeals to our memory of the tales and legends we heard as children, and if we consider the structure of the stories, it undoubtedly serves as their modern manifestation.

As Jacques Le Goff said: "The Middle Ages never ended." In a great many respects, we remain quite close to the people of that time. The same things delight and captivate us, disturb and frighten us. For proof we need only look at studies of modern urban legends, such as those by Véronique Campion-Vincent and Bruno Renaud. Fantasy most likely owes its success to the reactivation of supernatural figures, myths, and beliefs that forge a link between this world and the beyond, between men and the gods or God, and which uphold the idea of transcendence. But the Christian Church no longer holds sway over people's minds; what was once demonized is no longer so; fantastic creatures are no longer the emanations of Satan, but have recovered their specificity and even their authenticity. In addition to a thousand other aspects, they symbolize alterity, omnipotence, justice, evil, and knowledge of the arcane mysteries while still remaining subject to fate—and thus they are not so far from human beings as was once thought.

PART II

BETWEEN MAGIC AND DIABLERIE
Ambiguous Objects and Beings

5

A Typology of Several Kinds
of Evil Dead

For centuries, people have believed in and feared the return of the dead. Revenants had a reputation for being dangerous, which explains why various restrictive funeral rites were established (lamentations, sacrifices, gifts, ritual burials, and so on). I have chosen to schematize things here somewhat by presenting nine types of evil dead from ancient times that are well represented in Germanic traditions. A closer look at the most recent accounts will reveal that mindsets have scarcely evolved on this plane.

THE SUMMONER

The dead can kill the living in a variety of ways. The first and one of the oldest is what we could call the "summoning," a technical term borrowed from magic, where it serves to designate the summoning of a supernatural being. A dead person appears in flesh and bone[1] and calls the living by their name, which soon brings about their death.

Walter Map was the first medieval author to relate the following, which he considered to be a miracle that took place sometime between 1149 and 1182 in the land of Wales. The knight William Laudun came to Gilbert Foliot, bishop of Hereford, and told him:

Master, I fly to thee for advice; a certain Welsh malefactor died
in my house not long ago, a non-believer; after an interval of four
nights he hath never failed to return each night, and hath not ceased
summoning forth, one by one and by name, all his fellow-lodgers. As
soon as they are summoned, they grow ill and die within three days,
so that now only a few survive. (*De nugis curialium*, II, 27)[2]

The deceased did not have an aura of saintliness and his death con-
formed to his life: wicked he was, wicked he shall remain. He returns
to kill his fellow villagers, and it is enough that he summons them
by name. The bishop suggests that a fallen angel has slipped into the
corpse, and indicates what steps to take: "Dig up the corpse, cut the
neck, and besprinkle the body and grave with holy water, and then
rebury it." These measures, however, have no effect whatsoever, because
this revenant is particularly tough and continues dealing out death.
Eventually, the villagers abandon their homes.

On a certain night, therefore, William himself, since now but a few
were left, was summoned thrice, and he, bold and active as he was,
knowing full well what the summons signified, drew his sword and
rushed out. As the demon fled he pursued it to the very grave, and
as it lay therein, he clave its head to the neck. From that hour ceased
the persecution from this ghostly wanderer, nor henceforth did
William or any other suffer harm therefrom.

We can note one contradiction in the text: decapitating the corpse
had no effect whatsoever but splitting it in half "kills" it once and for
all. A detail such as this reveals that Walter Map drew his inspiration
from a folktale, which remains indifferent to this kind of unlikelihood.
Another explanation is plausible: decapitating the dead man is useless
if no one takes the precaution of placing the head at the body's feet in
the grave in such a way that the corpse cannot grab it and put it back
in its rightful place. Archaeology has in fact taught us that this kind of
mutilation is accompanied by the removal of the head to a position by
the feet of the corpse.

Let us leap forward several centuries and look at what Karl Ferdinand von Schertz reports around 1706 in his little work entitled *Magia posthuma*.[3] Dealing with similar phenomena, he mentions a "shepherd from the village of Blow, near the town of Cadan in Bohemia, who appeared on several occasions calling several individuals, who did not fail to die eight days later." In 1751 Augustin Calmet cites a work by Leon Allatius that says:

> On the island of Chios, the inhabitants do not respond to the first voice that calls them, for fear that it might be a spirit or a revenant. But if they are called two times, it can never be a *broucalaca*,* which is the name they give to these phantoms. If someone responds the first time they are called, the specter disappears but the one it spoke to will inevitably die.[4]

THE KNOCKER

Another way of killing the living is by knocking on their door, an action that has almost the same function as the summons. Even if testimonies are rare, no doubt because they have been confused with the activity of a poltergeist, they speak volumes and go far back in time. Here is one, drawn from the *Flóamanna saga* (Saga of the People of Flói), written around 1300. The plot unfurls in southwestern Iceland some three centuries earlier:

> The weather was beautiful on Christmas day and people spent the entire day outside. On the second day, Thorgils and his men went to bed early; they were already asleep when Jostein and his companions noisily entered the hut. They went to bed. They had barely stretched out when someone knocked at the door. One of Jostein's men leaped up, saying, "It's undoubtedly good news," went outside, was taken by madness, and died the next morning. The same thing happened the next night: a man went mad,

---

*[Calmet is using a gallicization of the Greek term *vrykólakas*. —Ed.]

declaring he had seen and been attacked by the man who died the night before.[5]

An Icelandic tale collected in the nineteenth century recounts how a deacon of Myrká, in the Eyafjörður, drowns while trying to cross a river.[6] He is laid to rest one week before Christmas. Yet on the eve of the Lord's nativity, Gudrun, his wife, heard knocking at the door:

> Another woman, who was with her, went to the door but saw no one outside. Furthermore, it was neither light nor dark because the moon was going in and out of the clouds. When the woman came back inside, saying she had not seen anyone, Gudrun said: "It must be for me and I am going to depart now, assuredly."

Outside, she saw her husband's horse and a man she took to be her husband. She climbed into the saddle and they rode off. They reach the gate of the cemetery where the deacon ties his horse and Gudrun sees an open grave. Though terrified, she has the presence of mind to grab hold of the bell rope.

> At that same moment, someone seized her from behind and it was lucky she had not had time to put both her arms in the sleeves of her coat because she had been punched so hard that the coat ripped at the shoulder seam. The deacon jumped into the open grave, causing the dirt to fall back on him from all sides.

Gudrun returns home, but "that same night, when all were in bed and the light had been extinguished, the deacon arrived and harassed Gudrun. . . . For the next half-month, she could not be left alone and someone had to stay to watch over her every night." Finally, a sorcerer is called upon who forces the dead man back under the ground with his spells and then rolls a stone over the grave. Gudrun recovers, but "she was never the same as before." The text leaves no doubt as to the meaning of this knocking at the door: the dead person does not return in search of simply any individual. He comes in search of his wife, and the narrator emphasizes this detail because the deacon remains invisible to everyone else. Though Gudrun does not die, the experience does leave her scarred for life.

The *broucalaca* of southern Europe is a summoner and a knocker at the same time. He has a habit of pounding on the doors of houses and calling people by name. Whoever responds, dies on the spot.[7]

Beliefs have a hardy life. Around 1900, students told Józef Klapper of the following belief in Gleiwitz (Silesia):

> When a person dies, the night following his burial, someone knocks at his door. You should not open the door because it is the dead man outside. If you open the door, he will carry other family members to the grave.[8]

THE VISITOR

The visitor can be considered a variant of the knocker. The sole distinction between them is that it is not said whether the visitor knocks on the doors of the houses he visits. In the beginning of the eighteenth century, a dead man described as a vampire sowed disorder in the Moravian village of Liebava. The canon of Olomouc Cathedral was charged with investigating the matter in the company of a priest, to whom we owe the following narrative:

> The depositions of the witnesses stated that a certain notable inhabitant of Liebava had often bothered the living people of said place during the night; that he had come out of the cemetery and appeared in several houses; that his unwelcome visits had stopped because a Hungarian stranger, passing through the village at the time of these rumors, had boasted that he could rid them of the vampire. To satisfy his promise, he climbed up into the steeple of the church and watched for the moment when the vampire left his tomb, leaving around the grave the linens in which he was buried when he went to the village to distress the inhabitants.
>
> Having seen the vampire leave his grave, the Hungarian promptly

descended from the steeple, snatched up the grave linens and carried them with him back up into the tower. The vampire on return from his travels and not finding his linens, shouted loudly against the Hungarian who was beckoning to him from the top of the tower: if he wanted his linens back, come get them. The vampire began climbing the steeple, but the Hungarian knocked over the ladder and cut off his head with a spade. This was the end of the tragedy.[9]

This dead man was no vampire; he was only a simple revenant! In fact, it is never said if he caused more deaths, and not a single allusion is made to any bloodsucking activity. He is called a "vampire," however, which is evidence that this word was first used describe revenants before being applied to bloodsuckers. The author of this report is thus interpreting a haunting in accordance with rumors that had been spreading in Europe for several decades and therefore contributed to establishing the myth. In fact, the Liebava revenant is similar to the one that William Laudun expedited *ad patres* . . .

On the other hand, some revenants clearly are vampires. The thirty-seventh of the *Jewish Letters*, published in 1738, does present a vampire visitor:

there died in the village of Kisilova . . . an old man who was sixty-two years of age. Three days after he had been buried, he appeared in the night to his son and asked him for something to eat; the son having given him something, he ate and disappeared. . . . Two nights later, he showed himself and asked for something to eat. They know not whether the son gave him anything or not, but the next day he was found dead in his bed. On the same day five or six persons fell suddenly ill in the village, and died one after the other in a few days. . . .

They opened the graves of those who had been dead six weeks. When they came to that of the old man, they found him with his eyes open, having a fine color, with natural respiration, nevertheless motionless as the dead; whence they concluded that he was most evidently a vampire. The executioner drove a stake into his heart; they then raised a pyre and reduced the corpse to ashes.[10]

THE FAMISHED

It was around the eleventh century that the famished dead made their first appearance in the literature. The *Russian Primary Chronicle* or "Tale of Bygone Years" reports a strange event that took place in 1092 in the Ukrainian village of Polotsk. While the different versions agree on the event, the one known as the *Radziwiłł Chronicle* includes a noteworthy observation that the others leave out:

> A loud noise was suddenly heard in the street, with devils galloping about there like human beings. If someone tried to leave his home, the devils would afflict him, invisibly, with a wound from which he died. No people dared to leave their houses. Next, these devils began appearing in the day on horses and there was no means to see them directly; people could see the hooves of their steeds. Thus they distressed the people of Polotsk and the surrounding region and for that reason people say: "The residents of Polotsk are being devoured by the dead."[11]

The authors waver between calling them demons or the dead. According to the version in the *Laurentian Codex*, the event reported in the *Chronicle* would have actually taken place in reality, not in the imagination, and it was revenants that caused the huge loss of life. We should note, incidentally, that these devouring dead form an Infernal Hunt[12] and arrive mounted on horses whose hooves alone can be seen.

Another testimony, in this case Scandinavian, transmitted by the *Gesta Danorum* of Saxo Grammaticus (beginning of the thirteenth century) and by the *Saga of Egil Onehand and Asmund Berserkerbane* (*Egils saga einhenda ok Ásmundar berserkjabana*),[13] tells us of the hunger of the dead. Asvit succumbed to his wounds and was buried in a mound with his horse, dog, and some food. Asmund had himself buried with him because they were sworn brothers.

> Coming back to life, Asvit began rending them with his fingernails, pulling his horse apart with his teeth and swallowing the dog in his mouth. But the steed and dog were not enough for him and he tears

open Asmund's cheek and takes off one of his ears. Asmund decapitates him and impales the evil corpse with a stake.

This sort of decapitation is confirmed by archaeological finds, and the use of a stake to affix the revenant to its grave is well vouched for by ancient Scandinavian laws that have a precise phrase for this: "to bury beneath the stake" (*staursetja lik*), and a passage from *Eirik the Red's Saga*[14] says that this was done in Greenland when the priest was absent and could not bless the grave.

This stake was commonly used to fasten the dangerous dead to the ground, and around 1007, Burchard of Worms admonished women who, on the death of an unbaptized infant, "carried its cadaver to a secret place and pierced its body with a rod. They declared that if they did not do this, the child would return and cause harm to many people." Burchard added: "If a woman does not manage to give birth to her child and dies in labor, then in the very grave itself the mother and the little one are pierced by a rod that nails them to the ground."[15] What underlies this is the belief that the mother and the child could transform into evil beings who will cause others to die—in other words, behave exactly like vampires *avant la lettre* or like the evil dead I am describing here.

Indirect testimonies show that it was believed that the dead could eat. In the Middle Ages, murderers were identified by binding them limb by limb to the murder victim. If the person was truly guilty, the deceased would devour the living person, and one text cites the case of a man whose nose and mouth were eaten by his victim.[16] The Greeks and Turks believed that the corpses of the *vrykólakas* ate at night and that the proof could be seen by disinterring them: their bodies were rosy and if cut open, would let flow rivulets of fresh blood.

If we take a look at the German memorates, we can find a number of folk names that imply hunger and eating: *Nachzehrer*, from the verb *zehren* meaning "to devour"; *Gierhals*, whose first element, *Gier-*, expresses "greed" and the compound word "greedy mouth or jaws"; there is also *Gierfraß*, from the verb *fressen*, "to eat like an animal."*

---

*In eastern Pomerania, we find the *Gierrach*, *Gierhals*, *Begierig*, and *Unbegier*.

THE NONICIDE

The "nonicide," meaning "nine-killer" (*Neuntöter* in German), is a revenant whose wickedness is confined to causing the death of nine (*nonus*) people close to him. It was believed that he would attract those whom he particularly loved, or that some mischance occurred at his death: a cat had been allowed to walk over his body; his eyes refused to stay shut; the headscarf of the woman performing his funeral ablutions had brushed his lips, and so forth. Obviously, our ancestors explained his misdeeds in their own way by stating that this kind of dead man loved his family so much that he wanted to keep them around him.

The oldest account of the nonicide is, to my knowledge, a newspaper article dated July 31, 1725, that Michael Ranfft inserted in his treatise on *The Mastication of the Dead in Their Graves*.[17] A certain Peter Plogojowitz died and nine people followed him to the grave shortly after. He lay on top of the living and squeezed their throats. He was exhumed and blood gushed from his corpse. He was then stabbed with a stake and cremated.

Peter Plogojowitz was simultaneously a nonicide, strangler, and nightmare. It can be seen that Plogojowitz prompted the desertion of his village, exactly like the revenant who was beheaded by William Laudun.

THE *APPESART*

Until the nineteenth century, a European belief spoke of a "spirit" that jumped on people passing through certain places—cemeteries, crossroads, abandoned chapels, forests, swamps—perching on their backs and making them carry it a good distance. It would only abandon them when they reached home. This "spirit" was often described as a dead man, but an explanation for its actions was not supplied. What can be gathered is that the *appesart*'s* victims remain in a greatly weakened state, as if a vampire had sucked out their vital substance, and are a

---

*I am using this word from medieval French, one of the designations for nightmare, because it corresponds exactly to the German *Aufhocker*, *Huckupp* in dialect, which designates this kind of figure.

finger's breadth away from death. In all likelihood, the *appesart* is the pure product of the fear that invades a person when passing near what were once called the "uncertain places" (*loca incerta*), the forests that served as havens for souls in torment, the unknown graves that were stepped on inadvertently, and so forth. Gerolamo Cardano informs us that a Milanese man returning home at three in the morning tried to escape from a revenant, but the latter hurled him to the ground. They fought and the man was finally rescued by some passersby, but he died eight days later.[18] These accounts give us the archetype, so to speak, of the *appesart*, a wicked dead man who hurls himself on you.

THE NIGHTMARE

In ancient times the nightmare [French *cauchemar*] was an entity that encompassed quite a few different realities: the witch's double that would come and sit oppressively on one's chest; a spirit (*mar*) that weighed down or trampled (the verb *caucher*) its victim; or even a dead person.[19] It is closely linked to the *appesart* but has one important distinction: it attacks sleepers, whereas the *appesart* hurls itself on travelers and passersby. It strangles men and sits on them with a crushing weight—like the cobbler who killed himself in 1591, whom we will discuss in the next section—and even sucks the blood of its victims.[20] From the end of the sixteenth century to the eighteenth century, the vampire conducted itself like a nightmare, smothering its victims, but this detail was lost in the flood of information concerning the vampire's behavior and violent acts, to the point that it was no longer perceptible. The collusion of the vampire and the nightmare, already pointed out by Ernest Jones, is well illustrated by the Czech *mora* and the German *Alp*, two nightmarish entities that suck blood.

THE STRANGLER

On January 7, 1732, three surgeons of the Austrian army handed in a report about a harmful revenant. Stanoicka, the wife of a *hajduk* [infantryman] of Medvegia in Serbia, died at the age of twenty after a three-day illness. Eighteen days after her burial, the doctors J. Fluchinger, J. H. Siegel, and J. F. Baumgarten performed an autopsy and found that her face was rosy red like that of the living, and that she had been strangled by Milloe, the hajduk's son. When they opened this grave, the village community discovered that the deceased was a vampire. The body was resting in an inch of blood, although there was no mention of any bloodsucking activity. The strangler is therefore already a vampire even if it does not always bear that name.

Karl Ferdinand von Schertz gives a good example of the strangler in his *Magia posthuma*.[21] A woman died after being given all the sacraments and returned four days after her burial:

> The village inhabitants saw a specter that sometimes appeared in the form of a dog, sometimes that of a man, not one person but several, and caused them much suffering, clutching their necks and compressing their stomachs until they suffocated; it even broke their bodies and reduced them to states of such extreme weakness so that they were visibly pale, thin, and exhausted. The specter even attacked animals, and cows were found struck down and half dead.

Von Schertz does not tell us how they got rid of this scourge that lasted several months, but he discusses whether people have the right to incinerate such revenants.

It will be noted that the stranglers often behave like the *appesarts*, as shown by the following anecdote:[22] In 1591, a cobbler slit his throat in a famous Silesian town. We don't know why he committed suicide. His wife said he succumbed to an attack. After six weeks, a rumor began circulating through the town: A ghost resembling the cobbler was attacking and crushing sleepers. At the same time another rumor was spreading claiming that the cobbler had committed suicide. The dead man's relatives opposed the exhumation of his body, but the dead man was hurling himself on the beds of sleepers where he would grab hold of them and try to strangle them. He weighed on them so heavily that pale marks could be seen on their bodies the next morning and even the marks made by fingers for hours after. Finally, the terrified populace had the body, which had been in the ground from September 22, 1591, to April 18, 1592, exhumed. The corpse was found completely intact and quite swollen, and the skin of its feet had sloughed off, but new skin had grown back. After a period of twenty-four hours, the corpse was reburied, but in an ignominious spot. However, the dead man continued his evil acts until his head, limbs, feet, and hands were cut off on May 7, 1592. He was cut open from the back and his heart was found intact, similar to that of a calf that had just been slaughtered. A pyre was made, and his body incinerated. Watch was kept over the ashes during the night so that people could not make off with any for criminal use. The next day they were placed in a sack that was hurled into the river. After that, the community was peaceful.

THE CHEWER

What most impressed our ancestors was the sound of moving jawbones coming out of graves,[23] as if the person buried there was eating something. Calmet gives us one of his era's definitions of the vampire, which confirms its kinship or even total identification with the chewer: "It is said that the vampire experiences a kind of hunger that causes him to eat the grave cloths he finds around him."[24] Latin texts call this type of dead person *manducator*, a neutral term that merely describes the phenomenon, while the Germans use the aforementioned term *Nachzehrer*. There is an immense corpus of relevant material that spans the period between the fifteenth and nineteenth centuries, so I will only give a few representative examples. We should note from the outset that the chewer is a passive vampire, for it never leaves its sepulcher and causes death from a distance through sympathetic magic. As it eats or swallows its shroud, its close relatives die.

The first account comes from the inquisitors Jacob Sprenger and Heinrich Kramer, charged with the repression of sorcery in the Rhineland during the last quarter of the fifteenth century:

Here is an illustration. One of us inquisitors found that a certain town had been almost depopulated through the dying of the inhabitants, and the rumor was widespread that a certain buried woman was swallowing bit by bit the shroud in which she had been buried and that the plague could not stop unless she ate the shroud entirely and swallowed it into her stomach. After there was a consultation about it, the chief judge and the burgermaster dug up the tomb and discovered that almost half the shroud had gone down into her stomach through her mouth and throat. Agitated at the sight of this, the mayor drew his sword, and after cutting off her head, he threw it out of the grave. With this, the plague suddenly stopped.[25]

It is this particular type of dead person that provided the principal foundation for the vampire myth in later centuries. The phenomenon was almost always connected to an epidemic of the plague, although we do not know exactly what the latter term designated.

The inquisitors' account is perhaps not the first concerning this kind of event. In fact, according to the *Czech Chronicle* (1541) of Václav Hájek of Libočany, parts of which are based on the one that Abbot Jan Neplach of Opatovice wrote around 1370, a case concerning a chewer took place in the Polish village of Lewin Klodzki. While Neplach does not refer to a "witch," Hájek makes that leap:

In 1345 the following events took place in the Bohemian town of Lewin. A potter named Duchacz lived there, married to a certain Bradka, who was a witch. When this became known, the priests urged her to turn away from such spell-casting, and although she publicly abstained she continued practicing her craft in secret. One day when she summoned all her spirits, she died brutally, and no one could say if she had died a natural death or if the spirits had slain her. For this reason, no one wished to bury her among pious Christians and she was interred at a crossroads. It was quite quickly observed that she had come back, often joining the shepherds in the fields by taking the shape of various animals. She terrified the shepherds and chased off their flocks, which caused them many problems. Sometimes she appeared as she did when still alive. Next, she began often coming back to the same town and surrounding villages, entering houses in various guises, speaking to the folk, while terrifying some and slaying a large number. The neighbors in town and the peasants of the surrounding area allied and had her body exhumed by a local skilled in such matters. When this was done, all those present could see that she had eaten half of the veil that had been over her head, and it was pulled from her throat all covered with blood. An oak stake was planted in her chest and blood gushed from her body at once, like from a steer, which surprised more than one person, and she was then reburied. A short time later, she began appearing again and much more often than before, terrifying and killing people, then trampling those she slew. For this reason, she was once more disinterred by the same man who then found that she had removed the stake that had been planted in her body and was holding it in her hands. Because of this, she was removed from the grave and burned along with her stake, then the ashes were tossed back into the tomb, which was then resealed. For several days a whirlwind was seen where she had been cremated.[26]

This is a complete report and the individual named Bradka shows herself as wicked and tenacious. She was predestined to play this nefarious role because she was a witch, and her death was quite suspicious. Not only did she eat her veil, which is the distinctive characteristic of the chewer, but she left her grave to wander wherever she liked. Bradka combined in herself features that are well confirmed among common revenants: the ability to change shape, the ability to speak, and a deadly nature. Finally, the account clearly tells us that stake planted in the chest is not a panacea and that only incineration could put an end to Bradka's wanderings.

Martin Luther himself was confronted by the problem posed by these beliefs in the evil dead. His *Table Talk* reports that "A pastor named Georg Rörer wrote from Wittenberg that a woman living in the village died and, now that she was buried, she was devouring herself in her grave, the reason for which all the inhabitants of this village were facing sudden death. He asked Luther to give him advice," but Luther replied that it was simply a diabolical trick and salt would put an end to it.[27]

The text shows that the chewer phenomenon had spread almost everywhere in the German-speaking regions. Luther's explanation is that of the medieval Church: everything is a diabolical illusion. According to the Annals of the city of Wroclaw (Breslau) in Silesia, large-scale mortality occurred in 1517:

> From Saint Michael's Day to Saint Andrew's Day around two thousand people died. During this time a shepherd was buried in his clothes in Gross-Mochbar; he devoured them and while doing so made the noise of a sow's jaws. He was therefore disinterred and his blood-covered clothes were found in his mouth; his head was then lopped off with a spade and his body thrown out of the cemetery, at which point the deaths stopped occurring.[28]

This presentation of chewers would be incomplete if I omitted a particularly illuminating text, as it allows us to establish with certainty the role that these unusual dead played in the crafting of the vampire myth. The Jesuit priest Gabriel Rzaczynski confirms the existence of the belief in Poland during the years 1710–1720, which shows that the chewer epidemic was spreading in Europe, thus providing favorable conditions for the development of what would become a veritable myth. He tells us the following:

> I have often heard said by trustworthy witnesses that not only have corpses been found that had long remained uncorrupted, supple, and rosy, but also those whose eyes, tongue, and mouth moved, who had swallowed the shroud in which they had been inhumed and had even devoured parts of their own bodies. In the meantime, news of a similar corpse had spread, one that has emerged from its tumulus and wandered by crossroads and in front of houses, showing itself sometimes to this person and sometimes to that, and attacking more than one to strangle them. If it involves a man's corpse, the folk call it *upier*; if that of a woman, *upierzyca*.[29]

Rzaczynski goes on to say that these corpses were beheaded to prevent such attacks. Starting in 1730, the authorities began to grow alarmed at these repeated exhumations and profanations of graves, which were accompanied by "barbaric acts." In that year the authorities of Alsfeld in Hesse forbade the disinterment and impaling of a dead person heard chewing in his or her grave. In Austria-Hungary, a writ of Maria Theresa in 1755 provided the legal basis for the prohibition of posthumous executions.

REVENANTS IN ANIMAL FORM

We have already encountered several examples of the dead who change shape. Many animal forms are possibilities in this respect. In the *Chronicle of the City of Frankenstein*, Martin Koblitz notes for the year 1605:

> In spring and summer . . . a monster has shown itself, often in the shape of a dog, sometimes that of a calf, during the night before and after midnight. This animal is called the Rothe or the Drothe. It has persecuted people terribly on the road that leads from Baumgarten to Frankenberg, near the woods. It has shown itself to travelers in full daylight and rolled upon them like a large club; it has violently tormented passersby to such an extent none dare take this road; when the miller, Martin Riedeln, took it, he was molested so savagely that he died from it three days later.[30]

We should not be led astray by the word "monster" in this account. It means "revenant" and is equivalent to the Latin *monstrum*, which has the same meaning. In German folk beliefs, this revenant that leaps upon passersby is also called *Aufhocker* (*appesart*). Its weight is almost intolerable and the person who was attacked remains for some time in a greatly weakened state that can be fatal. The evil dead creature of Neustadt assumes various shapes, but this is nothing new, since from around 1210 we have encountered shape-shifting revenants. Accounts of them increase even more in the fifteenth century. The most common animal shapes at this time were the dog, the goat, the crow, and the horse. Other forms it could take included a ball of fire or even a burning bush. Each region of Europe developed its own representations. In more recent periods, it was claimed that these revenants could also appear in the form of fleas, lice, and ticks—parasites that are, of course, vampiric.

This presentation offers an overview of the combination of elements; a revenant eventually accumulates several of these features. It remains to be seen whether we can find the same phenomena in every country of Europe. The typology that I have established with the survey of the examples provided here encourages a positive response, but one that should nevertheless be made more precise.

6

Grimoires and
Their Ancestors

The word "grimoire" is a corruption of *grammaria*, "grammar," which originally designated a book written in Latin but quickly took on the meaning of a "magic book." These books were given the name of *Physica*, which has survived to the present day in rural areas in the form *Phigica*. Whereas the Romance languages have preserved "grimoire" (*grimorio*), the Scandinavian languages use words like the Danish terms *svartbog* ("black book"), *sorte bog* ("book of spells"), and *lackerbog/laagebog* ("book of remedies," cf. Old English *læceboc*), and magic is designated by words like Swedish *frikonst* and *läkekonst* ("healing art"). In the German-speaking regions we have two names, *Zauberbuch* ("book of magic") and *Höllenzwang* (lit. "coercion of hell"), and black magic is called *Schwarzkunst* (nigromancy, lit. "black art") as opposed to white magic, *Zauber*. In Britain the terms "book of spells" and "magic book" are sometimes replaced by "grimoire."

A grimoire comes across as a mélange, a compilation of various recipes for curing certain ills as well as for summoning or invoking demons, obtaining some kind of advantage, crafting talismans and amulets, and casting or lifting spells, and so on. Some manuscripts indicate they contain extremely ancient knowledge that the sages, foreseeing the Flood, had had carved on marble in Hebron.

The old grimoires came in essentially two formats: the first is a duodecimo, twenty to fifty pages long,* a truly pocket-sized book intended for consultation when the sorcerer or mage was called by whoever required his services. The other was the folio, a monumental work for consultation and study at home. The latter type of grimoire was never printed and is only found in the form of manuscripts in library collections, and it is much richer than the sort that might be found at *bouquinistes* (secondhand book stalls) and antiquarian shops, which is more akin the Ghent grimoire described below.

During the demolition of a chimney at a mental asylum dating from the sixteenth century in Ghent, Belgium, a chest was found walled into the chimney containing the manuscript and the tools of an astrological sorcerer.[1] Although heavily damaged by humidity, which has left the upper part illegible, we have a good overview of its composition. In it we find the astral magic treatises by Thebit ben Corat; the Pseudo-Ptolemy; Behencatri,[2] who may be identical to the Behencacin cited by Trithemius;[3] Bayelis; Geber of Seville, in other words, Jabir ibn Hayyan, a twelfth-century Arab astronomer; and Hermes, as well as some anonymous works.

For a long period of time, the language used in grimoires was Latin—a disjointed Latin with faulty spelling and syntax. They are written in abbreviations in an error-ridden macaronic Latin, studded with summarily Latinized words from the vernacular and a mix of very corrupted Greek and Hebrew words that are often incomprehensible.

Magical treatises were in existence long before the appearance of the word "grimoire"—a generic term that designated highly diverse works whose one commonality is that they belong to a kind of writing anathematized by the Church. To get a better overview, we may consult the work of several medieval authors who, from the thirteenth to sixteenth century, drew up lists of these manuals. The nomenclatures

---

*The *Vinjeboka*, which was discovered in 1796 beneath the floorboards of the choir in the Vinje church and dates from the end of the fifteenth century, has twenty-seven pages. The *Lacker Bog* found in 1732 has forty-eight pages, containing thirty-five magic spells and uses a method of coding in which vowels are replaced by the numbers 1 to 5 and the consonants l, m, n, and r by those of 6 to 9.

are interesting because they clearly show that the essential portion of Western magic comes from the Mediterranean world, which was itself subject to even more remote influences, for example from India. Thanks to these authors, some of whom have been identified by name, we can see that there is a channel leading from ancient Babylon to Greece, then to the Arab world, and finally to western Europe.

The first author is Albert the Great (Albertus Magnus, 1206–1280), assuming the *Speculum astronomie* is truly his. This treatise mentions "abominable images attributable to Toz the Greek, Germath of Babylon, Belenus, and Hermes," images of planets that can be invoked by addressing, for example, the fifty-four angels that accompany the moon in its course. He speaks of *caracteres*—in other words, magic signs and symbols—and the "detestable names found in the books of Solomon on the four rings and on the nine candle holders, or in his *Almandal.*"[4] Raziel's *Book of Institutions*[5] is full of necromantic figures, in Albert's opinion. Toz the Greek left a treatise, *The Four Stations of the Worship of Venus*, a *Book of the Four Mirrors* for the same planet, and another with images of it. Hermes and Solomon have the lion's share of works attributed to them.

Roger Bacon (1214–1294), renowned for his *Mirror of Alchemy* and his treatise *Concerning the Marvelous Power of Art and of Nature and Concerning the Nullity of Magic*, works that earned him the reputation of a magician over the course of time, wrote the following in a letter to William of Paris:

> One must be exceedingly cautious in this matter; for man errs easily, and many err on both sides, some denying the whole business altogether and some inclining to the magical interpretation.
>
> In short, there are many books which are devoted exclusively to magic, to symbols and characters, incantations, conjurations, sacrifices, and to things of that sort. Such for instance are the books *de Officiis spirituum, de Morte animae*, the book *de Arte notoria*, and an infinite number of others . . .[6]

We should note that the second of these works has another title, *The Storehouse of Necromancy*, and that in 1679, Jean-Baptiste Thiers mentions *The Notory Art* in the following way: through this art, the demon:

> promises the acquisition of certain sciences through infusion and with no pain, provided one has practiced certain fasts, recited certain prayers, and revered certain figures, and observed certain ridiculous ceremonies. Those who make a profession of this art, swear that Solomon is its author, and it was by this means that he acquired in one night that great wisdom that made him so famous throughout the world. And that he held its precepts and method in a small book that he used as a guide and model.[7]

The most exhaustive of all the authors is Johannes Trithemius (1462–1516), the famous abbot of Sponheim, a Benedictine abbey located between Bad Kreuznach and Mainz.[8] In his *Antipalus maleficorum* (I, 3) he gives a list of eighty-nine titles, which represents a real library for his day. In it we find the authors cited by Albert the Great, and others such as Zeherit the Chaldean, Zahel, Messala, Roger Bacon (!), and Pietro d'Abano.

Trithemius proffers his opinion on these books, all of which he had read. *The Book of Four Kings* is "pestiferous" and "they dare attribute these cursed works to Saint Cyprian."* Trithemius cites the *Storehouse of Spirits* by a certain Rupertus, which is also known as the *Treatise on Necromancy* as it instructs how to command the obedience of evil spirits. *The Elucidation of Necromancy* by Pietro d'Abano (thirteenth century) "contains nothing healthy." *The Secret of the Philosophers* "is perfidious and stupid." The *Bond of the Spirits* "contains numerous orisons and conjurations with which vain men and lost souls can bind themselves together." The *Book of Illusions*, by a certain Thomas, "promises great wonders and deals with rings crafted in accordance with the thirty-eight houses of the moon, their *caracteres*, and their vain suffumigations." Balenitz wrote a *Book on the Inclusion of Spirits into the Rings of the Seven Planets*.

---

*Saint Cyprian has remained famous, fittingly, for having been a great magician before repenting. In the Scandinavian countries, his name is attached to the most popular grimoire.

So, it is upon similar treatises that the printed grimoires, which began to be produced in the sixteenth century, were based. Since that time, they have demonstrated a remarkable vitality. The Catholic Church put these books on the Index, and censorship forced their printers to endow them with fanciful records of their place and date of publication. The oldest to be mentioned is the *Thesaurus necromantiae* (Storehouse of Necromancy) of Honorius from before 1376. Countless grimoires have been printed since the sixteenth century, among which we should mention the *Enchiridion Leonis papae serenissimo imperator Carolo Magno* (Rome, 1525), which the pope gave to Charlemagne; the *Grimoire of Pope Honorius, with a collection of the rarest secrets*, printed in Rome in 1670; the *Grimorium verum, or the Veritable Clavicules of Solomon*, allegedly published in Memphis by Alibek the Egyptian in 1517; the *De magia Veterum* (On the Magic of the Ancients) of Arbatel published in Basel in 1575; and the *Clavis maioris sapientiæ* of Artefius (Paris, 1609).

Also belonging to the category of grimoires are the collections of medical prescriptions intended for the man in the street. With an appeal to the supernatural, pagan or Christian, these chapbooks offer some odd recipes. Here I should mention *Le Bastiment des Receptes* (The Structure of Recipes), printed in Lyon by Jacques Bouchet in 1544, then by Jacques Lion in 1693, in Troyes in 1699, and reprinted until 1824 (!) as *Le Médecin des Pauvres* (The Medicine of the Paupers; Troyes, 1722).

In France today, the most famous grimoires are *Le Grand Albert* and *Le Petit Albert* (The Great Albert and The Little Albert), which can still be found in esoteric bookstores. The first known edition of the *Petit Albert*, whose true title is *Le Secret des secrets de nature* (The Secret of the Secrets of Nature), dates from 1706. It was republished by Jacques-Antoine Garnier (Troyes) in 1723, and has appeared in many other popular editions.[9] Repeatedly reissued over a good many years, some grimoires have been reassembled in collections with piquant names, such as *Le Véritable Dragon Rouge* (The True Red Dragon), which is a treatise on the art of commanding infernal, aerial, and terrestrial spirits; summoning the dead; reading the heavenly bodies; discovering treasures and mineral sources; and so on. We also have *La Poule Noire* (The Black Hen), an edition augmented by the "Secrets of the Queen Cleopatra, secrets for turning invisible, secrets of Artephius," and so forth, with the mark of Astaroth on the 1522 edition.

In 1854, Victor Joly noted that these works were called "evil books" and that many families owned a "black book" (*neur lîve*), a collection of beneficial and malefic spells and incantations.[10]

In the German-speaking world, the *Romanus-Büchlein* (Little Book of the Roma), the *Geistlicher Schild* (Spiritual Shield), and *The Sixth and Seventh Books of Moses* enjoyed great popularity; the latter of these is still in print!* A Freiburg publishing house publishes the *Egyptische Geheimnisse* (*Egyptian Secrets*), falsely attributed to Albertus Magnus, and the *Geheimnisvoller Heldenschatz* (Mysterious Treasure of Heroes) by Staricius.[11] In both France and Germany, *The Lesser Key of Solomon* (*Clavicula Salomonis*) is still one of the primary references.

Some grimoires achieved a truly legendary status, such as the *Agrippa*, which took its name from the renowned Heinrich Cornelius Agrippa von Nettesheim.† It was claimed that this book could not be disposed of either by fire or water, or by selling it—in which case the owner would die in a state of damnation.‡ The book was allegedly the size of a man and had to be chained to the main beam of the house, and it had to be beaten if one wished to master it. The *Agrippa* is an enormous book. Its pages are red and its letters black. For it to be effective,

---

*It was even translated into French and is available in some Parisian bookstores.

†In Tréguier, it is called *Agrippa*; in the Châteaulin region, *Egremont*, for which there is a variant, *Egromus*; in the area around Quimper, *Ar Vif*; in the Upper Léon region, *An Negromans*; in Plouescat, the *Livre de l'igromancerie*.

‡Loizo-goz, of Penvénan, had one that inconvenienced him greatly and he offered it to a farmer of Plouguiel, who accepted it. One night, a dreadful din could be heard over the entire countryside. It was Loizo-goz taking his *Agrippa* to Plouguiel by pulling it by its chain, but no sooner than he had returned home, the book was already back in its old place. He made a large fire with gorse and hurled it in, but the flames drew away from it. Loizo-goz climbed into a boat, headed into the open sea, and cast it in the ocean weighed down with large stones, but returning home he could hear the noise of a chain on pebbles. It was the *Agrippa* that had managed to rid itself of the large stones. Loizo-goz saw it pass him by, as quick as an arrow. Once home, he found it hanging from its customary beam. Its cover and pages were dry. It seemed that the water of the sea had not even touched them. (Told by Baptiste Geffroy, known as Javré, Penvénan, 1886; see Anatole Le Braz, *La Légende de la mort chez les Bretons armoricains* [Paris: Champion, 1923], 373–74.)

the devil has to have signed it. Whenever one doesn't need to consult it, it should be kept closed with a large padlock. It is a dangerous book, so it should never be left within arm's reach. It is hung by means of a chain from the strongest beam in the room reserved for its use. The name of this book varies from country to country. The book is alive and it resents being consulted. One must be stronger than the book to wrest its secrets from it. As long as it remains untamed, one will just see red. The black letters only appear when coerced by a thrashing, such as one might give to an unruly horse. It is obligatory to fight with it, and the struggle can sometimes last for hours. One comes away from this fight soaked in sweat. The man who owns an *Agrippa* cannot rid himself of it without the aid of a priest and then only when he is at death's door.

Initially, only priests owned *Agrippas*. Each had his own personal copy. On the day after their ordination, they would wake up to find it on their night table with no clue where it came from or who brought it there. During the French Revolution, many ecclesiastics left the country. Several of their *Agrippas* fell into the hands of simple clerics who had learned how to use it during their time at school. They passed it down to their descendants. This explains the presence on certain farms of the "strange book."

The clergy know how many *Agrippas* were misappropriated, and which laypeople own copies. An old rector of Penvénan said:

> In my parish there are two *Agrippas* in places where they should not be. The priest pretends not to know as long as the owner is alive but when death approaches and he is called to his bedside, after he has heard the dying man's confession, he speaks to him like this: "Jean or Pierre, or Jacques, you have a very heavy weight to carry beyond the grave if you do not get rid of it in this world." The dying man asks in surprise: "What is this weight?" "It's the weight of the *Agrippa* in your house," the priest replies; "Give it to me—otherwise, having such a burden to drag behind you will ensure that you never reach heaven."*

---

*[As with the tale in the preceding note, this report comes from Le Braz (*La Légende de la mort*, 370–71). —*Ed.*]

It is rare that the dying man does not immediately surrender the *Agrippa*, but then the grimoire tries to make mischief. It caused quite a ruckus throughout the whole farm, the priest exorcised it until it remained quiet. He then ordered the people there to go fetch a piece of gorse wood. He lit it on fire himself and reduced the book to ashes that he collected and put in a small bag, which he then tied around the dying man's neck while saying: "May this be light for you!"

It is difficult for a rector to sleep easily so long as a single copy of the *Agrippa* remains in the hands of anyone other than him or his vicars. One need not be a priest to know when someone outside of the profession owns an Agrippa, as he emanates an odor of sulfur and smoke. Thus, people will steer clear of him. And then he doesn't walk like everyone else: he hesitates with every step he takes, for fear of trampling a soul. The *Agrippa* always returns home.

The *Agrippa* contains the names of all the devils and teaches how to summon them. It is possible to know by means of it if a dead person is damned. The priest who just performed a burial will immediately consult his *Agrippa*. When their names are called, all the demons come running. To dismiss them, the priest again calls them by name, but starting with the name of the one who arrived last, and so on.[12]

Other grimoires are on sale today, but they simply disseminate previously published material, often in a corrupted form. Their authors, who often hide behind exotic pseudonyms, imbue them with an air of mystery by stating that one grimoire was found chained up in the cellar of a monastery; another is written in blood or phosphorescent ink, sealed with the imprint of a skull; while yet another is presented in the form of a pocket bible with a black cover and red pages.[13]

In short, grimoires were the product of scholarly milieus and, from the Middle Ages to the Renaissance, they are part of an intellectual tradition that carried on via the stream of medical and astronomical manuscripts. They gradually spread to other domains, notably through the intermediation of priests who were the real sorcerers of the countryside. Norway provides us with a good example, where these churchmen are named:

Petter Dass (1646–1707), priest of Alstahaug
Christian Holst (1743–1824), priest of Røyken (Buskerud)
Ephraim Jaeger (1737–1799), priest of Bygland (Aust-Agder)
Hermann Ruge (1704–1764), priest of Vestre Slidre in Valdres
Søren Schive (1623–1705), priest of Bjelland (Vest-Agder)
Jon Mogenssøn Skanke (ca. 1570–1618), schoolmaster and priest of
  Innvik (Sogn og Fjordane)
Peder Strøm (1682–1741), priest of Borgund (Møre og Romsdal)

The *Galdrakver* (Little Book of Magic),[14] a seventeenth-century
Icelandic grimoire, belonged to Hannes Finsson (1739–1796), bishop of
Skálholt, but we don't know whom he obtained it from. In 1919, it was
said that Nils Dorph in Norway owned grimoires "like all the priests"
and that he had studied at the Academy of Wittenberg.

A TYPOLOGY OF MEDIEVAL GRIMOIRES

If we try to classify grimoires according to their primary content, we
will see that they can be sorted diachronically into several categories
within four major traditions, while recognizing that there are overlaps,
especially in the use of seals and images (amulets and talismans).

An intellectual tradition, it is (for the medieval West) the oldest
confirmed and consists of several facets.

Astral Magic/Hermeticism

These grimoires appeared during the second half of the twelfth century
and are essentially translated in Spain from Arabic,[15] while some are
based on Greek works. They deal with the crafting of planetary, zodia-
cal, and decanic talismans and amulets, make large use of *karacteres*
(magical signs, planetary seals), coded symbols of the stars and constella-
tions. The Arab authors attributed them to Hermes, Ptolemy, Aristotle,
or Plato. These grimoires tell us which orisons should be made to the
celestial bodies, which suffumigations to make, and what ingredients to
use (perfumes, metals, stones, inks, and so on). Here are some samples
from this family:

Hermes: *Liber Lune, Liber Solis, Liber Mercurii, Liber Veneris, Liber Martis, Liber Iovis, Liber Saturni*; *De septem annulis septem planetarum*; *Liber praestigiorum*; *De compositione imaginum* (also attributed to Belinus); *Liber Hermetis* (discusses the houses of the moon, the Zodiac, and their angels); *Liber secretorum Hermetis Hispani* (a collection of conjurations and *karacteres*); *Liber de imaginibus et annulis VII planetarum* (also attributed to Messala).

(Pseudo-) Ptolemy:[16] *De imaginibus*; *De componendis imaginibus, annulis et sigillis XII signorum*; *De compositione atque virtutie imaginum*; *Liber Hermetis* (by Alburabeth ben Feliz), with forty-five decanic talismans.

(Pseudo-) Aristotle: *Secretum secretorum* (translated by Adelard of Bath, and later by John of Seville); *Liber de mansionibus lune* (cited by Petrus de Prussia in the *Vita beati Alberti*, chap. 9).

(Pseudo-) Plato: *Liber vacce* or *Liber aneguemis/Liber neumich*, in other words, *Kitâb al-nawâmis*, translated in Spain during the eleventh century.

Enoch: *De XV stellis, XV herbis.*

Toz the Greek (Thoos, Tuz): *De stationibus ad cultum Veneris*; *De XII annulis Veneris*; *Liber Veneris*; *De quatuor speculis.*

Thetel (Techel, Cethel, etc.): *Liber sigillorum.*

Belenus (Beleemus, Balaminus, Balenus, Balemiz, Belemich, identified as Balinas,[17] in other words, Apollonius of Tyana): *De sigillis planetarum.*

Thebit ben Corah (Thabit ibn Qurra, 835–900): *De tribus imaginibus magicis.*[18]

al-Kindi: *De radiis* (ca. 1240), in which the powers held by each *karacter* are listed.

Other Books:

Picatrix (seventeen complete Latin manuscripts), which Trithemius described as a "volume consisting of four books . . . , it was translated from Arabic into Latin in 1256. In it many superstitious, frivolous, and diabolical things are found. . . . It provides orisons for the spirits of the planets, as well as images and rings with numerous and varied *caracteres.*" In 1456, Johannes Hartlieb, the personal physician of Albert III, duke of Bavaria, reviewed this book as follows: "There is another very noteworthy book in the necromantic art, which begins this way: 'To the glory of God and the very glorious Virgin Mary.' It bears the title *Picatrix* and is the most complete book I have ever seen on this art. . . . It is larger than three psalters."[19] The book enjoyed great success, as is evident from its translation into French,[20] Italian, English, German, and Hebrew.

Libro de astromagia (1279–1280),[21] which includes books dealing with each planet and their talismans, inspired by Utarid.

Libro de las formas et de las ymágines, by a certain Abolays (Abu Ali al-Khayyat),[22] translated in Spain between 1277 and 1279.

Book of the Twelve Signs of the Zodiac, mistakenly attributed to Arnaldus de Villa Nova (ca. 1240–1311),[23] indicating that the seals should be carved on metal and accompanied by magical phrases and prayers.

Black Magic

Rupertus Lombardus: *Thesaurus spirituum,* a treatise of necromancy making it possible to summon spirits outside the magical circle of the spell-caster.

Liber praestigiorum, by a certain Thomas, perhaps the same book that is attributed to Hermes.

Flos Forum, a collection of demon conjurations, including numerous names and *karacteres.*

Elucidarium necromantiae, attributed to Pietro d'Abano (died 1315–1316).

Vinculus spirituum, whose orisons and conjurations compel the obedience of demons.

Liber fantasmatum (cited by Roger Bacon).

Liber de morte anime (attributed to Aristotle).

Liber de sortilegiis, by Algabor Arabis and the work with the same title by Albedach.

Liber Simoni mago, which "promises much, thanks to demons."

Liber officiorum, in which the demons are divided up into four emperors, four kings, and so on.

Liber Razielis, which discusses spirits; the *Puritatum dei,* which contains the unknown names, orisons, and *karacteres*; and the *Liber institutionis* or *Liber de virtutibus et secretis*, all by Raziel.

Ars calulatoria Virgilii, which permits, through calculation, to discover the names and *karacteres* of the good and evil spirits.

Thesaurus necromantiae of Honorius, before 1376.

Medical Magic

Lacnunga, a collection medical texts and prayers, in Old English and Latin, compiled in England at the end of the tenth or the beginning of the eleventh century.[24]

Læceboc, a ninth-century Old English recipe collection.[25]

Costa ben Luka (Qusta ibn Luqa, active in Baghdad at the end of the ninth century), *De physicis ligaturis*, translated by Constantine the African (died ca. 1087).

Jabir ibn Hayyan, *Flos naturarum*, extracts of which can be found in the *Picatrix*, II, xii, 39–57; III, xi, 58–112; IV, vii, 23.

Tractatus ad faciendum sigila et ymagines contra infirmitates diversas, attributed to the physician Bernard de Gordon, active in Montpellier at the turn of the fifteenth and sixteenth centuries. The author seems to have been inspired by the *Surot Shneim Asar Mazalot*.

De sigillis, retitled as *De XII imaginibus Hermetis*, attributed to Arnaldus de Villa Nova, which depicts twelve seals with therapeutic and protective properties.

Liber Kyrannidorum,[26] a total of four books in which we learn how to craft remedies and talismans. It has a less pronounced astrological orientation than the *Picatrix*, and its magic is alphabetical. According to the theory of emanation (cf. *De radiis* by al-Kindi), the potency of the planets is dispersed through nature. By regrouping the elements received by nature, in other words, by rejoining the links of a chain of sympathy, hence a planet, a stone, a plant, a bird, a quadruped, and a fish, we can in fact obtain an effect that greatly surpasses the natural properties of each element. The choice of elements is based on the first letter of each one. The oldest example is a Latin manuscript dated 1272. It is a translation made in Constantinople in 1169 from a lost Greek original.

Solomonic Magic (Ars notoria)

This magic aims at compelling spirits. It can be called religious as it essentially consists of orisons to God, angels, demons, and so forth, in order to obtain protection, powers, and knowledge—and exorcisms. It was greatly influenced by Jewish and Christian writings.

Solomon: *De quatuor annulis*; *De novem candariis*; *De tribus figuriis spirituum*; *De sigillis ad demoniacos*; *De figura Almandal*; *Clavicula Salomonis.*
Liber sacratus, also called *Liber iuratus.*
Schemhamphoras.
Verus jesuitarum libellus.
Enchiridion Leonis papae.
Ars notoria.

POST-MEDIEVAL GRIMOIRES

The post-medieval grimoires are heteroclite collections of magical recipes borrowed from the scholarly tradition concerning apotropaic and medical magic, and from the Solomonic traditions reduced to their simplest expression with regard to orisons, names, and cabalistic words that are found in charms and prescriptions.

While astral magic was predominant in the texts of the sixteenth to seventeenth century, it was gradually reduced to only a few of its elements—for example, the signature of the planets—surviving in other treatises such as the *Herpentil*. If folk tradition as such remains hard to discern before the fifteenth century, it particularly flourished in the seventeenth century judging by the surviving evidence. Folk grimoires then took the form of household booklets owned by the head of the family—booklets that gathered together everything useful for the protection of humans, animals, and property, such as crops. Included with these were several black-magic recipes and some frankly marvelous spells that made it possible to open locks, make oneself invisible, walk without getting tired, and more, including some that relate to sex and love, and games of chance (dice, cards). Depending on the grimoire's origin, spells for good hunting or fishing could also be found there.[27] The Norwegian *Book of Kvam* (*Kvamsbok*), which dates back to the very beginning of the nineteenth century, is representative of the black books (*svartbøker*) of these countries.[28] Victor Joly estimates the number of volumes that circulated among the French and Belgian agrarian communities around the year 1850 to be 400,000. He cites a list of works from which I have extracted the following titles (given here in translation):[29]

> *Admirable Secrets of Albert the Great*; *The Red Dragon* followed by *The Black Pullet*; *Enchiridion Leonis papae*; *Grimoire of Pope Honorius*; *Red Magic*, magical works of Heinrich Cornelius Agrippa followed by *Secret of the Queen of the Hairy Flies*; *Wondrous Secrets of the Little Albert*; *Treasure of the Old Man of the Pyramids*; *Veritable Keys of Solomon* followed by the Great Cabala known as the *Green Butterfly*; *True Black Magic, Complete Manual of Demonmania, Phylacteries or Preservatives against Illness, Curses, and Enchantments*; *Grand Etteila*.

Several grimoires essentially relate to a religious mindset like the *Enchiridion* of Pope Leo and the later and abridged versions of the *Lesser Keys of Solomon*.

In Scandinavia, the *Cyprianus*, first printed in Stavanger in 1699, was the most famous and widespread grimoire. We have manuscript and print versions, often bearing fanciful dates (1509, 1529, 1699, 1719, 1793). The surviving examples inform us that they were owned by priests, schoolmasters,* and even bailiffs. Legends abound about it, the most recurrent saying that it was discovered in 1722 at Academy of Wittenberg, headquarters for the exploits of Doctor Faust. It then disappeared before being rediscovered in Copenhagen in a marble chest. Its pages were alleged to be black, covered with red or white writing. It is impossible to get rid of it for it always returns to its place, nor can it be burned. According to the accounts collected by Reidar Thoralf

---

*For example, O. Aasmunstad; T. R. Risdal; F. C. Mülertz; S. E. M. Driesen; and John Flood, chaplain in Hedrum.

Christiansen, a person can obtain a grimoire and by going to a cross-roads for three Thursdays in a row, he or she can summon the devil. A proper grimoire (*rigtig svartebok*) must be written in one's own blood and have a piece of the devil's claw attached to it.[30]

The internal characteristics of folk grimoires can be summed up as follows: the complicated rituals and suffumigations are no longer present; the Christian element is markedly stressed. Jesus, the saints, apostles, the three magi, and so on have replaced the old gods and spirits—a phenomenon that was already well underway in the Middle Ages. Here are two examples found in fourteenth-century grimoires from England:

1. Sint medicyna mei pia crux et passio Christi,
Vulnera quinque dei sint medicyna mei!
Virginis et lacrime mihi sint medicamina trina,
Her mihi portanti succurrant febricitanti! Amen
† A † g. † l. † a. † Jaspar † Melchysar † Baptizar †

2. Boro berto briore † Vulnera quinque dei sint medicina mei †
Tahebal †† ghether ††† guthman †††††

Pious medals replaced the talismans and amulets,
such as this Saint Benedict medal.

The number of named demons has diminished, mythological figures have disappeared, and it is rare to encounter a spell like this:

> To be good at fighting, take a human bone and draw this sign on your shoe or on the toe of the limb you fight with, while saying, facing northwest: I send the devil into the chest and bones of my adversary, in the name of Thor and Odin.[31]

7

Big Bells and Little Bells

Beliefs and Magic

Bells—made from iron or bronze, alone or in a carillon, and in all sizes, ranging from chimes and hand bells to ship's bells, campanas, and church bells—played an important role in the life of medieval people, and they were everywhere. They provided rhythm to the day; accompanied feast days, births, deaths, and weddings; and sounded the alarm. They warned of the coming of lepers. And let us not forget the small bells, for example the one rung by the bell ringer who marched at the head of the funeral procession, or that of the town crier who traveled the streets on the night before All Souls Day, Christmas, and other holidays, requesting people to pray for the dead.

Casting bells and taking care of them (the work of a bell founder) or ringing them (the task of the bell ringer) was considered an honorable trade, as shown by more than twenty-five surnames formed from the word "bell" (*Glocke*) in German-speaking regions.* There was a Nuremburg poet of the early Middle Ages named Georg Glockendon. In 1350, the bell tower was an ecclesiastical building; in early medieval England, people swore more on a bell than on the Gospels, but often did both together (*swear tō bōcan and bellum*), and breaking this oath could

---

*Such as Glockshuber, Glockner, Glockenmeyer, Glöckel (-le, -len, -ler, -ner), and Danzglock.

Left to right: church bell with iconography, Venice (ca. 1411); bell from Saleby, Västergötland, with runic inscription (1228); molds of the four evangelists for bell casting (England, 15th century)

incur a terrible punishment.[1] Courts and assemblies were convoked *per pulsationem campanae* (at the striking of the bell).[2] There is a legend concerning Charlemagne recorded in Jans der Enikel's *Weltchronik* (World Chronicle; circa 1277), the *Reimchronik* (Rhymed Chronicle), and other texts. He had a bell placed on a column outside his palace. Whoever came seeking justice could ring it. One day a snake rang it because a toad had moved into its nest. Charlemagne condemned the toad to be burned. In gratitude, the snake brought the sovereign a precious stone the next day.[3]

The bell served as a measuring unit for hops and as a heraldic charge. In the technical realm we have the diving bell, and in botany we have *campunula*, the bellflower. They appear in fairy stories (Tinkerbell) and we also find them in comic operas like Robert Planquette's *Les cloches de Corneville* (The Bells of Corneville; libretto by Louis Clairville and Charles Gabet) from 1877. In short, bells are omnipresent and not only to be found in steeples, belfries, and campaniles. Bells and clocks have even become the symbol of certain cities like Bordeaux with its Big Bell; when the king sought to punish the city, he had its bells and clocks removed. Everyone knows London's Big Ben, but we also have the Tsar

Bell of the Kremlin in Moscow, which was too large (445,166 lb.) for Napoleon to carry away; the large bell of Rouen; and Philadelphia's Liberty Bell in the United States. Bells are used in complicated mechanisms like the one at Strasbourg Cathedral, and in somewhat simpler automatons like the Jacquemart (bellstriker) of Dijon and the Clock Tower in Venice.

Bells are also present in place names. In Holland, for example, we can find Klokmoerke, Klokkeheide, and Klokkeven.[4] In France, twenty-seven place names are coined from *cloche* (bell) and appear in 216 different locales. For example, there is Clochemont, Clocheville, Clocheret, Malacloche, Montecloche, and so on. But none of these is as famous as *Clochemerle*, the title of a novel by Gabriel Chevallier (1956)!

In literature, bells are featured in proverbs such as the one we find in the work of Hugo von Trimberg (born ca. 1230, died after 1313): "A cracked bell has a poor sound."[5] Or in a more recent proverbial turn of phrase: "The infirmities of old age are the stroke of a bell that brings us death." Bells are featured in comparisons. In his *Sermons*, Jacobus de Voragine compares Christ, the apostles, the Virgin, and all creatures to bells.[6] The priest Conrad wrote the following in his exegesis of the architecture of a cathedral: "The windows and the bells represent all the spiritual teachers who with good words and good works present the good teaching to Christians."[7]

The *Eckenlied* (Song of Ecke, circa 1250), indicates that the giant of the title, Ecke, wears a helmet that reverberates like a bell when he is running in the forest and hits a branch with it.[8]

In Heinrich Wittenwiler's *Der Ring* (The Ring), the poet draws up a portrait of the hideous Mätzli Rüenrenzumph: "She was so humpbacked that a bell could be cast on her back."[9]

More recently, Pierre-Jean Bérenger wrote in the eighteenth century: "Power is a bell that prevents those who set it in motion from hearing any other sound."[10]

The importance of bells is evident from language, sayings, and expressions. In France the "gentlemen of the bell" (*gentilshommes de la cloche*) are the descendants of mayors and aldermen; "ringing the big bell" (*sonner la grosse cloche*) means implementing major measures, and "casting the bell" (*fondre la cloche*) means to make an extreme resolution. When someone is surprised to see that something one was counting on is missing, they are described as "sheepish as a bell caster" (*penaud comme un fondeur de cloches*). When someone cannot do two things at the same time, people used to say: "You can't ring the bells and go in the procession" (*On ne peut sonner les cloches et aller à la procession*). "Not being subject to the tolling of the bell" (*N'être pas sujet auch coup de cloche*) means being free to do what you like with your time, and "to move at the wooden bell" (*déménager à la cloche de bois*) still means to leave without paying.

In the German-speaking countries, "the bell is cast" (*die Glocke ist gegossen*) means "it's decided"; "to ring the big bell" (*die große Glocke läuten*) is to knock at the right door; "to run to the big bell" (*an die große Glocke laufen*) means to make a matter public; and "to hang something from the big bell" (*Etwas an die große Glocke hängen*) means to divulge something. The expression, "he is going to go into the bell" (*er kommt bald in die Glocke*) means "he is close to death" and "the bell has already been cast over me" (*die Glocke ist schon über mir gegossen*) means "I am already practically condemned." "It's unheard of" is expressed as "Now the bell strikes thirteen" (*jetzt schlägt die Glocke aber dreizehn*), and to describe "an ongoing case" people say "the bells are still ringing" (*die Glocken tönen noch*). Corresponding to the French expression "*ils n'être jamais sorti de son trou*,"* the German says, "*er hat nie eine andere Glocke gehört als die seines Dorfes*" ("He never heard any other bell than that of his village"). One amusing thing: "to speak salaciously" is expressed by the phrase "*mit der Sauglocke läuten*" (to ring the sow's bell). In England, to be superior in something was "to bear away the bell" or even "to ring the bell."

German historical texts of the Middle Ages, chronicles, and even police regulations mention six different bells:

---

*[The French idiom here, which literally means "he's never left his hole," would correspond to the English expression "he's been living under a rock." —*Ed.*]

Die mortglocke, which is rung during uprisings;

Die sturmglocke, the tocsin;

Die viurglocke, which is rung in the event of a fire;

Die torglocke, which announces the opening and closing of the city gates;

Die wahteglocke, the watchman's bell;

Die winglocke, which is sounded to announce the closing of taverns.

The texts give us a nice compound word, *glockenspîse*, "bell food," as a term used for metal. The use of bells in churches appears to have been introduced by Saint Paulinus of Nola (died 431). They started being hung in churches in the seventh century. Religious texts mention bells sounding the hours such as *die mettînglocke*, which rang for matins, and the death knell (*die todtenglocke*). Guillaume Durand, bishop of Mende, who died in 1296, devoted a chapter to bells in his *Rationale divinorum officiorum* (Rationale for the Divine Offices)[11] that tells us every religious building—church, chapel, monastery— had a bell with an easily identifiable peal, which allowed the lost traveler or wandering knight to know where they could find a place to stay.[12] In convents, there were five kinds of bells: that of the refractory was the *squilla*; the cloister, *cymbalum*; the choir, *nola*; the steeple, *campana*; and the towers, *signum*. But this sound also signified a wondrous place: "Near Carlisle in the British Isles," Gervase of Tilbury tells us, there is a forest in the midst of which is a valley surrounded by mountains: "There, every day at a certain time, a melodious carillon of bells can be heard."[13] In Ulrich von Zatzikhoven's *Lanzelet* (v. 3902–8), there is a small brazen cymbal (*êrin zimbel*) also called a *glockelîn* (small bell); when struck three times with a hammer it summons Iwaret to combat.[14]

We should note in passing that writs of parliament during the Ancien Régime restricted the use of bells and that they were forbidden by the Revolution. The Consulate restored to churches the right to ring their bells.

Bells are treated like individual persons; they are baptized and given names—the first mention of this is a bell crafted on orders of Folcuin, the abbot of Lobbes (965–990)—that had a godmother and godfather according to the Sarum Pontifical, and even a voice.[15] The most widespread bell names in Germanic regions are Anna, Susanne, and Margarethe. They can act on their own accord. Jacobus de Voragine states that all the bells of Rome rang spontaneously during the election of Pope Gregory, and Stephen of Bourbon maintains that others did the same at the death of Simon de Crépy.[16] In the traditional ballad "Sir Hugh," a bell is mentioned that rings with the intervention of human hands:

> And a' the bells o merry Lincoln
> Without men's hands were rung,
> And a' the books o merry Lincoln
> Were read without man's tongue,
> And neer was such a burial
> Sin Adam's days begun.

Long after the Middle Ages it was still thought that if a bell made a mournful sound or continued to vibrate long after it was rung, it was announcing a death. The independence of bells is made clearly visible in a belief from the Côtes-du-Nord region of France: they refused to ring for the baptism of an illegitimate child.[17] Numerous accounts tell us that bells resisted being moved by jumping into water[18] or burying themselves in the ground. Once sold, they returned. In Spain, the bell of Villela rings by itself on the eve of a misfortune.[19] It is therefore believed that they announce the future.

The personification of bells has earned us some beautiful verses by Marceline Desbordes Valmore (1786–1859):

> *La cloche pleure le jour*
> *Qui va mourir sur l'église,*
> *Et cette pleureuse assise*
> *Qu'a-t-elle à pleurer? . . . L'amour . . .*

The bell weeps for the day
About to die over the church
And this seated weeper
What does she have to cry about? . . . Love . . .

And let us not overlook these beautiful legends like the one about the bells traveling to Rome for Holy Week, from which they brought back gifts for children, or the one of the bells of drowned cities that still ring to remind us of their existence,[20] or even come back to the surface like the one of the Black Lake in Oisans.[21] Sometimes a buried bell is found by an animal.[22]

Ethnographical studies tell us that the water in which the clapper of a bell has been dipped heals a stich in the side; that writing your name on a bell cures hoarseness and earaches;* and that scrapings of their metal are good for epilepsy and fever. The magical nature of bells also extends to the bell rope, which relieves fevers; if small pieces of a bell rope are cut off and put in a little pouch hung around the neck of an infant, it helps teething; and finally, with a piece of this rope, a person can draw to themselves milk from all the cows within earshot of the bell.[23] Touching the rope at certain churches will make sterile women fertile. The sound of bells heals toothaches and, during the sixteenth century, helped in giving birth.[24] But it prevents witches from leaving for their Sabbat, and if they are already in flight, it halts them;[25] consequently, they call bells "barking dogs" (*bellende Hunde*).[26]

Moreover, the dozens of legends collected over the last two centuries tell of the departure of dwarfs and other subterranean dwellers (*underjordiske*), because they couldn't stand the sound of bells.[27] Near Hagelsberga, in the Westmanland region of central Sweden, stands a hill topped by a stone surrounded by a low wall and called the Chamber of the Nisse (*Tomtenissens stuga*). A spirit could be seen there at night, but it always vanished at daybreak when it heard the bells of Odensvi.

---

*It is believed that if someone writes his name on the large bell of Degerloch, near Stuttgart, when he is hoarse or has lost his voice, he will be healed (*Württembergisches Jahrbuch* 1857, vol. II, 151).

I would like to mention something curious: in the English ballads "The Cruel Mother" and "The Maid and the Palmer," a woman has murdered a child. Her punishment is transformation into the bell or clock of a church for seven years.[28]

In courtly romances, small bells worn as clothing accessories or affixed to harnesses or furniture were symbols of luxury, wealth, and nobility. In Wirnt von Gravenberg's *Wigalois*,[29] the masterfully carved and worked little gold bells on the equipage of Lady Elamie, chimed and tinkled (v. 9200). The horses' reins were richly adorned with little golden tinkling bells (v. 10650), and an artfully woven mosquito net is covered with little gold bells hanging from its lower edge (v. 10389). This is how the *Saga of Thidrek of Bern* (*Þiðrikssaga af Bern*) describes King Erminrek's banner:

> the outer part of the standard was made of silk as black as ravens, the next part was silk as bright as gold, and the third part was green as grass. Around the outside of the standard were seventy tinkling bells of gold. This standard rings and rattles so that it can be heard all around the army whenever it is carried by a rider or blown by the wind.[30]

We should note in passing that the *iele*, cruel Romanian fairies sometimes confused for good fairies, instead called the Beautiful Ones as a euphemism, wear bells on their feet, and the mouth of the *balaur* [Romanian dragon] is full of bells that whistle joyfully like a young man in love.[31]

Sometimes the little bell is given a particular shape and power. Allusions to the magic nature of bells are easily found in twelfth-century literature. In the *Garel vom blühenden Tal* (Garel of the Flowering Valley, v. 2456ff.) by Der Pleier, a little bell in the shape of a dog caused one to forget, and in the anonymous *Lohengrin*, the bell of the Grail Castle in Inde began ringing nonstop when Elsa of Brabant needed a champion. An inscription would then appear on the Grail defining Lohengrin's mission to some extent.[32]

Now that we have set the scene, let us look at the magical nature of bells, which is already sketched out in what I have described above. Let us start with the baptism of bells, which involves Christian magic and was gradually imposed. A capitulary of 789 (*Duplex legationis edictum*) mentions these baptisms along with a restriction: One must not baptize bells—in this context I think little bells are intended—so that they remain effective against storms.[33] We will revisit this subject. The cast iron of the bell and the steeple were blessed, we are told by the pontifical of Reims (twelfth century).[34]

The baptism, or rather blessing, of the bells was mentioned for the first time by Alcuin in the eighth century,[35] but the custom was established under John XIII, pope from 965–972. The eleventh-century *Liber Ordinum* provides us with their baptism ritual[36] and provides one major piece of information: the priest exorcised the bell that had just been installed. Here is the relevant passage:

> I conjure you, harmful and impure spirit, by the invincible name of the divine majesty, so that you acknowledge the desire of our humility and that, by the power of Christ, whom we call, you shall flee at once from this metal to which God the Creator has given sound and strength (*atque fugias ab hoc metallo cui Deus condens indidit sonum et fortitudinem*). . . . You know full well that you did not contribute to the creation, so be gone from it with your flaws so that it may be purified and serve to honor He who by His word made what has form.[37]

In his *De antiquis Ecclesia ritibus*,[38] the Benedictine historian Edmond Martène (1654–1739) mentions another spell close to this one:

> Make it so, Lord, that the sound of this bell serves to summon the faithful to the bosom of our mother the Holy Church, to repel far away the snares of our enemy, the ravages of hail and the impetuousness of storms; may your powerful hand impose silence on the hurricanes; may they tremble at the sound of this bell and flee at the sight of this cross carved on its edges.

In ancient times, the foundry, just like the forge, possessed a magical nature because mastery of the art of fire as well as the transformation of minerals into metals required, in the eyes of the common folk, supernatural powers, as Mircea Eliade has shown so well in *The Forge and the Crucible* (1956).

Baptism was therefore used to purify the metal, to replace a pagan magic with a Christian magic, to expel the demon from the metal so it could be used religiously as an instrument of worship and a means of defense against evil spirits. You should realize that metal, like salt and water, is a creature in the mind of liturgists, and that all these creatures have to be exorcised before Christian use. The baptism of bells was indispensable. Numerous legends tell how the devil sought to destroy or steal unbaptized bells because he knew he had no power over them afterward. If he did not manage to carry one off, it remained burning hot for a long time.[39]

Once it was Christianized, the metal transformed into the voice of the Church, if not that of God himself. The following inscription can be read on a bell from the church of Roskilde, Denmark: "My voice is a terror for all evil spirits." In Tulle, France, a bell was named Sauvo-Tero ["Land Saver"] "because it was believed that it protected the harvest from storms."[40] An inscription on a bell of Frickenhausen, Germany, and of Beuren read: "Anna, Suzanna, you have to hang for eternity / you have to remain there for eternity / you have to repel the [bad] weather."[41] In Ariège (France), Mariouno, the name of the bell of the church of Larcat, protected young people from the *Dragas*, malevolent fairies who would otherwise have torn them to pieces,[42] and it is common knowledge that the dwarf people vanished from our lands because they could not tolerate the sound of bells.

We can now comprehend why bells were rung when storms threatened. Meteors were believed to be sent by demons, and later by the *malefici* known by the name of *tempestarii*.*[43] Pope John IX is said to have ordered bells rung as a defense against lightning around the

---

*[Latin *malefici*, "witches"; *tempestarii*, "magicians who could control the weather by magic." —*Ed.*]

year 900. The sacristan of Hirsau had the bells rung against storms, and also used relics and crosses to dispel them, we are informed by the *Constititiones Hirsaugiensis* (II, 35). Rhineland inquisitors noted that they were rung:

> against the wind. There are two purposes for this. The first is that the demons should withdraw from their acts of sorcery as if on account of trumpets consecrated to God, and the second is that the congregation should be roused to invoke God against the storms.[44]

In Romania, the *Solomonari* or the *Pietrari* send hail, and they can be avoided by ringing the bells of the church.*[45]

For the bell to become an actual phylactery, however, it must have symbols and/or words carved upon it.[46]

> Engrave these words on a bell:
> *Dum turbor procul cedant ignis grando tonitrua*
> *Fulgor fames pestis gladius Satan et homo malignus*
> When you ring the bell, it will send fleeing the storm, lightning, plague, Satan, and evil men.[47]

So, it should come as no surprise to find legends recounting the devil's attack on a bell. There is a bell in Muhr, in the Salzburg region, whose edge is heavily nicked and on the inside there is the mark of the sorcerer who tried to bring it down on the orders of the Evil One.[48]

Small bells had the same properties as the large ones. Saint Sadalberga of Laon, who died in 655, is reputed to have been given a small bell by a doe for her daughter, Anstrudis, who feared storms. When a possessed person being exorcised began gesticulating wilding, little blessed bells would be rung (*cum spiritus in motu, tunc pulsetur campanella*).[49]

---

*[In Romanian folklore, the *Solomonari* are sorcerers and the *Pietrari* are their magical opponents. —*Ed.*]

We should also note that a bell may be used to summon spirits. The Pseudo-Paracelsus tell us:

> I cannot pass over in silence about a very great miracle I saw performed in Spain by a certain Necromancer. He had a bell that weighed no more than two pounds. Every time he struck it, he could conjure and summon specters, visions of numerous varied Spirits. When it pleased him, he inscribed several words and symbols on the inner surface of a bell, then started shaking and ringing it, and he would make appear a Spirit of the shape and appearance he wished. With the sound of this same bell, he could draw numerous other apparitions of Spirits near or send them away. . . . Every time, however, that he did a new work, he changed the words and symbols.[50]

It is worth knowing that some bells of medieval religious buildings have the particular feature of fragments of prayer being carved on them. On an Irish hand bell dating from the ninth century, we can read: "A prayer for Chumascah, son of Aillil." A bell from the Moissac Abbey bears the inscription *Salve Regina mater misericordiae* accompanied by medallions, a cross, and a human head surrounded by entwined wings. On a bell in the fifteenth-century Rakkestad church (Norway) we find the spell *help* ⊕ *got* ⊕ *vnde* ⊕ *maria* ⊕ *bi* ⌠ s.

They were also engraved with cryptograms, such as in Ammerbach and Salzbach, and various symbols, the examination of which clearly reveals Christian magic. The church bell in the Hvaler Church near Oslo bears a runic inscription. Ronald Grambo informs me that often the inscriptions are written backward and that they are magic spells and conjurations. These inscriptions are quite difficult to understand because they are often abbreviated and filled with grammatical and spelling mistakes.

In a study that has unfortunately gone unnoticed, which was published in an anthology in 1979, Kurt Köster examined bells with alphabet inscriptions and drew up a catalog of them.[51]

There we find the four evangelists, portrayed as the masters of meteors; the three Magi; Christ; angels; saints; and *nomina sacra*—their presence should come as no surprise if we recall the words of the Gospel according to Luke (10:17):

> "Lord, even the demons are subject to us in your name," pilgrimage seals, and, quite frequently, α ω/Ω. But the most striking thing is that these alphabets are mixed with these figures in medallions and whose presence is a priori inexplicable if we don't know that they are magical in the sense that they hold all the names of all the deities.[52]

It so happens that these alphabets on bells are complete or partial (the chapel of Örlishausen Castle in Thurgau, circa 1300), entirely repeated (Saint Laurentius Church of Flachslanden, Bavaria), or partial and in disorder (Battenfeld Church in Hesse), sometimes using both lower- and uppercase letters, read from left or right or right to left (Setzingen, near Ulm in Baden-Württemburg), the letters are upside down (Biel, canton of Bern, fourteenth century), or else are seen as if in a mirror (Älgarås, Sweden), or are set in parallel to the edge of the clock (Saint Martin's Church in Landshut in Lower Bavaria). All these games have nothing to do with Christianity and they are comparable to the signs and spells that were inscribed on apples, hosts, or bread that were given to the ill to eat in the context of magical healing.[53]

When the alphabet appears normally on the bell, it has nothing to do with magic. But when all the variants cited above begin, it is safe to say that we are leaving the Christian context and going back to ancient pagan practices. In some cases, when the alphabets are out of order and partial, it is valid to wonder if each letter might represent the first letter of a word with the whole thing forming a magic spell. We have examples of this with ANANIZAPTA, for example, the spell for a magical antidote. The mixing of Latin, Greek, and even Hebrew letters in alphabets, such as on the Diemeringen bell (thirteenth century, Lower Rhine) exactly matches what we find, for example, in English charms from before the year 1000.

The magical intent is clear when we find the initials for the phrase *Christus vincit, Christus regnat, Christus imperat* on the bell of

Fontenailles, which dates from 1202 and is now housed in the Bayeux Museum. Its inscription reads XV XR XIPAT and the date MCCII.[54] This phrase taken from Holy Scripture is one of the most frequent in Christian magic, the others being:

Christus natus est † *Christus passus est* † *Christus crucifixus est* †
Christus lancea perforatus est[55]
Vincit leo de tribu Juda, radix Dauit, alleluia*

In short, the carvings on bells present a blend of pagan and Christian elements. They aim at giving a bell the maximum supernatural power with a shameless combination of religion and magic, which I would again like to remind you is exactly the same as in charms and benedictions. Obviously, the individual is not entirely confident in the total efficacy of crosses, saint medallions, and so on, so the fruit of secular beliefs is added.

The aforementioned Pseudo-Paracelsus left us detailed instructions for making a magical bell. They are as follows:

Begin by noting the day of your birth and what day of the week it is. If the Sun is in Leo, Taurus, or Virgo, in ascension on the IVth, Vth, VIth, VIIth, XIIth, XIVth, XVth day, and the Moon in Aries, Gemini, or Libra, and Saturn in Virgo, Taurus, or Sagittarius, in the east up to the thirteenth or fourteenth degree, and when Leo and the Dragon's Head are in a good aspect.

Whatever week it is, take two ounces of gold, one of silver, half of mercury, half of lead, half of tin, and six of iron. But take one additional ounce of the metal corresponding to your birthday. When all has been alloyed, have a bell cast. Once it is ready, inscribe

---

*In the Vinje (Norway) grimoire, the phrase reads: † *De viro vicit leo* † *de tribis Judae* (72, nr. 14). The phrase—which can be found in the *Geraldus falconarius* (thirteenth century); in a hippiatry treatise for protection against worms; in a medical book from Liège; and on the Stavelot triptych—even offers protection against thunder! Cf. B. Van den Abeele, "De arend bezweren. Magie in de middeleeuwse valkerijtraktaten," *Madoc: Tijdschrift over de Middeleeuwen* 11 (1997), 66–75.

ADONAY on the clapper, and THETRA GRAMMATON on the lip, and JHESU on the crown. Next, keep it clean and in a clean place, for it is a secret of God, and you need no more names than these three.

When you wish to use this bell, prepare yourself ten days before, be chaste, eat and drink in moderation, pray, and put on new clothes. You must begin on a Friday. At night, make your way to a secret room so that no one knows where you are. Set up a table, cover it with a beautiful green or yellow tablecloth, and cover all the chairs around it. Place three fine wax candles in a candle holder made of silver or copper, prepare an ink as I have indicated to you, and, with a new goose feather that you must sharpen with a new knife, write the names of the spirits or planets you desire, each in its color. When that is done, say: "O God Tetragrammaton, Adonay, I, X, your creature, I pray that you compel these spirits to reveal to me what I wish. Next, ring the bell while saying: "Spirit X! I wish you to appear immediately." Repeat this three times and ring the bell three times. They will appear. Command them to sit while calling each by name, and say: "I, X, I ask you—and you shall name the spirit of the planet—that you tell me and write what I desire."

Here the bell draws its power from the configuration of the sky, the alloy of the metals that reflect it, and the names inscribed upon it. The quotation, a veritable convocation of spirits, follows a precise ritual and takes place in a secret place. All the details are important. This is why the color of the ink varies with each spirit: the *Picatrix* (II, 3)[56] devotes a long examination to this and says, for example, one must take red ink for the spirit of Mars and green for that of Jupiter. By the virtues of the names of God, the spirits will have to submit to the commands of the spell-caster.

We also see quite clearly how close magic is to religion: What is different in the crafting process here from that of Christian bells that also carry inscriptions? Only the submission to an astral configuration and the alloy. In fact, gold is ruled by the Sun, fire by Mars, and lead by Saturn.

To sum up: once blessed or engraved with cabalistic signs, the bell becomes an actual protective amulet. On the large bell of the church of St. Moritz, cast in 1419, it can be read: "My name is Saint Anne of God's cell, / May God protect all that I ring over / May God guard the beautiful valley / As far as my peal can be heard." An instrument of music, communication, and signaling by its types of peals, bells have been given a particular place in the daily life of the people of yesterday, and even if the literature of the Middle Ages only offers a glimpse, a long-term study reveals all their importance.

8
Weyland the Smith

The first literary account of Weyland the Smith comes to us from England in a text copied down in the *Exeter Book*, which was compiled around the years 950–1000. This anonymous poem written in Old English was given the title of "Deor" or "Deor's Lament," because in it a poet of this name depicts the sufferings of various heroes before bemoaning his own fate.[1] Based on the language of the poem, scholars believe it was composed between the sixth and seventh centuries. It attests to the spread of the legend and includes elements that are absent from the Norse texts that refer to Weyland. The first two stanzas concern Welund,* the prisoner of Nithad:

> Welund knew misfortune near the serpents
> Stubborn earl, he endured woe;
> He had as his companions sorrow and longing
> And winter-cold misery; he often knew anguish
> After Nithad set him in restraints,
> Supple sinew-bonds on the better man.
> Everything passes over, this shall too.

---

*[In this essay, Weyland's name appears in different forms, depending on the tradition and language cited: Old English Welund~Weland, Old Norse Völundr, continental Velent or Willant, and so forth. The name is also often rendered in modern English works as Wayland. —*Ed.*]

> Beadohild had for her dead brothers
> less pain than for herself,
> When she fully realized
> That she was pregnant. She could
> Never understand what happened.
> Everything passes over, this shall too.

While it is easy to recognize the main plot lines of the story—King Nithad had the imprisoned Welund crippled who got his revenge by raping Beadohild—the first hemistich of the first verse (*Welund him be wurman*) poses a serious problem because it lends itself to different interpretations,[2] some four in all: "near the" or "snake's home," would first be metaphors designating Nithad and his men. Or "snake" (*wurm*) could be metaphorical name for a sword or ring;[3] this would then refer to a lost part of the legend. Robert E. Kaske believes that the serpent is a symbol of Welund's works.[4] He bases his conjecture on *Virginal*, a Middle High German romance about the adventures of Dietrich von Bern, written in southern Germany in the thirteenth century, in which the son of a blacksmith, named Witege, has a hammer, tongs, and a serpent:[5]

> Witege had a splendid banner
> On a field of sinople
> Stood out an amazing emblem,
> That of the valiant knight:
> A hammer and tongs of red gold,
> A serpent of light silver
> As his father Weyland had commanded him.

In *Biterolf und Dietleib*, a heroic legend written between 1254 and 1260 in southern Germany,[6] Witege carries a shield adorned with a serpent. Another Middle High German text, the *Eckenlied*,[7] is particularly interesting because its versions include a variant. Version E7, whose manuscript dates from 1472, recounts the meeting of Dietrich von Bern (Theodoric of Verona) and the giant Ecke, who seeks this confrontation. Ecke says (stanza 80, 1–3):

Gallant knight, agree to fight;
The helmet I wear
It's Willant who forged it as it should be.

But version E2 says: "Dwarfs embellished it" (stanza 78). If we juxtapose the two texts, it establishes a connection between Weyland and the dwarfs. The former would have forged the helmet and the latter would have engraved it.

To support his theory, Kaske points out that stanza 17 of the Norse *Völundarkviða* offers the verse: "His eyes shined like those of a serpent" when speaking of Weyland. We may simply envisage the idea of Weyland's captivity in a pit of snakes like the one suggested by the figures carved on the two stone crosses of Parish Church in Leeds, which date from the tenth century and complement one another.[8]

Figures carved on the two stone crosses of the
Parish Church (Leeds) dating from the tenth century

The sculptures depict a man holding a woman by her hair and the bottom of her dress; a long ribbon girds the woman's waist and seems to bind the hands and legs of the man. At the latter's feet are tools, apparently those of a smith.

A series of bracteates discovered in eastern Frisia, Denmark, and Great Britain not only offer images that could be interpreted as referring to the legend of Weyland, but one of them, the Schweinsdorf bracteate, even includes the runic inscription WELADU, in other words Weyland(u). Heinrich Beck, who has closely studied these numismatic pieces of evidence, sees Weyland in a snake pit on this solidus. On the Harlingen solidus, he sees a flying female figure turning toward our blacksmith,* and on that of Fakse (Denmark) there is the crippled Weyland before Nithad, holding a pike while a creature holding a ring seems to be flying. On the solidus there remains a fragment of a runic inscripton, *undR*, which can be completed as Völundr.[9]

What is so interesting on these bracteates is the depiction of the arms of the central figure. They terminate with or in tools. The strange position of the legs might well depict a crippling injury and brings to mind the legs of the Titans whose limbs were snakes, or else a people "whose legs were like straps" (*loripedes*) that Pliny the Elder mentions in his *Natural History* (VII, 25). The connection to snakes must be quite ancient and Indo-European, as traces of it can be found, for example, in the legend of Erichthonius, the son of Hephaestus and the Earth.[10] The smith attempted to rape Athena who wiped his semen off her thigh with a scrap of wool, which she tossed on the ground. A child was then born. She hid the child in a small box, which she gave to the daughters of King Cecrops. They opened it and saw the child guarded by two serpents. According to some accounts, the child's body even terminated in a snake's tail. According to others, once the basket had been opened, it escaped in the form of a serpent.

Scholars have long noticed a strange kinship between the story of Weyland with a Gascon folktale collected by Jean-François Bladé (1827–1900).[11] To my knowledge this is the sole tale in the European

---

*This also bears a runic inscription, HADA, "combat" or "imprisonment."

Schweinsdorf solidus; Harlingen solidus

Fakse bracteate; Danish bracteate
(National Museum of Denmark, Copenhagen)

corpus of stories featuring blacksmiths that introduces an adventure in which a snake and captivity play a role. Although Kaske's interpretation has been rejected by many researchers of the past century, it should not be entirely dismissed when seeking to shed light on the background of a mythical creature. It would be helpful to spend a moment considering the folktale of the "Golden Feet." A blacksmith once lived in Pont-de-Pile, a hamlet located on the banks of the Gers in the commune of Lectoure. He was a pagan living by himself and he had no equal when it came to working iron, gold, and silver, with only a wolf for his assistant. A poor young man offered to be his apprentice. The smith tested his abilities before hiring him on the condition he never stay or eat with him. The young man hid and watched what the smith did once his day's work was done. He saw him go outside and imitate the chirping of a cricket while saying: "Come, my daughter. Come, Queen of Vipers," and she appeared. She told her father that she had seen the apprentice and had fallen in love with him.

The young man followed the smith, who next headed toward the Gers River, where he stripped naked, hid his clothes in a hollow willow tree, tore off his skin from head to toe, and appeared as a large otter. He jumped into the water, ate a fish, and came back out. He then put on his human skin and clothes and returned home.

The apprentice saw the same thing the next two nights.

When he was sent to the home of the Marquis de Fimarcon to forge jewelry, the daughter of the marquis fell in love with him. He fell in love with her and made her a wondrous necklace that he dipped in his blood, then dipped it again while the young woman stripped off her clothing to the waist. He then put the necklace on her, and it became one with her flesh.

The blacksmith visited the young man and gave him a drug to put him to sleep. He then bound and gagged him and offered him his daughter's hand. The young man refused, at which point the blacksmith took a saw and cut off his apprentice's feet and burned them in the forge. He then repeated his question and received the same rejection. He took the young man to a high tower that had no roofing, and no doors or windows. He called for his daughter and they both called upon the eagles of the mountain to carry the apprentice to the top of the tower.

In secret, the apprentice forged a steel ax, an iron belt equipped with three hooks, a pair of golden feet, and a pair of large wings—tasks that took him seven years to complete. Every evening the viper queen visited the young man through a hole and offered herself to him. Once he had finished forging the objects above, he agreed to be her husband.

When the viper queen entered through the hole in the wall, he crushed her with his golden foot, cut off her head, and attached her head and body to the hooks on his belt. He then adjusted his wings and flew to a spot where he could see the hamlet and the Gers River. Once the blacksmith had gone to the river and hidden his skin in a hollow willow tree, the apprentice stole it and hooked it to his belt. He then hailed the smith: "Your daughter is in two pieces, head and body, hanging from my iron belt. . . . Go look for your skin in the hollow willow. . . . I have it hanging on my iron belt. And now you are an otter forever."

The conclusion of the tale is not relevant to our study.

The kinship of this story with the Parish Church cross sculptures clearly emerges if we slightly revise the interpretation this cross has been given. What looks like a snake pit corresponds to the imprisonment of the apprentice in a high tower with no roof, windows, or doors, and which is only accessible from above. This is the reverse image of the pit. Eagles carried the young man into it. The snake or snakes in fact give concrete expression to the smith's daughter. As she appears on the cross, she seems to be subjected to poor treatment from the man beneath her. He is holding her by her hair and her dress.

The Gascony tale offers other parallels with the Weyland story. Like him, the apprentice is a skilled blacksmith; like him, he is maimed; like him, he forged wings; and like him, he has a woman as his adversary. Let me explain this last point. In the Norse tale from the Eddas, the antagonist is not so much Níðuðr as his wife, who figures out Völundr's intentions and orders her husband to have his tendons cut (stanza 17). Their daughter Böðvildr appears as the victim of the master smith's revenge.

The tale also provides some troubling details that give a glimpse of a Germanic source or remembrances of Germanic elements that would trace back to the Migration Era. When the smith of Pont-de-Pile strips off his clothes and his skin, he is an otter. It so happens that in the Eddas, the dwarf Andvari, guardian of the giant Hreiðmar's treasure, has the habit of bathing beneath a waterfall in the form of an otter, and the Germanic dwarfs are blacksmiths. The apprentice is also a magician who forges a magic necklace that has the ability to indicate his fate—it will turn red if misfortune befalls him—at the same time that it has the ability to put the young woman in a state of suspended death.

Would the Weyland legend therefore have been known in France and left a memory strong enough for it to appear in a false tale? The last point of the research on the subject inspires a positive answer. The legend came into [what is now] France with the Franks at the time of the great invasions; the philological analysis of the ancient testimonies reveals a significant West Germanic substratum. A further piece of evidence is how widespread the name of Weyland in Romanized forms became starting in the Carolingian Era. As a proper name, Galen and its variants appeared in Dijon in 877, Cluny in 878, in Metz in 952, and in Savigny (a diocese of Lyon) and Paris in the middle of the tenth century. In Italy, we find a Guelantus in Farfa between 802 and 815, and a Walandus in Pavia in 996. We should also note place names such as Walantiegum near Evreux, around 872–875, and a Guallancort, near Corbeil, between 992 and 1012.

If the proper name shows that Weyland was sufficiently known and esteemed for this name to be given to both clerics and laypeople, literature provides us with additional evidence. Out of 203 French and Provençal chansons de geste, our smith appears in twenty-two. Weyland/Galen emerges, for example, in *The Romance of Thebes* (v. 1676ff.), written in southwest France around 1150–1155; and in *The Song of Antioch* and *The Song of Jerusalem*, composed in Picardy in 1125–1150 and 1180–1200, respectively.

In Spain, *La Gran conquista de ultramar* written between 1295 and 1312, mentions "Galen, maestro do Toledo." French historiography doesn't overlook Galen: Ademar of Chabannes mentions a sword made by "Walandus faber" in his *Chronicle* (from the first half of the eleventh century).

Weyland traveled from Romania into Germania while keeping his main mythical features, then from there into Norway, where he was transformed into a hero and his story was interpolated with some foreign elements.

England's position as a relay into Ireland is demonstrated by the place names and proper names as well as by fragmentary texts. Our blacksmith turns up in the *Poetic Edda* and in the *Karlamagnus Saga* (I, 40), which calls him "the smith of England." Like the legend of Siegfried, the legend of Weyland is certainly Frankish in origin, which makes it easier to better comprehend its survival in the form of a *topos* of the epic.

The early diffusion of the legend of Weyland into England[12] is attested by the Franks Casket, or Auzon Casket, named after the place in the Upper Loire where this small chest with whale-ivory plates was found in the nineteenth century.[13] It measures 9 inches long by 7.5 inches wide, and it is 5.125 inches high. Created in northern England, most likely Northumbria in the seventh century, it is akin to two other small chests, one also in ivory that must have belonged to Gandersheim Abbey, while the other is preserved in the church of Mortain in Normandy. The Auzon Casket has inscriptions in Old English in runic writing and in Latin.[14] Several identifiable scenes are carved on it: one is the conquest of Jerusalem by Titus; a second shows the she-wolf nursing Remus and Romulus; a third, the adoration of the three Magi; and an episode from the Weyland legend.

The runic inscription consists of a short poem about the whale.

It is necessary to examine the scene depicted in detail, which is found on the left side of the casket's front panel (see image below).

On the left, we see Weyland. The position of his right leg suggests a handicap. He is holding tongs in his hand that are clasping a skull and with the other hand he is extending a cup to a woman accompanied by another female figure. She appears to be giving him a ring. The second woman is carrying a small bag or purse out of which pokes the top of a flask. We can see a decapitated body at the smith's feet. On the right, behind the two women, a man is catching birds. There is—as is frequently the case in the Middle Ages, where images are used to tell

Franks Casket front panel with scenes showing:
(left) the legend of Weyland; (right) the adoration of the Magi

stories—a juxtaposition of different scenes, since the image is dynamic: the murder of the children; the use of their bones; the visit of Böðvildr/Beaduhild, who is going to drink a soporific potion; and the capture of the birds, most likely by Egill, in order to give Völundr/Welund the means to fly. Because this "bird catcher" is so small, some have thought it was one of Níðuðr's/Nithud's children, whereas the figure's size is due to a technical restriction, leaving space for the keyhole of the chest.

The whole thing is therefore an interpretation, as only the *Thidrek's Saga* speaks of the manufacture of wings, but is it just as possible that the very elliptical *Völundarkviða* omitted this, which would assume that everyone knew what's what and tends to prove that this manufacture belongs to the oldest strata of the legend.

The runic poem poses immense difficulties of interpretation and Ralph Elliott suggests the following translation, with which scholars seem to be in agreement: "The flood lifted up the fish on to the cliff-bank; / the whale became sad, where he swam on the shingle."[15] These verses are understandable because the plates are made of whale ivory, but on the left the term *hronæsban* can be read vertically. Some interpret the term as meaning "whale bone" and others as "whale charm." This latter interpretation of the word as a magic spell should be correct because the Old English *bēn* means "prayer, conjuration." "Whale bone" does not make any sense, whereas the second translation corresponds to the text whose magical character is evident, firstly because the two verses are based on alliteration, and secondly because the initial runes are significant:

ᚠisc ᚠlodu ahof on ᚠergenberig

warþ ᚷa:sric ᚷrorn Þær he on ᚷreut giswom

This spell is intended to cause a whale to go around on the shore and it is comparable to the fishing charms found in Scandinavian countries.[16]

ᚠ, which reads as *feoh*, "livestock," refers to wealth. ᚷ, *gyfu*, means "gift." The combination of the two runes means "largesse" and what result from it, "reputation and honor." Now we can understand the presence of the adoration of the Magi on the right side: they are bearing gifts. What the Magi and Weyland share in common are knowledge of magic and the bearing of riches. Perhaps it is even possible to see it as a symbolic depiction of the image of the smith, transforming ore into metal and creating wealth.

PART III

NATURE AND THE ELEMENTS

Between Awe and Terror

9

The Magnetic Mountain

The Magnetic Mountain[1] first appeared in medieval literature around 1200, in the medieval German romance *Herzog Ernst* (Duke Ernst). A storm drives the hero's ship within proximity to this mountain. His boat gets stuck there, his crew dies of hunger, and griffins carry away their corpses. This gives Ernst and his loyal vassal Wetzel the idea to have the last surviving sailor sew them into hides. The griffins jump upon this prey and carry them off to their nest on another eastern mountain. Various elements of this episode can be seen in the earlier legend of Saint Brendan[2] from 1150 but they had not then been woven into a coherent narrative whole. *The Voyage of Saint Brendan* informs us that the Magnetic Mountain stands close to the Congealed Sea, which is, in fact, the mythical vision of pack ice and has been given several locations that have no connection to the Arctic.

Those who have studied this theme have said it was taken from Pliny the Elder's *Natural History* (2, 211),[3] which is not entirely correct, however. So let us retrace the history of the Magnetic Mountain starting with classical antiquity.[4]

THE TRADITION IN CLASSICAL ANTIQUITY AND IN THE EAST

Pliny is indeed one of the first to speak of two mountains near the Indus: one attracts iron; the other pushes it away. We should note that these mountains are quite far from the sea! This observation was not the source of the medieval tales for a good reason: this passage is missing in Solinus's *Collectanea*, which is the relay between Pliny and the learned literature of the Middle Ages, a source from which Isidore of Seville took a bit of material. In his *Etymologies* (16, 4, 1), Isidore is satisfied with merely saying that the magnet is called "Indian stone" because it was discovered there originally, and that it attracts iron objects and weapons. Around 1115, Honorius Augustodunensis, and another important relay of the legendary traditions of antiquity, simply states: "India where the magnet is born, the stone that attracts iron" (*De imagine mundi*, 1, 13).

Pliny's source was likely an Eastern tale, a trace of which we find in *The Marvels of India*, a treatise written around 950 by Buzurg ibn Shariyar:

> A sailor told me that between Khanfu, which is the main city of Little China, and Khomdan, the main city of Big China, the more important of the two and where lives the Grand Baghpur, there is a powerfully flowing riving of soft water that is as large as the Tigris in Basra. At certain spots along this river, magnetic mountains can be found that are so strong that it is impossible to sail on this river on a boat that carries any iron for fear it will be drawn to them. The horsemen that ride among these mountains do not shoe their horses.[5]

The similarity of this information with Pliny's note is conspicuous: we have a river, magnetic mountains—I stress the plural—and horsemen that do not shoe their horses, whereas Pliny mentions nailed shoes.

The sole echo of Pliny's tradition is found in the *Roman d'Enéas* (Romance of Aeneas), written between 1150 and 1200, in which Carthage is surrounded by three rows of magnets that attract and repel all the iron-clad (v. 433ff.):

> All around three rows of magnets
> Had been made with great precision
> From stone so terribly hard;
> The nature of the magnet is such,

That any man in armor coming near it
Is drawn toward the stone;
Thus, anyone with a halberd who approaches,
Will immediately be pulled to the wall.[6]

The geographer Ptolemy represents the other conduit for traditions from classical antiquity. In the second century, he mentioned the Magnetic Mountain, which he situated close to the Maniole Islands, on the sea route between India and the unknown lands south of the Equator at 142 degrees longitude by 2 degrees latitude. The Greek author states that Indian sailors would not allow any iron objects on their ships for fear of being attracted to that mountain.[7] Let me state at once that Ptolemy is the source from which the majority of medieval authors drew directly or indirectly.

At the beginning of the fifth century, a passage from the *Commonitorium Palladii*, attributed to the Bishop of Helenpolis (363?–430), follows Ptolemy. Near Taprobane—in other words, Ceylon—there are islands called the Manioles, which have a wealth of magnets that attract iron, so the boats sailing in these waters do not carry any, otherwise the strength of the magnets would hold them prisoner.[8] The legend is almost created; we should note and keep in mind that the *Commonitorium Palladii* was part of the legend of Alexander the Great, so it enjoyed wide distribution. Ptolemy is also the source for a passage from *The Persian Wars* (I, 19) by Procopius, who does not add anything new.[9]

I cannot state with certainty if the Arab geographer al-Edrisi (ca. 1099–1164) got from Ptolemy his information about the Magnetic Mountain, which he calls Murukein and situates on the eastern coast of Africa south of Bab-el-Mandep, when he writes: "No boat with iron nails sails alongside this mountain without being pulled and held fast, so much so that it can no longer get free."[10]

Another Arab geographer, Abulfeda, cites the Alkherany, located south of the Mount Melende so well known to travelers. It juts out into the sea for one hundred miles and a magnet mine is located there, and on the mainland fifty miles south there is an iron mine.[11]

It is perhaps because it was inserted into the geste of Alexander the Great that the Magnetic Mountain gained a place in medieval Arabic literature. Because of the imprecise dating of the *One Thousand and One Nights*, we can't say if the Magnetic Mountain went from geography into literature or if the geographers repeated a sailor's fable. However, this latter hypothesis seems the most likely to me. Whatever the case may be, Ibn al-Djazzar (died 1004) seems to have been the first to introduce the following motif that we find in a medieval translation of his *I'timad*: "Aristotle says in his lapidary that when the ships drew near this mountain, all the iron parts flew off of the boats, and this is why sailors make ships without iron nails."[12]

Before looking into this point more deeply, I would emphasize that in the learned literature there are two traditions: the source of one is Ptolemy and tells how the boats are attracted; the other mentions the nails flying toward the Magnetic Mountain and the sinking of the boats.

Qazwini (1203–1283) echoes the first tradition in his *Cosmography* and writes: "The Magnetic Mountain is near Egypt. It's a mountain on which the magnet that attracts iron can be found. All the boats used on this sea are built without iron for fear of it."[13] The mention of Egypt should not lead us astray; Qazwini is speaking of the Red Sea islands.

Let us now take a look at the tradition of the Pseudo-Aristotle. Aristotle has been attributed with the paternity of an Arab lapidary going back to Greek sources with insertions of other materials. The oldest manuscript of the Pseudo-Aristotle, completed on November 5, 1329, by Muhammad ibn-Mubârâk ibn 'Utmân is in the French National Library in Paris, but as it was already mentioned in tenth-century works it seems accurate to date this lapidary's tradition to at least the ninth century.[14] The Arabic text reads: "The Magnetic Mountain is in India, and when a ship carrying iron passes nearby, the vessel is drawn toward it, and if it is carrying a lot, it is carried away."[15]

The Pseudo-Aristotle was known in the medieval West since the eleventh century; Constantine the African (died 1087) refers to him in his *Liber de gradibus* (Book Concerning Degrees): the mountain is located in India, the local sailors build ships without iron; if they contain any, they are pulled toward the mountain.[16] Constantine's words are found again in Bartholomaeus Anglicus around 1240, Vincent de Beauvais (ca. 1250), Pierre Bercheur (fourteenth century), and in the medical literature,[17] mainly from the Salerno school. So, we can find it in the work of Platearius, a physician who settled in Salerno around 1140. It says that the Magnetic Mountain pulls out all the iron nails from ships, which then fall into pieces and sink.

The *Circa instans* of Platearius[18] enjoyed wide distribution and was translated into several languages.* In the Germanic regions, the oldest dates from 1180, and the center of its diffusion was the Lower Franconian area, the same area where *The Voyage of Saint Brendan* and *Herzog Ernst* were created. In France, the first translations date from the beginning of the thirteenth century. Platearius is therefore an important vehicle for the legend of the Magnetic Mountain, even of the manuscripts contain significant variants, some not mentioning the sinking of ships. The *Circa instans* is one of the sources of Johannes de Cuba's *Hortus sanitatis* (Garden of Health) via which the legend traveled into an expanded German translation, the *Gart der Gesundheit*.[19]

Around the end of the eleventh century, Serapion the Younger was inspired by Platearius in his *Liber de medicamentis simplicibus* (Book of Simple Medicaments), translated into Latin by Stephanus of Saragossa in 1233. He tells us that the iron nails flew toward the Magnetic Mountain and remained glued to it whenever a ship approached, which caused it to sink.

To be as complete as possible, I would like to point out that the Pseudo-Aristotle was translated into Latin and Hebrew, and that a fourteenth-century manuscript states explicitly that it is impossible to remove the ship from the mountain that attracted it. This detail is present in the lapidary of Ahma al-Tifashi (died 1254) who, like Muhammad al-Idrisi (1100–1165), speaks of several magnetic mountains in the Indian Ocean and the Red Sea, and it reappears in the 1282 lapidary of Baylak al-Qibjaki.

---

*[Platearius's *Circa instans* is a treatise on medicinal herbs. It was later translated into French as *Le Livre des simples medecines* (The Book of Simple Medicines). —Ed.]

Let us make a first assessment. The medieval West essentially owes its knowledge of the Magnetic Mountain to the *Commonitorium Palladii*, which follows the Ptolemaic tradition, and to the Pseudo-Aristotle whose lapidary is known thanks to the Latin translations from the eleventh and twelfth centuries. An ongoing interaction occurred between the scholarly literature and the legends and romances, which we can summarize as follows: the medieval legend was enriched with the motifs of the congealed sea and the rescue by griffins. The first motif is well known and was passed down by Pliny the Elder, Solinus, and Isidore of Seville; the second motif comes from Eastern sources and owes its popularity to the *Roman d'Alexandre* (Romance of Alexander).

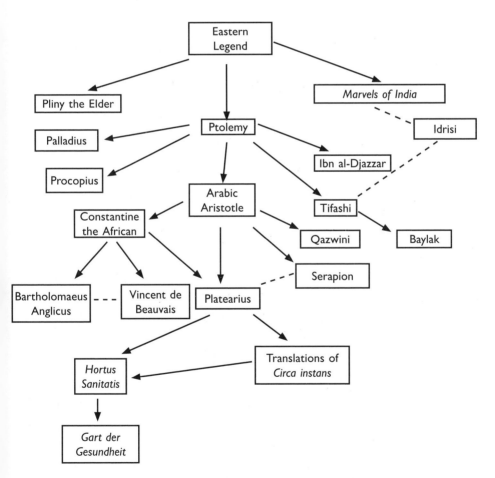

The diffusion of the Magnetic Mountain legend in the learned literature

THE TRAVELERS' TALES OF THE MEDIEVAL WEST

Situated at the convergence of scholarly literature and legendary traditions, travelers' tales occupy an important place. *Mandeville's Travels*, a compilation well known to medievalists, twice notes the existence of the Magnetic Mountain: first, in the Indian Ocean and the Strait of Ormuz, based on Palladius; and second, in the context of the legend of Prester John. There, Mandeville exploits the motif of the boats stuck at the foot of the mountain whose rotten wood gave birth to a forest. The cartographers repeated it in Andreas Walsperger's map, which dates from 1448 and situates the Magnetic Mountain north of Iceland and includes the following caption: "None sail in this vast sea because of the magnet."

At the end of the fourteenth century, Johannes Witte de Hese repeated the legend but confused magnet for "diamond," a common mistake. Among the works based on traveler's tales I would also like to point out those of Felix Fabri (1438–1502); Ali Aziz Efendi of Crete's (1749–1798) *The Story of Jewad*, a Turkish narrative; the *Sirat Sayf ibn Dhi Yazan*, a popular romance of the early Middle Ages; the *Schilte Haggiborim* by Rabbi Abraham ben Hamase; and the *Gelilot Erets Ysra'el* by Rabbi Gershon ben Eliezer (seventeenth century), inspired by Palladius.

THE LEGEND IN THE LITERATURE OF LEISURE

Let us first look at the Eastern accounts. The first traces of the Magnetic Mountain can be seen in the voyages of Sinbad the Sailor, which are based on *The Wonders of India* by Buzurg ibn Shahriyar al-Ramhormuzi. In the sixth voyage, Sinbad's vessel is carried away by a sea current to a mountain where it breaks apart. This current was gradually replaced by magnetic attraction. The mountain forms an island whose ground is covered by bones and wreckage, the stones of this place are gems. His sailors dying of hunger, Sinbad finds a river that vanishes beneath the vaulted ceiling of a cave. He builds a raft, loads with it with precious stones and other goods, and departs. Nearly all of these details also appear in *Herzog Ernst*, but in a different arrangement.

One Thousand and One Nights expressly speaks of the Magnetic

Mountain in the tale "The Porter and the Three Ladies." A storm sends the boat of Agib off course and an ocean current carries it to the Magnetic Mountain. A sailor says: "The boat is going to break apart and all the nails are going to fly to the mountain and be glued to it." A copper cupola on top of ten pillars stands on the mountain. It is topped by a horseman on a copper horse. One can only escape if the horseman is toppled from his mount. Various elements here have clearly been borrowed from medieval learned literature, but the rescue is achieved by means of magic and not by griffins.

Agib's adventure resurfaces in the Turkish tale of Qara Khan, which dates from 1796–1797, as well as a horror story from twentieth-century western Europe. It does not retain the specifically Arabic elements, nor does it name the hero or the time and place. The hero learns the means for rescue from a dream and not the ship's captain, and we find borrowings from Mandeville and the legend of Saint Brendan. The horror story was collected in the 1960s from Roelf Piters de Jong, born in 1905, who heard it from his grandfather, Abram de Groot—this is a fine example of the oral tradition at work.

Rescue by magic is specific to the Arabs and reappears, for example, in the *Voyages of Abulfawaris*.[20] The horseman is replaced by a drum. As soon as someone strikes it, the boat comes loose; on the second strike, it starts sailing away, and on the third, it resumes its correct course. But the person striking the drum must remain there. One additional detail: the Magnetic Mountain is high and steep; it looks like polished steel, and glistens and sparkles.

In medieval Europe, the translations of the legend of Saint Brendan into Middle Dutch, Middle German, Bavarian, and Eastphalian form one of its most important avenues of transmission.[21] These texts say the following: After passing the island of Avares, Saint Brendan was driven northward by a storm and came to the Congealed Sea.[22] Brendan saw countless masts there that he thought looked like a forest. A divine voice warned him not to continue his voyage for a stone that attracted all iron stood in the middle of this sea. Only the Bavarian version called this stone a "magnet" (*Mangnet*). A favorable wind carried Brendan far from this danger.

The second text that contributed to the spread of the Magnetic Mountain legend is *Herzog Ernst*, which was translated into Latin (as the *Ernestus*) by Odo von Magdeburg around 1212–1218. It is now known as version E. An anonymous version in prose, called version C, was retranslated into Middle High German designated by the initial F. F and C include a digression concerning the Magnetic Mountain that says it possesses a radiance strong enough to set the masts of ships on fire.[23]

The third conduit for the legend of the Magnetic Mountain is the legend of Virgil the magician.[24] Several poems with important variants among them tell how he made his way to the Magnetic Mountain. Synthesizing the information that these poems contain, the story can be reconstructed as follows: Aristotle heard about the Magnetic Mountain (*Agetstein*). A noble family that had fallen into poverty learned that many ships carrying great wealth were stuck at the foot of this mountain. They asked Virgil to bring them to them. Virgil agreed because a document he wanted was located on that mountain. He knew the winds and the dangers of sirens, and he set off with enough provisions for a year and four oxen. The voyage lasted for fourteen months. The sailors heard the song of sirens, crocodiles made off with sleepers, and griffins also carried away their prey. One day they saw a forest of masts and a high mountain. The magnet attracted the four oxen chained together. Here the story of a spirit named Melian has been inserted: he found a stone that nullifies the effect of the magnet. Virgil frees the oxen using the stone, loads the boat with riches, and throws the oxen overboard. A whale seems to devour them and pulls the boat away from the mountain, but the ropes break and the travelers also lose their anchor. Virgil disembarks, finds a path, and explores the mountain where he finds a fly in a glass vial. The fly asks the enchanter for help: if he frees him, he will show Virgil the book he is seeking. So, Virgil frees him and learns there is a bronze statue with a document in its head and a club in its hand. The fly—in other words, the spirit—shows it to him and Virgil takes the book and imprisons the spirit back in the vial. He then slips into a hide and griffins carry him to the high stone where Saint Brendan was in great torment. He opens the book with a key, reads it, and can return to Rome.

Heinrich von Mügeln recounts another version of this legend. Venetians in search of wealth left for the Magnetic Mountain (*Achtstein*) with a scribe named Virgil and two griffins tied to the boat with ropes so as to keep it from the magnet's fatal attraction. But the ropes break; Virgil goes ashore to the mountain, finds the spirit in the vial, frees it, and learns what he needs to know to take possession of the book. He opens it and eight thousand devils spill out, but he manages to seal them back in the book. He frees himself from the Magnetic Mountain and returns to Venice with his companions.

Explanations for these rather obscure elements are provided by *Reinfried von Braunschweig*,[25] a Middle High German courtly adventure romance written after 1291: only Virgil and his companions are able to leave the mountain; the book belongs to the necromancer Savilon, and King Solomon has banished the devil in the vial.

All these works with Virgil use and recast elements coming from different sources. The oxen tied to the ship are an imitation of the griffins that Alexander the Great used to ascend into the air; the devil in the vial comes from Eastern traditions and the same is true for the bronze statues. The writers were familiar with the romance of *Herzog Ernst* and *The Voyage of Saint Brendan*. This allows us to see how the legend evolved.

The Magnetic Mountain finds its way into the legend of Henry the Lion, and three accounts should be considered: a popular book from the Netherlands; the aforementioned romance of *Reinfried von Braunschweig*; and a Czech chapbook from the fifteenth or sixteenth century.[26] All were influenced by *Herzog Ernst*. The Dutch text recounts the following:[27] the Duke of Brunswick sets sail with his men for the Holy Land. A storm sinks all the ships but his, and pushes him into the Congealed Sea where stones attracted everything made of iron. A griffin living nearby circles the boat day and night, carrying off any who risk going on the bridge. The duke orders his men to sew him into an ox hide together with his sword. The griffin carries him off to its nest.

Reinfried von Braunschweig offers a completely different version of this adventure. While staying at the home of the Queen of the Amazons,

Reinfried hears about the Magnetic Mountain and decides to go there. The queen gives him a magic plant that can feed him and orders the construction of a boat without iron. Lastly, she recommends that he forgo wearing any armor. After various adventures, the hero reaches his destination. The boats stuck at the foot of the mountain are described at length. Reinfried scales the mountain, sees a bronze door guarded by a monstrous bronze statue, and looks around him. The mountain is surrounded by a square wall of bronze with four doors of the same metal. He finds a cave with the tomb of the wizard Savilon, reads the book that is chained there, and learns *grosso modo* what we already know via the legend of Virgil. Lastly, he leaves the island easily because his ship has no iron.

The anonymous author used *Herzog Ernst*, the legend of Solomon, and that of Virgil to reconstruct an adventure that teems with disjointed elements: the motif of a rescue with the help of a book of magic, a spirit, or griffins has vanished; the theme of the ironless boat suggests that he followed geographical texts.

The Czech chapbook is shorter. Bruncwig's ship is attracted to the Magnetic Mountain, his sailors devour each other, and the hero remains alone with a loyal knight. He has his knight sew him into a horsehide sprinkled with blood, and the griffins carry him to dry land.

Outside these stories, the long Middle High German poem of *Kudrun*, written around 1240, offers singular pieces of information about the Magnetic Mountain:[28] it is hollow and inhabited, the sand there is silver, and the walls of the castle are made of gold. Albrecht von Scharfenberg's *Younger Titurel*, written around 1250, tells how the Grail family came before the Magnetic Mountain and battled griffins. One new detail that appears in this text: the stuck boats have survivors—pagans whom the bishop Boniface baptizes.

Let us turn now to French literature. The several texts in which the Magnetic Mountain appears can be divided into two groups. On the one hand, we have writings that retranscribe the European version of the legend; on the other, we have accounts that are akin to the romance of *Reinfried von Braunschweig* and the legend of Virgil.

The first group includes *Esclarmonde*,[29] which is believed to date from the thirteenth century and forms the sequel to *Huon de Bordeaux*.

It seems to be inspired by the Latin translations of *Herzog Ernst*. At the same time, the influence of *The Voyage of Saint Brendan* is undeniable.

Huon slays two of the emperor's nephews, Raoul and Gualerant, and has to flee. He embarks from Bordeaux for Aufania. After eight days, the steersman has gone off course (v. 1055ff.); the captain climbs the topmast and says (v. 1017ff.):

> *Bien voi palagres de mer encargié m'a*
> *et que no nef tous jours avalera.*
> *Li aÿmans, je cuich, nous conquerra.*

> Indeed I see the open waters have blocked us
> and that our ship will sink forever.
> The magnet, I believe, will destroy us.

Whereupon they meet Judas (v. 1033ff.), who warns them about the magnet (v. 1086ff.). The sailors spy land and, from the top of the mast, the captain sees a forest of masts (v. 1091ff.), which indicates they are nearing the Magnetic Mountain (v. 1104ff.). They remain stuck at the foot of the mountain in despair and commend themselves to God, but the captain has an idea (v. 1127ff.):

> *Biax sir Hues, par la vertu nommee,*
> *de no vitaille iert droiture moustree:*
> *il est droiture parmi la mer salee*
> *que la moitié est au Seignour donnee.*
> *Puis qu'a tous jours soit li nave arrivee,*
> *tant c'on puet vivre li est abandonnee.*

> Dear Lord Huon, called by virtue,
> we will act in accordance with the law with respect to food.
> The law, when on the salty sea,
> is that half be given to the Lord.
> Ever since the ship arrived here,
> for so long as we live, it will be offered to Him.

They remain there for more than two months, provisions run out, and the men start dying one after the other. Huon prays and then he suddenly hears a loud noise. It is a griffin approaching who pounces on the dead men and carries them away (v. 1211ff.). Huon thinks that the bird can rescue him (v. 1225ff.). He takes his weapons and lies down near the corpses (v. 1261ff.). The griffin carries him to a mountainous island under the rule of Persia. There he finds a tree with the fruits of youth and a spring.

In the fifteenth century, in the fragmentary alexandrine chanson de geste known as *Charles le Chauve* (Charles the Bald),[30] which is set apart from the adventures of Huon de Bordeaux, a storm drives Dieudonné, the protégé of the fairy Gloriande, toward the Magnetic Mountain (folio 42r°), but he owns a wondrous horn with which he can call Gloriande. She doesn't wish to help him but permits the dwarf Maufuné to go to the mountain and gives him a boat without iron (folio 42v°) with which he saves Dieudonné.

We can see here that we have a compilation of different works, mainly geographical, and the boat without iron is reminiscent of the one the Queen of the Amazons procured for Reinfried von Braunschweig.

The second group of texts is represented by the alexandrine version of the *Roman d'Ogier* (Romance of Ogier the Dane),[31] which dates from the fourteenth century, and by *Bérinus*,[32] a romance in prose also from the fourteenth century. Let us first take a look at the former text. Driven to the foot of the Magnetic Mountain, Ogier and his men are dying from hunger. Soon the hero is the only one left. An angel appears to him and restores his courage. By passing from one boat to the next, Ogier makes his way to an island near the mountain where he discovers a marvelous castle. It is invisible by day but sparkles at night. He slays a gigantic reptile, eats fruit from an orchard, and gets rid of his leprosy.

The sparkling castle is distinctly reminiscent of Mount Karbunkulus of the Czech chapbook *Stillfried and Bruncwig*, and shows that an Arabic Alexander legend, traces of which we can find in Qazwini's *Cosmography*, was known in the West. Contrary to what Gédéon Huet suggests, the *Roman d'Ogier* does not seem to be inspired by *Esclarmonde*.

Bérinus is perhaps the most interesting romance when we study the

Magnetic Mountain. It contains Eastern motifs in fact, notably the rescue by virtue of magic and human sacrifice. The passages that concern us can be summed up this way: The rulers of Rome, Bérinus and Cleopatra, have two children, Aigre and Romaine. As a result of an act of treachery, Bérinus is forced into exile with his wife and children. They set sail but come to the Congealed Sea (the dead sea where nothing moves) from which a current carries them away. They try to escape it by casting their anchor but lose it, and the next night they land by a forest. On seeing this, the steersman faints; when he regains his senses, he tells them they have come to the Magnetic Mountain, "from which none can leave." "The ship drifts in such a way that it is drawn to the magnet and stops against the other ships of which there is a great abundance" (p. 233). The author makes a short digression here to describe the Magnetic Mountain:

> This place, where this magnet is, lies in the ocean, but there is no nearby land to which one could arrive in less than fifteen days; it was in such wise that none could get there in one year, and is beside the Congealed Sea. This magnet was five rods long and equally as wide, and is of such a nature that three days' sail is as close as ships can get to it without it drawing them by its force, unless there is no iron in the boat, because it greatly loves and desires iron, which it can clearly sense some two leagues distance away.

All were weeping, crying, and praying. A man named Siliran climbed into the boat without saying a word (p. 235) and then told what had happened to him (p. 236). He declared: "I've walked around this stone several times such as it was before yesterday, and by chance, I found next to it a scripture." He brings Bérinus to that place. The hero reads the book and learns the different ways to get free:

> If there be any that Fortune has brought hither and they seek to depart, it is first necessary that they empty their boats of all that is silver and gold therein; do that but ensure you keep enough so you can return to your country. Once this is done, everyone on the boat will draw lots, and the one who is chosen by lot will go ashore

where he will find a ring lying on the ground, which he will cast into the sea. And as long as the sheep will have departed, the boat can sail away safe and sound with all its people save for him who threw the ring into the sea, compelled by force that he who drew this lot cannot by any spell escape it, for none could aid him otherwise in this task.

They then draw lots (p. 240) and Aigre has to remain there. He finds the ring and follows the instructions (p. 243). When he casts it into the sea, a storm rises and carries the vessel away. Aigre despairs but is visited by the sorcerer Mauchastre, who promises to help him. Aigre examines the other boats and finds a horse with which he shares his food. One day, a ship attracted by the magnet arrives. He tells the sailors what they must do, but this time someone else draws the short straw.

A conspicuous kinship is evident between *Bérinus* and "The Third Kalandar's Tale" of the *One Thousand and One Nights* and the *First Voyage of Abulfawaris* as well as with the legend of Virgil. The presence of a survivor and the casting of riches overboard are new, although this latter motif does bring to mind the words of the captain in *Esclarmonde* (v. 1127ff.).

We still need to cite the prose version of *Huon de Bordeaux*, dating from the fifteenth century.[33] This is a nonrhyming version of *Esclarmonde* in which the anonymous author incorporates details from other stories into the legend of the Magnetic Mountain.

The masts of the trapped ships are covered with foliage (fol. 130r°) as in *Mandeville's Travels*. A marvelous castle stands on the Magnetic Mountain (fol. 131r°) that can be reached by a staircase with 372 steps but is so narrow "that a man can only ascend sideways." This motif appears to be borrowed from the *Roman d'Ogier*, but I recall that "The Third Kalandar's Tale" also presents a wondrous building with a staircase. The episode in which Huon enters the castle, kills a monstrous reptile, and eats fruit is borrowed from the *Roman d'Ogier*.

We can now draw up a summary of the legend's evolution through the Middle Ages. The Western traditions can be distinguished from the Eastern ones by the following modes of rescue:

- being sewn into an animal hide that griffins carry away
- griffins pull the boat away
- a whale takes the boat away from the Magnetic Mountain

The Eastern traditions penetrated into the West during the thirteenth century and provided the romance writers with the motif of the magical rescue (for example in *Bérinus* and the legend of Virgil). As I cannot claim to have listed every account of the legend, it is useful to recall the distribution of motifs according to the texts, in order to facilitate the work of researchers who may discover new attestations.

Primary Motifs

Congealed Sea: only the Western legends connect this to the Magnetic Mountain—*The Voyage of Saint Brendan, Herzog Ernst, Virgil, Esclarmonde, Reinfried von Braunschweig.*

Shipwreck: only found in the Eastern legends and horror stories; it appears in the learned literature.

Rescue by griffins: this is only connected to the Magnetic Mountain in the West—*Herzog Ernst, Esclarmonde, Reinfried von Braunschweig,* the Czech chapbook, *The Voyage of Saint Brendan, Kudrun,* and the *Younger Titurel* mention the presence of griffins near the Magnetic Mountain; the motif is obscure in the legend of Virgil.

Magical rescue: 1. A man must sacrifice himself (*Bérinus, Abulfawaris*); 2. A spirit helps you (*One Thousand and One Nights, Virgil,* horror stories); 3. Magical stone (*Virgil*).

Ancillary Motifs and Developments

A single survivor: *Esclarmonde*; the other texts have two to seven (seven in *Herzog Ernst,* two in *Stillfried and Bruncwig*);

A boat without iron (this motif excludes other rescue methods): *Reinfried von Braunschweig, Charles le Chauve;*

The Magnetic Mountain sparkles and twinkles: *Abulfawaris,* version C of *Herzog Ernst;* in the *Roman d'Ogier,* this detail is replaced by a castle that has the same properties;

Another island is close to the Magnetic Mountain: the *Roman d'Ogier*, Czech chapbook;

A forest born from the worm-eaten wood of the trapped ships: *Mandeville's Travels, Huon de Bordeaux* in prose;

Magic: 1. Spirit/fly in a vial (*Virgil, Reinfried von Braunschweig*) or bird (*Bérinus*); 2. Automaton or statue (*One Thousand and One Nights, Reinfried von Brunschweig, Virgil*); 3. Marvelous building (*One Thousand and One Nights, Abulfawaris, Reinfried von Braunschweig*, the *Roman d'Ogier, Bérinus, Huon de Bordeaux* in prose).

Textual Accounts

Pliny the Elder, *Historia naturalis* (2, 211):

> *Duo sunt montes iuxta flumen Indum, alteri natura ut ferrum omne teneat, alteri espuat, itaque si sint clavi in calciamento, vestigia avelli in altero non posse, in altero sisti.*

Isidore of Seville, *Etymologiae* (16, 4, 1):

> *Magnes lapis Indicus ab inventore vocatus. Fuit autem in India ita primum repertus: clavis crepidarum, baculique cuspidi haerens, cum armenta idem magnes pasceret, postea et passim inventus.*

Commonitorium Palladii (ed. Kübler, in *Romanische Forschungen* 6 [1891]: 203–37, here at 211):

> *Sunt autem mille aliae insulae in rubro mari, quae sunt subditae ad istam praedictam insulam [= Taprobane], in quibus sunt illi lapides, quos magnetes nominamus, qui trahunt ad se ferrum. Etiam si qualiscumque navis advenerit, quae habuerit de ferro clavum, statim apprehendent eam et non dimittunt eam. Habitatores autem de illis insulis quando faciunt naves, non ibi mittunt clavos ferreos, sed tantum clavos ligneos, et semper cum illis vadunt ad illam insulam, ubi habitat ille rex magnus.*

Ibn al-Djazzar, *I'timad* (cited from Valentin Rose, "Aristoteles' De lapidibus und Arnoldus Saxo," *Zeitschrift für deutsches Altertum* 18 [1875]: 322–455, here at 410):

> *Minera huius lapidis in littore maris propre Iodiam. Ar[istoteles] dixit in libro de lapidibus quod quando naves applicant se huic monti, EGREDIUNTUR FERRA A NAVIBUS, et ideo naves illius maris fiunt preter clavos ferreos.*

Constantine the African, *Liber de gradibus* (cited from Rose, "Aristoteles' De lapidibus und Arnoldus Saxo," 380):

> *Aristoteles dixit esse lapidem in ripa maris Indiae inventum. . . . Dixit etiam in libro de lapidibus quod nautae non audent transire cum navi ferreos clavos habente aut aliquod artificium ferri in ea ducere. Nave etiam illis montanis approinquante, omnes clavi et quidquid ex ferro editum a montanis attrahitur cum proprietate quam habent.*

De simplici medicina dictus Circa instans (cited from Rose, "Aristoteles' De lapidibus und Arnoldus Saxo," 410):

> *. . . unde dixit Aristoteles quod invenitur in litore Indie et Oceani. Montes autem sunt ex talibus lapidibus confecti. Unde naves infixas clavis ferreis attrahunt et dissolvunt.*

Platearius, *Circa instans*, Middle Dutch version (fourteenth century) (*Een middelnederlandse versie van de "Circa instans" van Platearius*, ed. Leo J. Vandewiele [Oudenaarde: Sanderus, 1970], 182):

> *Van den zeylsteen: Hi heuet macht yser na hem te trecken ende men vinden des daghes by den ouer des mers ende montes Oceani dat siin berghe des lants siin van alsutken stenen verghadert. Dar omme trecken sy na hem scepe dar iseren naghel an siin ende verderunse.*

Serapion the Younger, *Liber de medicamentis simplicibus* (trans. Stephanus of Saragossa, cited from Rose, "Aristoteles' De lapidibus und Arnoldus Saxo," 411):

> *Minera huius lapidis est in maritimis partibus prope terras Indorum. Et quando aves appropinquant monti minere ipsius. NON REMANET ALIQUOD FERRUM QUOD NON EGREDIATUR A NAVE ETVOLET sicut avis usque ad montem et si est aliquis clavus taliter infixus quod non possit evelli, salit et evellitur donec adhaeret illi monti, et ideo naves illarum partium non clavantur cum clavis ferreis sed cum clavis ligneis. Nam si essent naves clavate cum clavis ferreis, quando appropinquarentur illi monti, DILACERENTUR omnes.*

Lapidary of Pseudo-Aristotle, Leiden manuscript (fourteenth century) (cited from Rose, "Aristoteles' De lapidibus und Arnoldus Saxo," 368):

> *Minera huius lapidis est in ripa maris propinqui terre Indie. Quando naves transeunt prope montem ubi lapis iste est, non potest in eis remanere. FERRUM QUIN SALIAT EXTRA et EVOLANS nunc supra nunc subtus NON CESSAT DONEC PERVENIAT AD MAGNETEM.*
>
> *Similiter clavi navium ERADICANTUR unde competit naves transfretantes per illud mare non coniungi clavis ferreis sed clavillis ligneis alioquin periclitarentur. aut enim DIRUMPERENTUR per clavorum eradicationem. Aut usque AD MONTEM TRAHERENTUR a quo IMPOSSIBILE EST NAVEM SEPARARI cum ferro postquam ei applicata fuerit.*

Lapidary of Ahma al-Tifashi (in *Fior di pensieri sulle pietre reziose di Ahmed Teifascite opera*, trans. Antonio Raineri [Florence: Mediceo-Laurenziana, 1818], 50):

> *Questa pietra ha una delle sue miniere in un monte, che resta sulla spiaggia del mare tra l'Hegiaz e l'Iemen, ed un'altra, in quest'ultimo paese presso Sana. Oltracciò, al dir d'Aristotile, trovasi pure nel mare una montagna intera della stessa pietra, la quale è cagione che tutte le*

navi, e le barche, che le si avvicinano, rimangon prive di quasi tutti i lor chiodi, imperocchè questi spiccandosi sine dal corpo interno di quei bastimenti se NE VOLANO a lei come altrettanti uccelli. Per tal motivo non s'inchioda mai con ferro qualsivoglia nave, o barca, che debba viaggiar per quel mare, ma si procura invece di cucirla con tralci, e filamenta di cocco. I Popoli dell'Iemen si servono di sbucciati ramoscelli di palma per cucire, e formare i proprj navigli. Quanto alla sovraccennata montagna tutta composta di Magnete, la quale esiste nell'India sulla spiaggia del mare.

Mandeville's Travels, Paris manuscript (B.N.F., ms. Fr. 5637, folio 51r°):

et si sont toutes leurs nefs faites de boys et de fut, sans fer ne clou, pour les roches des AYMANS, dont il a en mer la entour tant que c'est merveille, car se une nef passoit parmi ces marches ou il eust clos ou bendes de fer, tantost seroit perie; car l'aymant de sa nature trait le fer a luy, si trairoit la nef a lui pour la cause du fer, si que iamès ne pourroit departir.

(folio 83r°):

Et combien qu'ils eussent meilleur marchié en terre Prestre Jehan, si redoubtent il longue voie et les grans perilz qui sont sur la mer en telles parties y a, car il a en moult de lieux grans roches de PIERRES D'AYMANT, qui TRAIENT A EULZ LE ER de leur propre nature.

Et pour ce, se il y passe nulle nef ou il ait clos ne bendes de fer, tantost ces roches la traient a elles ne s'en pourroit jamès partir. Je meïsmes vi en la mer de loing ainsi comme une GRANT YLLE, ou il avoit arbrissiaux, espines, ronses et herbes a grant foison et nous dirent les maronniers que c'estoient toutes nés, qui estoient la ainsi arrestées pour les roches d'aymant; et de la pourreture qui estoit dedens les nés estoient creus et naissus ces arbrissiaux, ces ronses et celle herbe, a si grant foison comme on le pouoit veoir adonc.

Et de celles roches il y a en moult de lieux a entour. Et pour ce n'y osent les marchans aller, se il ne scevent moult bien le chemin ou ils aient bon couduiseur.

Petrus Berchorius (Pierre Bercheure), *Reductorium morale* (Venice, 1574) (11, 94):

> *In aliquibus partis maris sunt montes et scopuli de lapidibus magnetis, et ideo tanto impetu naves attrahunt propter ferrum quod ibi est, quod contra eos freguntur, et penitus dissolvuntur.*

Johannes Witte de Hese, *Peregrinatio* (text in Friedrich Zarncke, *Der Priester Johannes* II [Leipzig: Hirzel, 1876], 164):

> *Et mare iecoreum est talis naturae, quod attrahit naves in profundum propter ferrum in navibus, quia fundus illius maris dicitur quod sit lapideus de lapide adamante, qui est attractivus.*

Gesta Ernesti Ducis (= version E of *Duke Ernst*) (ed. Paul Lehmann, *Abhandlungen der Bayerischen Akademie der Wissenschaften* 32/5 [1927]: 3–38, here at 25–26):

> . . . *viderunt eminus montem precelsum supra mare, qui Mangnes appellatur, et diligencius intuiti contemplati circa eum naves et malos omni nemore opaciores ac densiores, cum aliter eis videretur.* . . . *sic premissa prece cum clamoribus in celum, cum iam monti propinquarent, ab eius ammirabili virtute per omnem navium illarum densitatem tam valide acti et attracti sunt, quasi nichil eis obsisteret.*

Historia ducis Ernesti (= version C of *Duke Ernst*) (ed. Moriz Haupt, "Herzog Ernst," *Zeitschrift für deutsches Altertum* 7 [1849]: 193–303, here at 221–23):

> . . . *et prospiciens a longe quasi ingentissimam molem montis prospiciebat in quo quasi silva pinuum densissima malorum multitudino se in altum porrigebat.* . . . *Interea loci trieris ipsorum magis et magis prolapsa et magneti lapidi, qui per naturam ferrum sibi attrahit, applicata capitur, tenetur. ibi eiusdem lapidis fulgor ad modum ignis de fluctibus coruscabat; quo fulgore multa vetusta navis,*

*quae in binas partes in medio dirupta est, summitati arenae, quae
est multo periculiosor quam maris unda, supernatat, malorum etiam
multorum ab illo fulgore confractorum moles ingentissima cadens
deorsum in trierim novorum advenarum mortificabat multos, et, ut
compendio utar, illa nobilissima iuventus praeter paucos inibi miserae
mortis diversis modis pocula gustabat.*

The Congealed Sea and Rescue by Griffins

Benjamin of Tudela, *Travels* (*Masa'ot Binyamin*, ca. 1170) (cited from
Haupt, "Herzog Ernst," 296):

*inde in Sinam, Orientis terminum, tendentibus quadraginta
dierum iter est, et maris quo iter faciunt nomen esse ferunt MARE
CONCRETUM, ubi sidus Orion dominatur procellarum ibi
ventum subinde excitans. itaque tum nullus nauta navi ob venti
vehementiam vehi potest adeoque etiam ventus navem in istud MARE
CONCRETUM protrudit ut e loco isto extricari nequeat. quo fit ut
homines illic donec commeatus absumatur haerentes postea moriantur.
quapropter multae naves hac ratione pereunt. verum enim vero
homines artem quandam excogitarunt qua ex huiusmodi funesto loco
evadere possent. nam sumptas secum iuvencorum pelles, si ventus ille
irruat eosque in mare concretum protrudat, arripiunt ac se iis inserunt,
gladium singuli manu tenentes pellesque intus consuentes, ut eo aqua
penetrare nequeat, posteaque sese in mediam aquam proiiciunt. quos
prospicientes magnae aquilae GRYPHES dictae iumenta esse putant,
et descendentes arripiunt eos atque in aridum exportant usque in
monte aut valle ad devorandum insident. sed homines inclusi festinant
et illas gladiis caedentes occidunt et e pellibus egressi incedunt donec ad
terram habitatam perveniant. mortalium multi hoc modo evadunt.*

Roman d'Alexandre, Venice manuscript (v. 7061ff.):

Trapped with his men in the Forest of Raan, Alexander made this
pact with a demon. He would free him if he told him how to get out
of the forest and swore to go to the Isle of Orion ruled by tumult

and where numerous demons lived. Alexander then speaks of a journey he once made:

> ... *unques hom n'i fut mais que sol cil dui gloton,*
> *sans moi, cui en porterent en volant dui grifon;*
> *de ce que je refis ressemblai je bricon,*
> *je entrai en une nef toz sols sens compaignon*
> *si i mis avec moi un moult tendre pollon;*
> *la mers retint la nef, fort tens fist environ,*[*]
> *la main mis a la spee que oi cente al giron,*
> *al pollet en trençai la gorce e lo menton,*
> *lo sanc en recuilli en la pel d'un leon,*
> *la pel en oi glüee, si sembla un sacon*
> *autresi me mis ens com feïs un bacon.*
> *Dui grifon de montaignes volant a un randon*
> *autresi m'i porterent com un petit peison.*
> *En volant mi porterent en l'isle d'Orion ...*

The Legend of the Noble Lord of Bruneczwigk (fifteenth century) (facsimile edition: Iris Dinckelacker and Wolfgang Häring, eds. *Michel Wyssenherre: Eyn buoch von dem edeln hern von Bruneczwigk als er uber mer fuore. In Abbildung aus dem Cod. poet. fol. 4 der Württembergischen Landesbibliothek*) (Göppingen: Kümmerle, 1977). English summary of the rescue:

Bruneczwigk's ship was stopped by a dead calm sea, the sailors died of hunger and the only survivors were the hero and a sailor. Bruneczwigk's horse was slaughtered and skinned, the hero slipped into its hide that a griffin carried off to its nest. Our hero cut open the hide with his sword and got out. He then killed the griffin and cut off its claws that he used to climb down the mountain. He came upon a dragon and a lion that were fighting; he killed the monster, henceforth the grateful lion now followed him. One day the hero

---

[*]This is a clear allusion to the Congealed Sea.

came to a river that encircled a mountain. He built a raft and set sail. The current carried him into a cave where he saw a carbuncle (garnet), which he took. When he emerged from the underground course of this river, he found he had reached the land of the crane-humans.

Czech chapbook of *Stillfried and Bruncwig* (ed. Václav Hanka, *Stára povest o Stojmíroví o Brunsvíkovi knízatech ceskych* (Prague, 1827). English summary of the second part:

Bruncwig set off on adventure on a ship with his companions. After three months of errantry, a storm pushed them close to the magnetic Mountain (*hora Aktstein*), whose attractive force cast them on an islet named Zelator where numerous boats had become stuck. The men were dying of hunger until all that remained were Bruncwig and his loyal servant, Balad, who advised him to have himself sewn into a horsehide that would then be sprinkled with blood. The hero did just that and a griffin carried him off to its nest. Bruncwig freed himself, slew the young griffins, climbed down the mountain, and eventually came to a valley where he saw a dragon attacking a lion. He slew the nine-headed, fire-breathing dragon and the lion followed him ever after. One day he spied far over the sea a castle, walked fifteen days in its direction, built a raft, sailed for ten more days, and came to Mount Karbunkulus, which sparkled like fire. He wrested off a piece that he used for a beacon in his sea voyage . . .

10
The Raft of the Winds
*Toward a Mythology of Clouds
in the Middle Ages*

Since the dawn of time, clouds, mists, and fogs have continually inspired the human imagination. Like all inexplicable phenomena from "elsewhere," they have the power to both pique our curiosity as well as unnerve our state of awareness at a given moment in our historical evolution. The existence of clouds has been linked to gods, demons, and to various spirits. In the Bible we see Jehovah leading the Hebrews in the form of a pillar of cloud to show them which route to follow (2 Exodus 13:21) and the poet Alfred de Vigny was thinking of how He revealed himself when he wrote:

> *Et, debout devant Dieu, Moïse ayant pris place,*
> *Dans le nuage obscure lui parlay face à face.*

> And standing before God, Moses having found a place
> In the dark cloud, spoke to him face to face.

In the *Iliad*, Homer presents clouds as a means used by the gods to intervene in human affairs. Hephaestus wraps Idaios in a thick fog to hide him from Diomedes; Aphrodite saves Paris by concealing him in a cloud; Poseidon hides Aneas in a fog and thus spares him from the blows of Achilles; Athena dispels the fog that covers Diomedes's eyes and he can then see gods and men. Other Greek authors inform us that Olympus and Mount Ida are covered in cloud when Zeus is staying there.

To the best of my knowledge, only Western mythologies describe the genesis of clouds. The Finnish Kalevala has this to say about their cosmogony:

> A goldeneye is looking for a place to build a nest and cannot find one. It spots the knee of the virgin impregnated by the foam crested waves emerging from the sea, lands there, and lays six golden eggs and a seventh an iron egg. But the Water Mother feels the heat on her knee and she moves causing the eggs to fall into the sea where they break and transform:

> the lower half of one egg into the earth beneath,
> the top half of another egg into the heavens above.
> The top half of one yolk gets to glow like the sun,
> the top half of one white gets to gleam palely as the moon;
> any mottled things on an egg, those become stars in heaven,
> anything black on an egg, those indeed become clouds in the sky.[1]

Another account comes from the mythology of the ancient Scandinavians, who see the world's creation this way. The sons of Buri slay Ymir, the primordial giant, dismember him, and form the world from the pieces of his body:

> And from his eyelashes the cheerful gods
> made Midgard for men's sons
> and from his brain the hard-tempered clouds
> were all created. (*Grímnismál*, st. 41)[2]

The text says nothing about "good clouds," but we can pick out the bond that united a giant, the personification of natural forces, the *numina* of nature, and clouds. Around 1060, the *Ezzolied* (Ezzo's Song, also known as *the Cantilena de miraculis Christi*), composed at the behest of Bishop Gunther of Bamberg, was inspired by similar traditions when it says that the human-microcosm is made of eight different elements, including clouds:

> God, in His omnipotence, made many things. He created the only man from eight parts: from earth he made his flesh; from the dew he made his sweat; from the stones, his bones; from plants, his veins; from the grass, his hair; from the sea, his blood; from the clouds, his mind (*von den wolchen daz muot*): from the sun, his two eyes[3] (v. 37–43; 45–50).

When reading this, there is good reason to wonder if certain expressions like "having your head in the clouds," or "brain fog" might not have originated in thoughts like these.

In the Middle Ages, little distinction was made between clouds and mists: the former floated in the sky and the latter hovered on the surface of the ground. Moreover, clouds were inseparable from the air of which they were an element. It so happens that in this era, air was regarded as the abode of demons; Christians based this belief on Saint Paul's Epistle to the Ephesians 6:12, and on the Church fathers Origen, Saint Ambrose, and Saint Augustine. Petrus Lombardus (twelfth century) explicitly states that demons come down from the air to lead men into temptation.[4] For pagans, clouds were connected to rain and hail and obeyed supernatural forces that were anthropomorphized early on, but these are more like demons in the Greek sense of the word (*daimon*) than major gods, even though the ancient North Germanic peoples established a connection between Njörðr and rain, and between Þórr and lightning. Nowhere is there any question of a god connected to clouds. A poem from the *Poetic Edda* gives us various metaphors reflecting the mindsets:

> Clouds they're called by men, and hope-of-showers by the gods,
> the Vanir call them wind-rafts,
> hope-of-dew, the giants call them, power-of-storms the elves
> In hell the concealing helmet. (*Alvísmál*, st. 18)[5]

These lines from the "Lay of Alvís (All-Wise)" create to a certain extent a synthesis of medieval beliefs and make it possible to discern the major poles around which these beliefs are organized:

- clouds are connected to the air, wind, and rain, whether beneficial or not;
- they are comparable to ships, which reflects the idea of the air being like the sea;
- they conceal (an extremely ancient idea).

Here I will attempt to present a "mythology of the clouds" in the Middle Ages using this typology.

THE CLOUDS AND THE SEA

Humans started comparing the fluffy appearance of clouds to the sea at a very early date, and this image persists. Even today, we talk of a "sea of clouds"—an expression that takes on its full power when one is on an airplane. But when the sky is clear and only a few clouds are lazily floating by, people tend to compare them to ships, to "wind rafts." To move from an image of rafts to fully rigged-out vessels was an easy step for the human imagination, which gave rise to a very odd legend recorded by Agobard, the bishop of Lyons from 816 to 840.

It was thought that some men, magicians or sorcerers called *tempestarii* (weather makers), could cause rain and hail, and it was said that ships carrying them came from a mythical land called Magonia. Sailing over the clouds, these boats carried away the fruits of the earth that had been struck by hail. The sailors paid the *tempestarii* for supplying them with this provender. One day, says Agobard, several people grabbed three men, bound them, and brought them before a sham tribunal to stone them, thinking that they had fallen from such a ship. They only changed their minds after much scolding.[6]

The idea that ships sail in the sky gave birth to another legend, whose first trace can be found in the *Otia imperialia* (Recreation for an Emperor) by Gervase of Tilbury (ca. 1152–1218):

> A strange event in our own time, which is widely known but none the less a cause of wonder, provides proof of the existence of an upper sea overhead. It occurred on a feast day in Great Britain, while the people were straggling out of their parish church after hearing high mass. The day was very overcast and quite dark on account of the thick clouds. To the people's amazement, a ship's anchor was seen caught on a tombstone within the churchyard wall, with its rope stretching up and hanging in the air. They were advancing various opinions on the matter to each other, when after a time they saw the rope move as if it were being worked to pull up the anchor. Since, being caught fast, it would not give way, a sound was heard in the humid air as of sailors struggling to recover the anchor they had cast down. Soon, when their efforts proved vain, the sailors sent one of their number down; using the same technique as our sailors here below, he gripped the anchor-rope and climbed down it, swinging one hand over the other. He had already pulled the anchor free, when he was seized by the bystanders. He then expired in the hands of his captors, suffocated by the humidity of our dense air as if he were drowning in the sea. The sailors up above waited an hour, but then, concluding that their companion had drowned, they cut the rope and sailed away, leaving the anchor behind. And so in memory of this event it was fittingly decided that that anchor should be used to make ironwork for the church door, and it is still there for all to see. (I, 13)[7]

It will be noted that the weather was cloudy, which suggests that the invisible vessel was floating over the clouds. This idea of an "upper sea" likely reflects a cosmological notion from Genesis (1:7) taken literally. What the Bible in fact says is that "God . . . parted the upper waters from the lower waters." Furthermore, Gervase of Tilbury recorded another extraordinary event:

There is a town in Gloucestershire called Bristol, a prosperous place, full of wealthy citizens. It is a port from where one can cross from Great Britain to Ireland. A native of that place once went on a voyage, leaving his wife and children at home. After covering a great distance in the course of a long voyage, when the ship was sailing in a remote part of the ocean, the citizen in question sat down to eat with the sailors at about nine o'clock one morning. After the meal he was washing his knife at the ship's rail when it suddenly slipped from his hand. That very hour it fell through an open window in the roof of the citizen's own home—the kind of window which the English call a skylight—and stuck fast in a table which stood beneath it, before the eyes of his wife. The woman stared at it in amazement, struck by the strangeness of this occurrence. She kept the knife, which she recognized from former days, and when, a long time afterwards, her husband returned, she learned from him that the day on which the accident occurred during his voyage coincided with the day on which she acquired the knife. (I, 13)[8]

CLOUDS, A CONCEALING VEIL, A FRONTIER

Perhaps more important than the legends cited above is a notion according to which the clouds are hiding something and therefore form a border, most often materializing the separation of our world from the dwellings of the beyond, which is not only the empire of the dead.

When Saint Brendan set sail on the western ocean in search of the earthly paradise, the *terra repromissionis*, he finally caught sight of an island surrounded by a wall of clouds. He and his companions spent an hour crossing through them before seeing the wall that surrounds paradise.[9] In another account of his voyage, this wall of clouds is so thick that it takes three days to cross it. Fortunately, the clouds abruptly end on either side of a narrow path, a phenomenon reminiscent of the Hebrews crossing the Red Sea. We learn that the clouds form a defense that only allows passage to the elect.

In the *Roman d'Alexandre* (Romance of Alexander), which might be called a medieval "bestseller," there is a Land of Darkness where the fountain of youth is located. While most accounts do not spell out what this darkness consists of, two texts expressly say that it is connected to clouds. Joseph ben Gurion Hacohen says the following in his *Sefer Josippon*, printed in Venice in 1544: "The area was so darkened by shadows and mists that they [Alexander and his men] couldn't see each other" (chap. 10).[10] Meanwhile, the great Persian poet Nizami, who wrote his *Sikandar Nama e Bara* around 1190, says that when Alexander the Great emerged from the Land of Darkness "the rays of the sun pierced the clouds."[11] Here again, the clouds concealed the vision of a borderland that is not that of men and not yet the otherworld. In fact, the Land of Darkness forms to some extent an antechamber of the Land of the Blessed, a kingdom of the dead forbidden to the living. In the Eastern versions of his legend, Alexander meets an angel named Israfil, who warns him not to push any further ahead. *Mandeville's Travels* (fourteenth century) indicates that beyond the land of Prester John, a mythical Christian sovereign whose kingdom was said to be next to Mongolia, where an expanse of shadow-haunted deserts bordered the earthly paradise, "in which Adam and Eve were put."[12]

Mandeville's Travels, a compilation of travelers' tales and geographers' writings, mentions another Land of Darkness called Hamson in the East, in the Kingdom of Labeyhas (Abkhasia): "Nevertheless men who live in the country round about say that they can sometimes hear the voice of men, and horses neighing, and cocks crowing, and know whereby that some kind of folk live there, but they do not know what kind of folk they are." The explanation given is interesting: the emperor of Persia was persecuting the Christians who sought refuge in a valley; cornered, they begged God to save them: "Immediately there fell a thick darkness which surrounded the Emperor and his army, so that they could not go away anywhere; and they still live in that darkness and always will."[13]

We can see, then, that darkness is also suggestive of the mythology of clouds: the terrifying expression of it that makes concrete the instant when sun, moon, and stars vanish; the moment when the individual can no longer get oriented; the time when he or she makes their way to the limits of the known world, beyond whose borders there is no return. This is why the otherworld, in all its forms, is frequently separated from our own world by clouds, but it is also bathed in a singular light. Around 1191, Gerald of Wales told the story of a young man who went there by following two dwarfs:

> They led him first through a dark underground tunnel and then into a most attractive country, where there were lovely rivers and meadows, and delightful woodlands and plains. It was rather dark, because the sun did not shine there. The days were all overcast, as if by clouds, and the nights were pitch-black, for there was no moon nor stars. (*Itinerarium Cambriae*, I, 8)[14]

In ancient Germanic mythology, clouds and darkness are inseparably linked in the word *nifl* (Latin *nebula*) that means "dark" and "cloud." Norse cosmogony tells us that before Creation there was Chaos, a depthless abyss: Ginnungagap. To its north was Niflheimr, "Dark World" or "World of Clouds." To the south was the "World of Fire," Múspellsheimr. A spring flowing in Niflheimr gave birth to all the original rivers, the *Élivágar*. The link between *nifl* and water is clear, as clouds are merely one form of water. It also appears in the Old High German word *uuolche*, "cloud," whose Indo-European root carries the idea of wetness. The afterworld for common folk is named Hel and according to the Icelandic mythographer Snorri Sturluson (thirteenth century), it contains nine dwelling places; the last one, the deepest and most terrible, is called *Niflhel*.[15] There are also the famed Nibelungen (Norse *Niflungar*). Their name consists of the root *nebel*, "cloud, fog," which is cognate with the Norse *nifl*, and the suffix *-ung/-ing* that serves to establish a lineage connection (for example in the name of the Merovingians, the "descendants of Merovech"). They would therefore be etymologically connected to darkness and clouds, which clearly indicates they belong to another world: in this case, the hollow mountain in which they live. But we must remember that in the Middle Ages, the hollow mountain was envisioned as an empire of the dead, a simulacrum of a burial mound.

Reduced to literary tropes and somewhat de-mythicizied, these notions fed the Arthurian imagination. In his *Lanzelet* (composed around 1190), Ulrich von Zatzikhoven portrays a certain Malduc of the Misty or Dark Lake (*Malduck von dem Genibelten sê*); he is a magician, and the borders of his castle are defended by the Wailing Marsh (*daz schrîende mos*).[16] The most explicit is Chrétien de Troyes, the illustrious poet who lived at the court of Marie de Champagne in the second half of the twelfth century. In his romance *Erec et Enide*, written around 1170, he was inspired by the notions we have been looking at. The knight Erec must succeed in finishing a trial called the "Joy of the Court" and, more poetically, "The Cloud Fence" in the medieval Welsh version of the tale.[17] It involves confrontation with a knight, Maboagrain, most likely a giant originally, who has chosen to live with his wife, a fairy described in a way to seem more plausible to the rational mind, in an orchard enclosed by a wall of air or clouds. For seven years, all those who attempted this trial have been killed. "The orchard," says Chrétien, "was surrounded by no wall or fence, but only by air. Air that by magic served as the wall all around this garden like iron, so nothing could enter it except at one single entrance. All winter and summer, there were flowers and ripe fruits." This is a major theme of paradise according to Celtic legend. "Its fruits were under a spell that they could be eaten inside the garden but not taken outside." There could be no better way to highlight the otherworldly nature of this orchard. Erec defeats Maboagrain, who had slain all the knights that had risked entering the garden and stuck their heads on stakes. He blew the horn there and the fence vanished. In *Geraint, Son of Erbin*, the Welsh tale, he is told: "Sound yonder horn," said he, "and when thou soundest it, the mist will vanish; but it will not go hence unless the horn be blown by the knight by whom I am vanquished." In a mysterious coincidence for which the old texts held the secret, we find behind these deeds a practice that survived in the Alps into the nineteenth century: a horn would be blown to drive away threatening clouds, a custom that had already been anathematized by the *Indiculus superstitionum et paganiarum* (Small Index of Superstitions and Paganism; §22) in the eighth century.[18]

Linked to the otherworld, clouds are also connected to magic and spells. In his *Wigalois* (*Gwi le Gallois*), written between 1210 and 1215, the German poet Wirnt von Grafenberg records a fine tale about a malefic fog.[19] To reach the Castle of Roaz, the usurper of the kingdom of Glois, it is necessary to cross the very singular swamp surrounding it: every morning, a pernicious cloud rises above it that is as thick as pitch or resin. It has the particular feature of killing anyone who enters it by literally gluing them solid (v. 6725–62). As Roaz is a pagan who signed a pact with the devil to help him in all his undertakings, we can safely assume that the cloud is diabolical. In *Wigalois*, it marks a border in which the forces of good battle the forces of evil, and where the knight fulfills his quest.

CLOUDS, DWELLINGS OF THE SPIRITS

Christianity makes a connection between God and clouds, as we have seen, and in the Middle Ages, a trace of this notion survives in the legend of Saint Christopher. In the ninth century, Ratramnus of Corbie recalls how, in a long letter addressed to Bishop Rimbert, charged with converting the Scandinavians, the cynocephalic giant Christopher lost his dog head and became a man like any other:

> In fact, we acknowledge as a member of the human race a figure whose life and martyrdom stand out by such brilliant qualities. It is believed that he [Christopher] even obtained from God the sacrament of baptism by the ministry [*mysterium*, "mystery," in the text] of a cloud spilling its water upon him, as is told by the tale.[20]

Clouds are therefore one of the forms in which God's intervention takes place.

In higher mythology (the one that is well organized by mythologists) it is rare to find traces of clouds in the Middle Ages. On the other hand, numerous texts give us important bits of information featuring supernatural beings. To the best of my knowledge, only one single text connects a god to clouds: the *Jómsvíkinga saga* (Saga of the Jomsvikings), written around 1200. Jarl Hakon confronts the Vikings of Jomsberg, but the naval battle turns against him. He goes to land

and enters a forest and comes to a clearing where he goes down on his knees and invokes his patron deity, the goddess Þorgerðr Hörðaröll— or Hörðabrúðr, Hörgabrúðr, or Hölgabrúðr. He offers to sacrifice his seven-year-old son, Erlingr, to her, and she accepts. Erlingr is put to death, Hakon returns to his ships sure of victory, "Now press the attack with all your might," he tells his men, "because I have invoked the two sisters Þorgerðr and Irpa to give us victory, and they will not let me down." They engage in a new new battle, and the following occurs:

> And thereupon clouds began to gather in the north and, as the day drew on, they soon covered the whole sky. This was followed by lightning and thunder, accompanied by a violent hailstorm. The Jomsvikings had to fight against the storm and the hailstorm was so fierce that men could hardly keep on their feet. . . . Hávarðr the hewer was the first to see Hölgabrúðr [= Hörðaröll] among Hákon's men but many others endowed with second sight saw her, too. When the hail let up a little, they saw that an arrow flew from every finger of the witch and each one found its mark." (chap. 33)[21]

Þorgerðr Hörðaröll is a guardian goddess of fertility; the name -brúðr ("fiancée, bride") is attached to Vanir gods, one of the two major families of Germanic gods, the other being represented by the Æsir. In the form Hörða, the first part of her name makes her a tutelary goddess of the inhabitants of Hörðaland (Norway), but if we use the variant Hörga, which is also attested, she would be connected to funeral mounds, hörgar, and therefore to the dead. Another goddess, Irpa, is always associated with Þorgerðr, but we know practically nothing about her.

With this splendid text we find ourselves at the heart of medieval beliefs concerning clouds. They are in the service of spirits, personifications of meteorological phenomena, that Christians call "demons." Shakespeare reflects this opinion in *Macbeth* (III, 5) in which one of the witches states:

> Hark! I am call'd; my little spirit, see,
> Sits in a foggy cloud, and stays for me.

And in *The Tempest* (I, 1), Shakespeare introduces Ariel, a demon of the air who tells Prospero, the duke of Milan:

> All hail, great master! Grave sir, hail! I come
> To answer thy best pleasure; be't to fly,
> To swim, to dive into the fire, to ride
> On the curl'd clouds . . .

Because clouds bring storms, rain, and destructive hail, attempts were made to protect oneself by driving them off, and even making them dissipate. People knew that God and his saints ruled over the weather, so many prayers were addressed to them. Often mentioned are Saints Colomban, Donatus, John the Evangelist, Oswald, and Catherine. According to Gregory of Tours, Saint Martin prevented a fratricidal war by sending a storm. When Queen Clotild learned that Childebert and Theudebert were marching against Lothar, she went to the tomb of the blessed Saint Martin and kept vigil there the whole night so that her sons would not slaughter each other.

> When day dawned a great storm blew up over the spot where they [Childebert and Theudebert] were encamped. Their tents were blown down, their equipment was scattered and everything was overturned. There was thunder and lightning, and they were bombarded with hailstones. . . . No drop of rain fell on Lothar, no clap of thunder was heard, no winds blew where he was. (*Historia Francorum*, III, 28)[22]

Bells are rung and processions conducted, which are often circumambulation rites.[23] In these, the marchers circumambulate the region they wish protected by walking around it with crosses and relics. In a more recent era, clouds were fired upon, and one day people saw a witch falling who, with her evil spells, had raised the storm . . .

All of these methods are merely Christian in appearance. Of course, the bells were baptized—although the *Duplex legationis edictum* of 789 forbids it—and it was believed that they drove away all spirits within earshot. An inscription on the Roskilde (Denmark) bell reads: "My voice is a terror for all evil spirits." Other methods were employed to amplify the magical powers of bells. For example, the alphabet—complete or incomplete, in order or disordered, repeated or not—was often carved on bells because it was believed to possess the power to express all things, therefore all forms of spells and prayers as well. Sometimes the images of saints and the emblems of their pilgrimages would be carved on them.

However, the Church never stopped fulminating against these beliefs. In 561, the First Council of Braga (Portugal) pronounced anathema on anyone who "believes that the devil himself . . . produces thunder and lightning, bad weather and drought, *sua auctoritate* (by his own authority)." In the year 600, the sixteenth anathema of Milan against the Manicheans targets those who "assert that rain, lightning, clouds, and hail would not happen on God's orders." But what do we read in the *Sacerdotale Romanum*, printed in Venice in 1585? A long incantation concerning spirits, clouds, and storm:

> Christ + conquers. Christ + reigns. Christ + commands you, clouds and storms, to dissolve without hurting anyone nor causing the loss of a man, of a beast, of the fruits of the earth, of trees, of a place or a dwelling. May God + the Father surround you! May God + the Son surround you! May God + the Holy Spirit surround you! May God + the father destroy you, may God + the son destroy you, May God the Holy + Spirit destroy you! Amen.
>
> May Saint Matthew +, Saint Mark +, Saint Luke +, and Saint John the Evangelist, who spread the Gospel to the four cardinal points, be able, by virtue of their merits and their prayers, to obtain from Our Lord Jesus Christ that this storm be driven and expelled from all the regions inhabited by men. . . . I command you, by virtue of the omnipotence and strength of God and Our Lord Jesus Christ, supreme sovereign and not by relying on my force and taking pride in it—unclean spirits, you who bring these clouds, I command you by the power of God . . . , by His terrible judgment and by his most holy cross . . . do remove yourselves from them and disperse them

in the forested regions where they can cause no harm to men, nor to beasts, nor to birds, not to fruits . . . + He commands it of you Himself, demons! You who move these clouds. He who from the shining cloud declared: "This is My beloved son" . . .

Then present the cross to the four cardinal points and say: "See + this sign of the most holy cross, flee harmful forces + because Our Lord Jesus Christ, son of God, supreme sovereign, Lion of Judah, scion of David, had defeated you as well as the world!"[24]

No Christian text could be clearer: clouds obey demons! Another spell, collected in Estonia around 1644, addresses the personification of thunder that has been almost deified and is apparently regarded as the master of clouds:

Dear thunder, we offer you [sacrifice], an ox having two horns and four hooves, and we pray to you, for our labor and our sowings, and so that our straw be copper-red and our grain be golden yellow. Push elsewhere all these thick black clouds, toward the swamps, the high forests, and the remote deserts! Give us, and to our laborers and sowers, gentle rain and fruitful weather! Holy thunder, protect our field so that it produces good straw at the bottom, good ears up high, and good bread on the inside.

It will be noted that the wild and uncultivated lands—swamps, forest, and so forth—are an otherworld toward which the evil forces of any form are expelled. In weather charms, the speaker regularly asks the demons of storms to go to such places that are deserted by humans.[25]

These demons are not always anonymous and, thanks to charms composed in the eleventh to fifteenth centuries, we know some of their names. In the Austrian-Bavarian region, we find a certain Vasolt. Mermeut or Meremunt recur several times in these charms. Here is how this demon was banished in the German-speaking regions of the eleventh century:

I bless you, air, in the name of the Lord,
I implore you, devil and your angels,

I implore you do not stir up
The storm or anything else,
And you have nothing to say
Because no one gainsays you.
God and the son of God forbid you,
He who is the source of all creatures.
Saint Mary forbids you.
I implore you, Mermeut, you and your companions
Who rule over the tempest,
I implore you in the name of the one who originally created
Heaven and earth,
I implore you, Mermeut, by this right hand
That shaped Adam, the first man, in His image,
I implore you, Mermeut, by Jesus Christ
Son of the one God,
I banish you, demon and Satan,
I banish you
to have no power
To harm in this place or this village,
To bring here the tempest,
To cause violent rain, . . . [etc.][26]

We also know of a certain Wiggo whose misdeeds Einhart of Fulda (circa 770–840) described in his *Translatio et miracula sancti Marcellini et Petri* (III, 14).[27] While a possessed young girl was being exorcised, Wiggo began speaking and revealed that he and his eleven acolytes, disciples of Satan, had devastated the Frankish kingdom by destroying grains, vines, and fruits, and killing livestock with epidemics. I would like to point out that, during the great plague of 1350, the mortality was attributed to the presence of a thick cloud carrying noxious air that had been sent by demons . . .

Just as a reminder I will mention the belief in the existence of certain men and women with links to the demons that ruled clouds, and who were called *tempestarii* (weather makers), *immissores tempestatis* (storm senders), *fruges perditrices* (fruit spoilers), and *malefici* (black magicians, witches). They were accused from the early Middle Ages of sending hail clouds using spells and various sleights of hand, such as sticking a broom into a pail and stirring it. The judicial means for dealing with them was set during the Synod of Freising in the year 800, which authorized their imprisonment and the use of gentle torture—in other words, moderate enough not to kill them. The ecclesiastical authorities made a provision for seven years of penitence, of which three were "on bread and water," and this in addition to the judgment of the civil authorities.

Tempestarii and other witches only used the power of the demon, their ally who stirred up clouds and utilized them as a means of transportation. This appears in a thirteenth-century exemplum:

> A wealthy miser of Milan asked his accomplice to place ten gold marks in his grave when he died, which was done. But his accomplice told the city judge about this, who, wishing to take this wealth, sent his servants to open the grave and take the gold. They were unable to do so because the dead man got up and sent them fleeing. The judge then went to the tomb, entered, and took the gold. But the dead man grabbed him and strangled him. The next day, a priest followed by a large crowd made his way there with relics and removed the gold from the grave, while exorcising the devil with his prayers. But the demon, soaring into the air above the tomb, began furiously shouting: "Take what's yours and leave me what's mine!" He created an enormous cloud around the tomb and into this mist he gathered the two corpses and carried them off with him.[28]

Having read the small dossier I have assembled here, you will realize that clouds reflect a much larger mythology, which includes both the weather and darkness, in both the literal and figurative senses of the word. Direct testimonies are quite rare, as is almost always the case for something that seems self-evident—at least for the people of a specific era. Therefore, people do not speak so much of clouds but instead of their effects. The conjuration of the *Sacerdotale Romanorum* is a rare example of a repeated mention of clouds. In fact, the entire Middle

Ages used figures of speech in this regard, and we can draw up the following equations:

1. clouds = darkness = demonism, evil spells, death, and catastrophes
2. clouds = a frontier of the otherworld, borders

I should also mention certain miracles linked to clouds, which are difficult to inventory given the breadth of texts that would need to be scrutinized. I will offer one example. In 1536, a certain Johannes Doltzburger, an astronomer in Medina (Hispania) saw a very black cloud arise on which stood two children, each holding a sword in the right hand and a buckler in the left. They fought and the one with a shield decorated with an eagle slew the one with the shield bearing a crescent moon and a star. The astronomer interpreted this sign as heralding the empire's victory over the Turks.[29]

In more recent times, literature and film have made wide use of clouds—here I am thinking of the Gothic novel or *cinema fantastique*, with their depictions of mist-enshrouded castles or an ominous moon that is partly veiled by clouds. Clouds also turn up in poetry, for example as a metaphor for thoughts that are constantly changing shape. And in "folk wisdom" we find expressions that refer to dreams ("to have one's head in the clouds," or the absent-minded hero of the French Professeur Nimbus comic books), serenity ("unclouded happiness"), and danger ("black clouds on the horizon").

11

The Masters of Weather

Tempestarii, Coercers, Defenders, and Others

Atmospheric conditions have always held exceptional importance for the people of earlier eras, especially in agrarian societies. Rain and sunshine are necessary for the fruits of the earth. For this reason, humans have established a relationship between weather and the higher or invisible powers called gods, demons, or spirits. Thor was the master of weather for the ancient Scandinavians according to the testimony of Adam of Bremen.[1] By blowing into his beard, he could cause the wind to rise, something that is also said of a certain Rauðr in the *Saga of Olaf Tryggvason* (chap. 78), by Snorri Sturluson (1179–1241). In the *Story of Burnt Njal* (*Njáls saga*), Thor unleashes a storm that destroys the boat of a Christian missionary. Olaus Magnus also mentions a certain Erik "Windhat" (Väderhatt), who had the power to raise a favorable wind thanks to said hat.[2]

THE DEMONS OF THE METEORS

With Christianity, a connection was made between bad weather and the demons who live in the skies. The first trace of this belief is found in Saint Paul's letter to the Ephesians (6:12) before it went on to feed the whole body of religious literature. The principal transmitters are Origen,[3] Augustine (*De Civ. Dei*, VIII, 22; *de gen. ad lit.*, III, 10), and

Ambrose (*In psal.*, 118).[4] Saint Augustine indicates that fire and air are subject to demons to the extent that God allows (*De Civ. Dei*, VIII, 15–22). This vision of things intersects with the native beliefs of what we call folk mythology, a domain with moving contours that is difficult to get a handle on. It is the expression of a worldview (*Weltanschauung*) that sees the universe inhabited by multiple forces, which it is possible to contact through the intermediation of specialist. In this sphere, we see that the high gods of the old pagan pantheons have practically vanished; the individuals presiding over the weather are entities that form a heterogeneous ensemble that can, however, be divided into two groups: supernatural beings and humans. The latter can, in turn, be divided into two subgroups: the living and the dead. The pagan and Christian visions of the weather masters—which were called "cloud leaders" (*meneurs de nuées*) in nineteenth-century France—combine with one another because they overlap. The presence of demons in the air is explained by the legend of the neutral angels—those who did not take part in the conflict between God and Lucifer, and were cast onto earth and into the sky to become demons. They were reputed to send hail, torrential rains, and storms—in short, the bad weather that threatens the crops of men.[5] Among the demons mentioned in the texts, we should cite Meremeunt (Mermeut)[6] or even the Wiggo about whom Einhart speaks in his *Translatio et miracula sancti Marcellini et Petri*. This demon admits to having destroyed with his eleven companions the grains, vines, and fruits of the Frankish kingdom for several years.[7] These demons would end up being literarily transformed into giants in the entertainment literature,[8] or into monsters.

According to the penitential texts and the old laws, there are individuals who can establish contact with these demons and make them act on demand, which most often means to raise storms.

THE NAMES OF THE WEATHER MAKERS

Since the eighth century, the penitential literature has called them *immissor tempestatis* or *emissores tempestatum*, thus "storm senders," and this name is commonly given as a synonym of *maledicus* and *maleficus*:

maledicus id est emissor tempestatis (*Poenitentiale Parisiense*, cap. XII, p. 413);

emissor tempestatis id est maleficus (*Poenitentiale pseudo-Theoderici*, cap. XII, 21, p. 598).

In general, the penalty leveled at the *tempestarii* was a penitence of seven years—three years of which would sometimes be on dry bread and water!

The Visigothic laws of Chindasuinth condemned "the tempest casters who, it was said, sent hail upon the vines and fields with certain incantations" (*immissores tempestatum qui quibusdam incantationibus grandines in vineis messibusque inmittere peribentur*).[9] In 963, Ratherius of Verona used the locution *immissor aut propulsor tempestatum*.[10] Isidore of Seville speaks of *malefici* who "agitate the elements, together through the power of demons in order to unleash hail storms and tempests" (*Etymologiae*, VIII, 9).

The term *tempestarius* is practically always used in the plural by the law texts, for example in the *Capitulare missorum item specialia* of 802–3. In 789, it appeared in the *Admonitio generalis* (cap. 65); in the synod of Reisbach-Freising of 799 or 800; in the *Dicta* (cap. 22) by Pirman of Reichnau (died 753); in the work of Herard of Tours (*Capitula*, cap. 3) in 858; and in *De grandine et tonitruis* (On Hail and Thunder) by Agobard of Lyon, from which I have drawn the following interpretation of the intentions of the *tempestarii*:

there is a certain region, which is called Magonia, from which ships come in the clouds. In these ships the crops that fell because of hail and were lost in storms are carried back into that region; evidently these aerial sailors make a payment to the storm-makers, and take the grain and other crops.[11]

These *tempestarii* come from Magonia, which is undoubtedly the "Land of the Mages" if we take into account the comment of Bernardino of Sienna (fifteenth century), who writes:

alii quoque, cum descendere viderint quamdam nubem, quam quidam
magonem vocant, quae solet de mari haurire cum navium periculo,
aquam illam evaginato ac vibrato ense quibusdam conjurationibus
praecidere quodammodo simulant.

And others, too, when they see a certain cloud descending, which
some call a *magon* and which is wont to draw up water from the sea
at the danger of ships, they feign to cut that water in a certain way
by unsheathing and waving a sword with certain conjurations.[12]

With regard to the formation of the geographical term *Magonia*
from *magus*, an analogue can be seen in *Narragonia* (the "Land of
Fools"), from *narr*, "fool," in Sebastian Brand's fifteenth-century alle-
gory *Das Narrenschiff* (The Ship of Fools). In the Germanic regions,
clouds became quickly compared to ships and a skaldic kenning
for them is *vindflot*, "wind raft" (*Alvísmál*, st. 18). Moreover, Hans
Sachs (fifteenth–sixteenth century) uses the term *nebelschiff*, "ship of
the clouds," which shows us that there truly was a tradition whose
first traces are the ships that arrive from Magonia through the sky.
A fourteenth-century manuscript also contains a poem of 160 Latin
hexameters titled *De rebus Hiberniae admirandis* (On the Wonders of
Ireland), in which a "ship in the air" is mentioned.[13]

The *Admonitio generalis* and the capitulary of 802–3 give us
another name for these men who influence the weather through the
intermediary of demons: *tempestarii vel obligatores*. The "obligators"
are so named because they have the power to force the demons to act
on their behalf.

The fact that these *tempestarii* are almost always referred to using
the plural form of the word suggests that we are dealing with a brother-
hood or a group.

Fortunately for human beings, there are individuals capable of
diverting bad weather and thwarting the evil actions of the *tempestarii*.
In the Middle Ages they were called *defensores*, the "defenders" or
"protectors"—in other words, "storm lifters" by analogy with the
"lifters of ailments" who are healers. But the texts give the impression

that the defenders are quite simply weather makers, thus sorcerers, and that their actions can reflect beneficial as well as malefic magic. We also find even more vague names in the Christian benedictions, for example *incantatores malorum* (conjurors of evils) and *ministres sathane* (servants of Satan).[14]

It has been noted that in the early Middle Ages, it was essentially individuals of the male sex who reportedly had power over the weather. My research has only yielded one account that alludes to women, that of the *Homilia de sacrilegiis* by the Pseudo-Augustine, which is preserved in a manuscript in Einsiedeln (Stiftsbibliothek, Codice 199, folio 487): *Tempistarias nolite credere nec aliquid pro hoc eis dare* (Do not believe *tempestarias* or give them anything for this).

A variety of individuals used magic to influence meteors—in other words, they used meaningful ritual words and actions, some for the good of the community, and others to harm it. This is not simply a legend: Agobard of Lyon castigates "the people of these regions—noble or not, city dwellers and country folk, young and old—who believe that men can make it rain or hail whenever they want," and he refers several times to the words spoken when people see lightning and hear thunder (they say: "Aura levatitia est" ["The air is raised"]).[15] Bartholomaeus Anglicus meanwhile mentions the people of Vinland (*Vvinlandia*)—perhaps the Wends—who have the ability to procure favorable winds for whoever pays them to do so. The local *tempestarii* make a ball of thread and form knots in it. The strength of the wind depends on the number of knots:

> *globum enim de filo faciunt et diversos nodos in eo connectentes . . .*
> *ventum maiorem vel minorem excitant, secundum quod plures nodos*
> *de filo extrahunt vel pauciores.*[16]

for they make a ball of thread and connect different knots in it . . . they excite a greater or lesser wind, according to which they pull out more or fewer knots from the thread.

The *tempestarii* of the fifteenth century were primarily sorcerers.

CALLING RAIN OR STORMS

A few scattered texts inform us of other practices, some intended to make rain, others to drive it away. Gregory of Tours describes a ceremony that took place in the sixth century, in the Massif Central region at the lake of Saint-Andéol:

> At a fixed time a crowd of rustics went there and, as if offering libations to the lake, threw [into it] linen cloths and garments that served men as clothing. Some [threw] pelts of wool, many [threw] models of cheese and wax and bread into it, as well as various [other] objects, each according to his own means, that I think would take too long to enumerate. They came with their wagons, they brought food and drink, sacrificed animals, and feasted for three days. But before they were due to leave on the fourth day, a violent storm approached them with thunder and lightning. The heavy rainfall and hailstones fell with such force that each person thought they could not escape (*cum discedere deberent, anticipabat eos tempestas cum tonitruo et coruscatione valida; et in tantum imber ingens cum lapidum violentia descendebat, ut vix se quisquam eorum putaret evadere*). Every year this happened this way, but these foolish people were bound up in their mistake. (*De gloria confessorum*, II, 6)[17]

At the beginning of the eleventh century, Burchard of Worms recorded a ceremony intended to bring rain. When there was no rain and they needed it (*dum pluviam non habent et ea indigent*), the women would pick a virgin, strip her bare, and bring her to a place where black henbane grew. There she was made to pull out the plant and its root with the little finger of her right hand and tie it to the little toe of her right foot. They then took her to a river where they sprinkled water on her with the help of rods (*Decretum*, XIX, 5, 194). This rite is very reminiscent of the *Dodola* ritual of the Slavs.

If we refer to *Ruodlieb*, the first romance of the Middle Ages, it is clear that the ashes of the dead played a role in atmospheric precipitation. An adulterous woman says the following before her sentence is carried out:

If you wish to hang me from a tree, cut off my long hair and make it into a rope to strangle me, as I've sinned so often because of it. But I beg you to take my body down after three days, to burn it, and to cast the ashes in the water so that the sun doesn't mask its shining, so that the sky refuses to rain, and so that people say hail is wounding the earth because of me (*ne iubar abscondat sol aut aer neget imbrem, / ne per me grando dicatur ledere mundo*, VIII, 45, 51).[18]

At the beginning of the thirteenth century, when speaking of a tall mountain with a lake at its summit, located in the Catalonian bishopric of Gerona (*Otia Imperialia*, III, 66), Gervase of Tilbury tells us that throwing stones into the lake will unleash a violent downpour. Thomas of Cantimpré also mentions stones tossed into a spring.[19] In both cases, the rulers of atmospheric phenomena are land spirits. At the lake of Saint-Andéol, it involved a propitiatory ceremony with offerings, in return for which they received rain. In the Catalonian lake, the rain was sent to punish an offense (*tamquam offensis daemonibus tempestas erumpit*). In both cases, however, supernatural beings play a role. The connection between land spirits demonized by the Church and bad weather clearly appears in a passage from the *Chanson des Chétifs* (Song of the Captives). Beaudoin de Beauvais slays a dragon living in a cave in Mount Tigris, the "demon" leaves the reptile's body in the form of a crow and unleashes a terrible storm.[20]

In the *Malleus Maleficarum* (II, 1, 15), a witch tells how to cause a storm:

"I was in my house and at noon the demon summoned me, telling me to take myself to the open country"—the "Plain of Kuppel," which is its name—"and to bring a little water with me. When I asked what work he wished to perform with the water, he answered that he wished to make rain. So as I passed through the city gate, I found the demon standing under a tree." . . . "The demon told me to dig a small hole and pour the water into it." . . . "I stirred it with my finger, in the name of that devil and all the other demons." . . . "It disappeared, and the Devil took it up into the air."

Another witch also describes her method:

"First, in the field we use certain words to beseech the Prince of
All Demons to send one of his subordinates to strike the person
indicated by us. Then, when a certain demon comes, we sacrifice a
black rooster to him at a crossroads casting it up into the air. Having
accepted it, the demon obeys and immediately stirs up a breeze. Yet,
he does not always cast the hailstorms and lightning bolts into the
places intended by us, but does so according to the permission of the
Living God." (*Malleus maleficarum*, II, 1, 15)[21]

The inquisitors gave other examples that head in the same direction, like that of a young girl who stirs the water of a stream and makes
it rain (II, 13; 15). They also indicate that hail and lightning can be
summoned by tossing a black cock in the air at a crossroads (II, 15).
According to other accounts, although admittedly much more recent
ones, the same results can be obtained by using one's own urine.

DIVERTING BAD WEATHER

The *Homilia de sacrilegiis* provides us with two clues regarding how
the *tempestarii* took action. It condemns all those who think they
can turn aside hailstorms by using lead tablets covered with incanted
writings or horns." The *Indiculus superstitionum* (tit. 22) refers to a
chapter "De tempestatibus et cornibus et cocleis" (On Bad Weather
and Horns and Snails). These mysterious *cochleae* ("snails") have to be
seen as noise-making instruments. The *Indiculus* is therefore alluding
to a very ancient practice, that of making noise to send demons fleeing—or even the dead who have come back—a practice inherited by
the Church as storms were "broken" by ringing bells, bells that were
at one time not only blessed but also covered with cabalistic signs and
symbols, which reinforced their protective power.[22] We can find con-
firmation of these facts in the *Manual of the Burgos Church* in 1497,
which says this: "when one sees a storm approaching, cymbals must
be played" (*dum viderit moueri tempestas, statim pulset cimbala*).[23]

In the thirteenth century, Guillaume Durand, the bishop of Mende, described the magical power of bells in the following way:

> The bells are rung in processions to put demons to flight, for when they hear these trumpets of the militant Church ring the bells, they are terrified. . . . This is the reason why, when a storm is brewing on the horizon, the church rings its bells so that the devils, hearing the trumpets of the eternal King, tremble, flee, and refrain from unleashing the tempest.[24]

Devising remedies for escaping storms, the authors of the *Malleus Maleficarum* (II, 2, 7) wrote the following:

> For this reason it is a universal or general practice in the Church to ring bells against the wind. There are two purposes for this. The first is that the demons should withdraw from their acts of sorcery as if on account of trumpets consecrated to God, and the second is that the congregation should be roused to invoke God against the storms.[25]

BLESSINGS AND CHARMS

Today it is difficult to rediscover these rituals, as practically everything that we have and which is concerned with opposition to storms—the conjurations, charms, and blessings—was initially transmitted by the clerical literature and is therefore heavily Christianized. Black magic spells for weather are only known through the literature of entertainment and historiography, and then, in the early Middle Ages, through the registers of the Inquisition.

When bad weather threatened, the defender used charms that are a mixture of blessing and spell, and an amalgam of Christian and pagan elements. The Christian spells for bad weather that we have at our disposal carry limpid titles:

Benedictio contra aereas tempestates
Benedictio contra tempestatem

Benedictio aure
Benedictio salis et aque contra fulgura
Benedictio aquae contra fulgura
Oratio ad depellendam tempestatem
Orationes contra grandines et tempestates
Ordo contra tempestates
Coniuratio contra tempestatem

It should be noted that the Latin *benedictio* should be taken in the sense of "charms," that holy water and blessed salt were used, and there were three distinct domains: the blessing of places one wished preserved; the blessing of the methods used; and the banishing of the storm (*oratio, coniuratio*). Holy water is expressly said "to drive away wandering and unclean spirits, and all the harmful forces of the devil, ghosts, thunder, and lightning" by purifying the premises (*purgatio et purificatio*) where it is cast.[26]

The traces of paganism contained in the benedictions clearly show that they had replaced autochthonous charms, but it should be acknowledged that the eradication of ancient practices and the condemnation of weather makers did not rest solely on the desire to spread the true faith and protect people. Agobard of Lyon informs us that the clergy were in competition with the *tempestarii*, and the people preferred to give them their meager pittance than to pay a tithe to the church.* This distrust or even outright hostility is clearly apparent in the Danes' behavior in 1080: they attributed bad weather and other evils to the priests![27]

FROM *TEMPESTARIUS* TO CLERIC

So the clergy replaced the *tempestarii*, which numerous theologians condemned violently at the end of the Middle Ages, especially because they were using the sacraments to divert bad weather.[28] Jacob Sprenger and

---

*The synodal statutes of Brixen were still advising priests in 1453 to avoid processions and circumambulations in the fields to drive away bad weather or to summon good weather.

Heinrich Kramer indicate that people carried out "the Sacrament to calm the wind" (II, 2, 7) and cited another remedy against hail and tempests:

> Hailstones are cast into the fire with the invocation of the Most Holy Trinity. The Lord's Prayer is added two or three times along with the Hail Mary. The passage "In the beginning was the Word," from the Gospel of John with the making of the Sign of the Cross is added against a storm all over: in front, in back and in every direction of the earth. In this case, when he repeats, "The Word was made flesh," three times at the end and then says, "May this storm be put to flight by the words of the Gospel," the storm will suddenly stop if it was in fact caused as a result of sorcery. . . .
>
> In addition, when a certain sorceress was asked by a judge whether storms stirred up by sorceresses could in some way be calmed, she replied, "Yes, through the following phrase. 'I adjure you, hailstorms and winds, by the Five Wounds of Christ and by the Three Nails that pierced His hands and feet and by the four Evangelists, Matthew, Mark, Luke and John, to dissolve into water and come down.'"[29]

We should also mention other rites, special masses, the use of relics* and processions that are suggestive of circumambulation rites. In 1240 or 1244, in the Liège region, a triple circumambulation took place with barefoot priests and laypeople, to ask for rain—it had no result because they forgot to invoke Mary. A new procession was made while singing the *Salve Regina* and it caused such a strong downpour (*tanta inundatio pluviae facta est*) that all those participating in it were soaked.[30] Recourse to weather saints was common and they were regularly invoked in Christian benedictions and spells. Their names vary depending on time and place, and their influence over the weather is regularly connected to a remarkable event from their lives, most often the diversion of a tempest due to a prayer. Let us cite as examples Remigius, Quiriace, John,

---

*Some are supposed to have protected Gregory of Tours from a storm (*In gloria martyrum*, 83).

Paul, Quentin, Columba, Cyril, and Donatus among the male saints, and Barbara and Brigid among the female saints. In the thirteenth century, Gervase of Tilbury tells of a man's encounter with Saint Simeon, who gave him a horn that granted protection against lightning.[31]

Some rituals have come down to the present day, such as the following charm from the fifteenth century:

> Begin by blowing three times toward the clouds and say in the shape of a cross:*
>   Downpour, hail,
>   I command you, by the three nails of Our Savior +++,
>   I command you, by the force of God, the heavenly father +++,
>   I command you, by the Holy Trinity of God +++,
>   I command you not to strike the earth
>   Before you become fruitful water,
>   Say five *Paternosters*, five *Ave Marias*, a *Credo*, three times each, and invoke God by His five sacred wounds.

The speaker addresses the *grando, procella, diabolus, satanas, angeli satane, angeli tartarei*, conjures them (him, her), and commands them to find dry and deserted places (*loca arida et deserta*).[32]

Storms can also be turned aside by planting a cross in the ground while reciting a conjuration. Here is what a ninth-century Latin manuscript tells us:

> You must inscribe the following prayer on the cross that is planted to divert storms:
>   I implore you, angels carrying the storm by saint [?] to not cast stones on the land of this servant named [———], but to go carry them into the uncultivated lands and the hidden mountain. As you have sworn to our fathers, go and may you be propitious. Remember, Lord! Say to the angel, striking Your temple to stay his hand. *Aios Aios Aios, Chiriale Chiriale Chiriale, Allalal*, from this village that is called (name it).

---

*In other words, toward the four cardinal points.

In the *Malleus Maleficarum* (1487), the inquisitors Jacob Sprenger and Heinrich Kramer discussing these words, accepting only those borrowed from the liturgy:

> because if there were any virtues inherent in certain words or Sacramentals or other blessings and lawful chants, they would possess such virtues within themselves, not as words but as a result of divine arrangement and ordination and as a result of the agreement of God, as if the Lord said, "Whoever does this, I will perform this grace for him." This is how the words in the Sacraments achieve what they betoken. . . .
>
> Regarding the other words and chants, it is clear from the foregoing that as words that are put together in groups or uttered or symbolized, words achieve nothing, but the invocation of the name of God and the obsecration, which is a very sacred public declaration of entrusting the result to the will of God, are beneficial. (II, 2, 7)[33]

Stones and plants hold a special place among the apotropaic measures that should be taken. The *Lapidary* of Damigeron/Evax (sixth–seventh century) mentions three stones that fall into this category: coral (VII, 7), emerald (VI, 3),[34] and ceraunia (XII, 4).

Lastly, the Carolingian capitulary *De villis* recommends that everyone keep Jupiter's Beard (*Barba Iovis, Donnerwurz*) in the home to grant protection against lightning, and the virtues of laurel are commonly known as it is the sole tree that is never struck by lightning.[35]

We should remember that everything dealing with atmospheric conditions forms a syncretic ensemble that testifies with great precision to the way in which the Church assimilated, covered over, and then eliminated very ancient rituals. Believers and unbelievers were united in the same faith, namely, that it is possible to cause rain, hail, and wind, or to drive them away; to bring down lightning or to send it away. This presumes a vision of the world that situates in the universe forces embodied by gods, demons, and spirits, and then saints as masters of bad weather and of sunshine.

12

Mythical Aspects
of the Mountain in the
Middle Ages

When reading medieval texts, we are struck by a bipartition of space that seems to exist without the writers consciously acknowledging it. On the one hand, we have wild nature—the savage world (*diu wilde*) represented by the sea, the forest, and the mountain, the deserts in travelers' tales—and, on the other hand, there is civilization: the world of cleared lands and plains, cities and towns. The highly inaccessible regions and those that are unexplored, remote, unknown, or misunderstood, are *a priori* disturbing. They are described with the aid of clichés: it is still the savage sea even when the boat lies at anchor in port,[1] the forest is dark (*vinster walt, vinster tan*) and tangled,[2] the mountain high and steep, carved by deep, silent valleys. In *La Chanson de Roland* (The Song of Roland) the tone is established when we read (ll. 814–15):

> *Halt sunt li pui e li val tenebrus,*
> *les roches bises, les destreiz merveillus.*

> High stand the peaks, the vale in shadow,
> Black the rocks amid the wondrous torrents.

All these places are the theaters for extraordinary manifestations: they are the domain of the marvelous.*[3] Here anything and everything is possible; it is the country of chivalrous and initiatory adventure. Here live monstrous men and fantastic creatures, and finally supernatural beings. I was inspired to seek out the reason for this and what follows are the fruits of my reflection on the matter.[4]

The mountain is an elevated place,[5] whose height is expressed by the size of the shadow it projects.[6] The mountain is often protected by a rampart of thick forests and forms primarily a mysterious and marginal world, a world that German scholars designate by the word *Tabulandschaft* ("taboo landscape"). It is ideal for exciting the imagination of people who have yet to pierce Nature's secrets and interpret in their own way the rumbling of avalanches, the fogs and mists of the mountain, and the strange forms created by erosion. For the latter, geology gives us the term "fairy chimneys," and Swiss maps, for example, show countless foothills and mountains that are named *Wilder Mann* or *Wilde Frau*.

How are mountains born? Various legends provide an answer to this question. In Iran, it was Ahriman who, cast beneath the earth, carved an underground tunnel like a mole.[7] In the land of Albret, it is said that the land was flat before the Deluge, but when the floodwaters receded, mountains appeared. Between 1235 and 1250, Thomas de Cantimpré and Vincent de Beauvais testify to a similar belief.[8] Among the ancient Scandinavians, Snorri Sturluson tells us that mountains were formed from the bones of Ymir, the primordial giant.[9] In antiquity

---

*Here, for example, are two legends that we find in the *Liber floridus*, which Lambert of Saint-Omer wrote in 1120: "There is another tomb in Britain at the top of Mount Cruc Mayr; whoever lies down next to it, whether he be large or small, the grave will adjust to his size. And every pilgrim that prostrates himself three times before the tomb will not be worn down by the fatigue of the journey. In Britain, there is a very admirable miracle: a stone that can be found in the Cheym Valley during the night and on the mountain during the day; When the folk there cast it into the water or bury it in the ground, in the morning it can always be found again at the top of the mountain, and in the valley at night" (Ghent Cod. 92, fol. 64v°). The source of these tales is the *Historia Britonnum*, in which we also find this short notice: *Secundum miraculum est ibi mons qui gyratur tribus vicinibus in anno* (Second marvel: there is a mountain that revolves three times a year).

it was believed that Mount Atlas was nothing other than a giant of the same name that had been petrified by Perseus.* The mythic character of the mountain is perceptible right from the start, even if the enlightened minds of the Middle Ages maintained that they were born due to earthquakes or because of the action of the winds.[10]

In this era, the names of the principal mountains of the *orbis tripartitus* (the tripartite vision of the earth, or better, the terrestrial surface) were known,[11] and the legend became attached to them, blended with more or less scientific observations. In the thirteenth century, people wishing to climb mountains were advised to take a water-soaked sponge to breathe through if they did not wish to suffocate;[12] the air there is indeed "subtle and penetrable," totally lacking in humidity, and most unhealthy.[13] It was claimed that bearded women lived in the mountains of Norway[14] and that people lived in the vicinity of Grand Saint-Bernard who were suffering from goiters that were the size of a gourd.[15] It was also believed that crystal was solidified snow or ice.[16]

Let us take a quick look at the inhabitants not of a particular mountain, but of all those mountains that haunted the medieval imagination. The Riphean Mountains, which the cartography of the time situated at the extreme northeastern border of the known world, north of Germania as well, are the kingdom of the griffin guardian of the emeralds and gold that can be found there in abundance.[17] The same fable pertained to the Caucasus and the mountains of India. In Wolfram von Eschenbach's *Parzival* (ca. 1210), it is said that Gahmuret's coat of mail is made from gold that these monstrous birds snatched from the mountains.[18] We should note that the Arabs place the roc (*rukhkh*) there and the Persians, the *simurgh*. It is truly a world out of the ordinary: Paul the Deacon (ca. 720–799) informs us that gigantic bison lived in the Alps; fifteen men would be able to stretch out on the hide of just one of them.[19] Alpine caves were home to numerous dragons, and the poems about the adventures of the deeds of Dietrich von Bern are full of descriptions of the battles that the

---

*But in the Middle Ages, Atlas was regarded as an astronomer (cf. Vincent de Beauvais, *Spec. nat.*, VI, 22).

legendary king of Verona and his companions (the Wylfinge) waged against them.[20] Such encounters could go terribly wrong and Ortnit, King of Lombardy, was eaten by a monster like this.[21] Centaurs could be found in the Tyrolean mountains,[22] and in the wondrous mountains of the East there lived serpents with the heads of women.[23] It must be noted, however, that monstrous men are more plentiful than the *bestiae* and the *beluae*.

At the beginning of the fourth century BCE, Ctesias of Cnidus described the pygmies living in the Indian mountains along with the dog-headed men.[24] Beton, Alexander the Great's head surveyor, reports that in this place they captured Opisthodactyls, in other words individuals whose feet were backward;[25] this is why Latin writers called it the "Antipodes." Other learned men inform us that the Amazons lived near Mount Caspios[26] and that Etna was home to the Cyclops.[27]

The ancient Scandinavians maintained that the world of the giants (Jötunheimr) was beyond the mountains (cf. *För Skirnis* in the *Poetic Edda*); the *Fornaldarsögur* (sagas of ancient times) tell how the giants live in a cold and wild land among mountains and glaciers. This is what gives them their name (*bergrisar*). This opinion is confirmed by the *Saga of Grettir* (*Grettis saga*) concerning Hallmundr, and by the story of Hálfdan the Black, which indicates that the giant Dofri gave his name to Dovrefjell, Norway. In the *Saga of Bárðr* (*Bárðar saga Snæfellsáss*) we learn that this giant was nicknamed the *áss* of Snæfell mountain.*

In Ireland, the giants erected a monument of Mount Killaraus (Kildare) known as the "Giant's Ring."[28] In Germany, they are frequently the denizens of mountains.

In Germanic literature, Der Pleier, whose literary activity took place between 1260 and 1280, gives a precise idea of the notion people had of the mountain's inhabitants. In his romance *Tandareis und Flordibel*, the queen of the dwarfs leads the knight Tandareis to Salvasch Montân (= Savage Mountain) where he saw "numerous wild men and women, large and frightening to see. . . . He also saw many large women who

---

*[Old Norse *áss*, "god," is the singular form of *æsir*. —*Ed*.]

were black and monstrous."[29] Among such individuals, we encounter
Fasolt in the Tyrol, the Cursed Hunter, who sometimes takes on the
features of an ogre named Orkîse.[30] A being covered in scales, Kolkan,
lives in the Galacides Mountains, in Grotimunt.[31] Men of fire appear
on Agremontin.[32] All the figures mentioned live in the open air. Let
us look at what goes on inside the mountains, because we should not
forget a widespread notion in Germanic regions, which maintained they
were hollow.

The dwarfs are at work inside the mountains for they have the
mission of extracting the gold, gems, metals, and pearls that are found
there in abundance.[33] We should recall that mountains are reputed to
have great wealth. Herodotus claimed that mountains had this reputation in antiquity (*Histories*, III, 16; IV, 13 and 27). The rivers flowing from them carried precious stones. In the land of Prester John, the
mythical sovereign whose kingdom was believed to be located beyond
the Islamic countries, there is a mountain as clear as crystal. The river
Idonus flows out of it, says the Middle High German poet Albrecht
von Scharfenberg, and its waters carry sapphires, emeralds, carbuncles,
topazes, sard, beryl, chrysolites, amethysts, and diamonds.[34] Flowing
not far from there in Mount Olympus is a spring in which eagles find,
in the month of May, gems with wondrous properties.[35] In the epic that
bears his name (*Herzog Ernst*), dating from the end of the twelfth century, Duke Ernst crosses through a mountain by sailing on an underground river. The depths of this mountain reveal many gems.[36] In the
adventure of *Reinfried von Braunschweig* it is also said that there are
mountains made of pure gold and onyx.*[37]

Here I would like to interrupt this overview of what medieval literature gives us. All these elements inspire me to ask a twofold question:
What does the presence of unusual individuals and animals signify, and
where do mountains get their reputation for wealth?

From the presentation of these details the primary function of
the mountain emerges: it is not only a natural frontier but a mythical
one, and I believe its different aspects in antiquity and the Middle

---

*This gold mountain stands not far from the Magnetic Mountain.

Ages stem from this function. And what would it be the frontier of, if not the otherworld, the beyond?*[38] By examining the texts from this angle, it is possible to draw a brief typology of the mythical mountain.

THE SACRED MOUNTAIN

From the most ancient texts onward, the mountain appears as an intermediary world between man and the gods, the demons, and their secularized forms: its summit abuts heaven and its base neighbors the empire of the dead. It possesses an undeniably sacred nature, which is first explained by it being the home of the gods and a place where supernatural beings congregate. The *Epic of Gilgamesh* informs us that gods held council on Mount Cedar.[39] The link between heaven and earth for the Babylonians was symbolized by a cosmic mountain or its replicas, the ziggurats. For the Altaian people the Ostyaks, there is a goddess seated on a celestial mountain with seven levels and she inscribes the fate of the individual at their birth on a tree with seven branches.[40] Greek mythology informs us that Mount Olympus was the home of Zeus, and then, as we know, Olympus lost all connection with the mountain of the same name.

Classical antiquity teaches us that mountains are a place where higher beings like to go. Helicon is the abode of the Muses of Boeotia; it is where the Hippocrene spring gushed out from under the hoof of Pegasus. This is where Athena and the nymph Chariclo bathed, where Pan's son Crotos lived as well as Eupheme, the Muses' wet nurse. Mount Pelion hosted the coupling of Cronos and Phylira, who gave birth to Chiron the Centaur; here also lived Poseidon's sons Syleus and Dicaeus. Let us take note of this alliance between sea and mountain as it occurs frequently during the Middle Ages. Greek legend therefore indicates the mountain as the abode of the gods, the demigods, and members of their retinues.

---

*I am employing the term "beyond" in contrast to our sublunary world, without any Christian connotations.

The same thing is true for Scandinavian mythology: the god Heimdall's seat is on the mountain Himinbjörg (*Grímnismál*, st. 13). The mountain called Hnitbjörg, the "Crashing Rock," is famous. Here is where Gunnlöð lives. She is the daughter of the giant Suttungr and guardian of the sacred containers (the cauldron Óðrerir and the vessels Són and Boðn) that hold the blood of Kvasir blended with honey: this beverage has the ability to turn everyone who tastes it into a poet (*skald*).[41] And then we have Helgafell, the "Sacred Mountain," which according to the *Book of the Settlement of Iceland* (*Landnámabók*, II, 12) was worshipped. The presence of a place name like Sólarfjöll (Sól's Mountains) in Iceland implies that mountains were the site of the worship of the goddess Sól. An eighth-century Carolingian catechism, the *Ratio de cathecizandis rudibus*, attests to the use of mountains in pagan worship.*[42]

Starting in the twelfth century, the mountain became the home of fairies and demons, an apt consequence of its pagan nature, and later witches would hold their sabbats there. It is therefore the meeting point between our world and sacred in both its positive and negative forms—isn't it worth noting that pagans built their temples there, as did the Christians with their chapels (such as in Le Puy-en-Velay)? It was on the mountain that Moses was given the Tablets with the Ten Commandments (Exodus 19:3–25).†[43] It is also where witches coupled with devils or had sacred communion with them there, and fairies had their fountain of youth.[44] This motif is one that really highlights the borderland nature of the mountain, a nature that is clearly visible in the Middle High German romance of *Friedrich von Schwaben*, written after 1314: a wondrous fountain is where the three rationalized fairies, Angelburg, Malme, and Malmelon recover their human

---

*It states: *Non auguriabis non ad montes, non ad arbores* ("You shall not go into the mountains to indulge in divination, nor among the trees"). A sixth-century spell clearly shows the assimilation of the ancient mountain gods into devils. The speaker addresses the devil that dwells in the forests, the passes, and the mountains (cf. Ferdinand Ohrt, *Fluchtafeln und Wettersegen* [Helsinki: Suomalainen tiedeakatemia, 1929], 3–16).

†We should also note that the Last Judgment will take place on a mountain and God will establish his paradise there (Isaiah 2:2 and 65:25).

shapes after having been metamorphosed into pigeons.[45] In *Lanzelet*, an Arthurian romance by Ulrich von Zatzikhoven from around 1190, the fairy who saves the child Lanzelet from certain death lives on an island consisting of a crystal mountain "round as a ball."[46] In *Seifrid de Ardemont* (ca. 1245–1255) by Albrecht von Scharfenberg, the mountain, which was protected by a burning moor and monstrous serpent, is the place where the fairy Mundirosa comes to wait for her future husband.*[47] We then have Gervase of Tilbury, the first folklorist of the Middle Ages, who recorded the legends concerning the demons on Mount Aiguille and Mount Canigou in 1214.[48] The demonic aspect of the mountain can be seen in the fact that dragons and giants, the forces of chaos, live there. In *Das Lied vom Hürnen Seyfrid* (The Song of Horn-skinned Siegfried), the flying dragon is a demon.†[49] This aspect also appears in the legend of Tannhäuser in which the fairy of the Venusberg (*mons Veneris*) was demonized by Christian culture.[50]

So, we can easily recognize the twofold nature of the mountain, its basic ambiguity—in a word, its ambivalence—which is fully expected since it participates in two different worlds as a frontier. This point seems particularly well illustrated in Iranian myths. In these, the souls of the dead are first led to the summit of the Elbruz where there sits a court of three divine judges who weigh these souls. Next the soul ventures onto the Tchinvat bridge that spans the gulf of hell. It is wide and easy to cross for the pure soul but shrinks when the wicked approach, tumbling them into the abyss.[51]

By virtue of this ambivalence, we have a balanced distribution of the various Christian and pagan myths concerning the mountain.

---

*The hero crosses a burning moor where a storm is raging, performs the feat of the *fier baiser* ("daring kiss"), makes his way to a high mountain that blocks one end of the moor, scales it, and meets the fairy Mundirosa who awaits him there and whose kingdom lies beyond the sea.

†The monster says in fact: *deyn vatter vnd deyn muoter / gesichst du nymmer mer, / noch auch keyn creatur / sichst du doch nymmer an, / mit leyb vnd auch mit seele / muost du zur helle gan* ("You shall never again see your father and mother, nor any creature; you shall descend into hell, body and soul").

THE SITE OF INITIATORY AND HEROIC PROWESS

In the mythological poem of the *First Lay of Helgi Hundingsbani* (*Helgakviða Hundingsbana* I), the battle between Helgi and the sons of Hundingr takes place at Logafjöll (Mountains of Flame). After the battle, it says:

> Then a light shone from Logafell (Logafjöll),
> And from that light came lightning-bolts;
> wearing helmets at Himinvangi [came the valkyries].
> Their byrnies were drenched in blood;
> and beams blazed from their spears.[52]

Then a valkyrie came to him who offered the hero her love. In my opinion, it is not helpful to dwell on the combination of different motifs. Let us take a look at a very medieval and non-mythological tale.

Living near Lac du Bourget was a monstrous cat that was so efficient at slaying men that soon the land was deserted. King Arthur went to the mountain where the cat had its lair and confronted the monster. According to *Le Livre d'Artus* (The Book of Arthur), he was victorious and, in remembrance of his battle the *mont dou lac* (mountain of the lake) was renamed the Mont du Chat (Cat's Mountain), which today is called the Dent du Chat (Cat's Tooth).* In the *Romanz des Franceis* (before 1204),[53] the poet André states that Arthur met his end.

The first branch of the legend shows King Arthur fulfilling his duty as sovereign by ridding the land of a monster, which is in fact the spirit of the place, and by restoring order. His victory proves that his

---

*The Cat's Tooth is a natural "reservoir" of legends. Theodor Mommsen points out the presence of an inscription to Mercury there. The Dominican Stephen of Bourbon (circa 1180–1261) recorded the passing of the *Chasse Artus* there and the existence of a lewd paradise reminiscent of the one in *Venusberg*: caught by surprise by the Mesnie Hellequin, a peasant is led into a palace where he takes part in a feast before going to bed where he finds an extremely beautiful woman; but all this is an illusion (cf. Albert Lecoy de la Marche, *Anecdotes historiques* [Paris: Renouard, 1877], 231).

sovereignty is legitimate. The second branch suggests that he was no longer worthy of ruling his land.

All the elements of the quest are bundled together in the legend of Hürner Seyfrid (Horn-skinned Siegfried): Seyfrid learns of his origin from the dwarf Eugel, confronts a man transformed into a dragon that seeks the damnation of the beautiful Kriemhild, wins his fiancée and a treasure, and becomes the suzerain of a dwarf people. All these adventures occur in the immediate proximity of a mountain named Drachenstein (Dragon Rock).

THE MOUNTAIN AS REFUGE

The mountain is a refuge, concretely at first in the legend of the building of Vortigern's tower on Mount Heriri (= Erir, the Snowdon),[54] and in that of the Seven Sleepers of Ephesus who hid from persecution in a cave on Mount Anchilus.[55] We should note that Alberich/Auberon built his castle on a mountain.*[56] But this refuge is also that of hope: those who sleep inside it will find salvation at the designated spot.[57]

I should point out that the mountain is also a place of perdition. Both aspects appear to me to be well combined in the legend of Pyrene, the daughter of King Bebryx. When fleeing from her father's wrath, she sought refuge in the mountains but was devoured by wild animals. This speaks to the ambivalent nature of this place.

THE MOUNTAIN AS A PLACE OF PERDITION AND RECONCILIATION

Next, the mountain is a place for punishment and atonement, but also reconciliation. After committing the first sin, Adam hastened to the peak that now bears his name in Ceylon.[58] Prometheus was shack-

---

*This is extremely interesting because it attests to a close relationship between Alberich/Auberon and mountains. It so happens that, during the Middle Ages, Alberich, the well-known dwarf, was one of the beings alleged to live in hollow mountains.

led on a mountain in the Caucasus for giving fire to humanity.* The disobedient valkyrie was punished by Óðinn to sleep on Hind Mountain (Hindarfjall) surrounded by a wall of fire.[59] Melusine imprisoned her father, the king of Albania, in a hollow mountain in Northumbria for breaking the promise he had made to his wife, Pressine, to not watch her when she was in labor.[60] Pressine condemned his daughter Palestine to guard her father's treasure on a mountain in Aragon.[†61] Lastly, a legend spread by the Church maintained that Dietrich von Bern, a heretic suspected of Arianism, had died after throwing himself into Mount Etna,[‡62] a fiery mountain.[63]

But the punishment can be only temporary, so it becomes atonement while awaiting redemption.[64] Palestine will remain imprisoned until, as her mother says, "the day a knight of your lineage comes to you to obtain the treasure in order to conquer the Promised Land and free you." However, monstrous lizards defend all access to the mountain and only the chosen one will pass the test.[65] In the romance by Jean d'Arras, we also see a purely Christian aspect, that of intentional atonement. Raymond of Poitiers became a hermit on a tall mountain to prepare his soul for salvation.

Atonement therefore brings about the reconciliation of man and the higher powers, and it is in this sense that I interpret the fact that God stopped Noah's Ark on the mountains of Ararat when the flood waters began to recede (Genesis 8:4).

THE MOUNTAIN: HEAVEN AND HELL

Lastly, the mountain is both heaven and hell for pagan and Christian alike. In the *Epic of Gilgamesh* and in the legend of Saint Brendan, hell

---

*We should note that the two mountains are defended by monsters: a giant in the first case, reptiles in the second.

†This motif is seen again in the Middle High German poem *Reinfried von Braunschweig* (v. 14129–48): Gawein (= Gauvain) spots a giant shackled to a mountain and surrounded by birds; a young girl at his side attempts to defend him.

‡It is striking to see here the frequently attested relationship between the dead and the mountain.

is located inside a mountain.[66] The *Visio Tnugdali* even adumbrates a precise topography of hell: it consists of mountains sundered by deep valleys.[67]

But hell can simply be the land of the dead: the Hittites placed this empire inside a mountain. In Sámi shamanism, the descent into the land of the shadows begins with a trance journey into a mountain.[68] The mystic journey of shamans for the Tungusic people of Manchuria led to a mountain. The shamans climb it before descending the other side into hell.[69] In the legend of Alexander the Great, the Land of the Blessed is located on a mountain that stands in the middle of the Land of Darkness, not far from the Fountain of Youth.[70] The symbolism here is crystal clear! In Iceland, the *Eyrbyggja saga* (chap. 4) explicitly states that the dead enter mountains to live in them. Other texts indicate that the dead go into Helgafell, the "Holy Mountain."

Allow me to present a hypothesis. I am struck by the constancy of a motif that recurs continuously in Norse literature: The mountain is the empire of the dead, and one may wonder to what extent one should not see in the construction of mounds and tumuli one of the forms taken by this belief. Would these mounds not be an extension and simulacrum of the mountain as an empire of the dead? This is an idea we can see again in the Celtic belief involving fairy mounds.[71]

This notion of the mountain as the realm of the dead peeks through, in my opinion, in the reputation of inexhaustible wealth connected with it. Heinrich von Neustadt offers support for this idea. In his romance *Apollonius von Tyrland* (Apollonius of Tyre), written around 1300, the name of the land of eternal spring is the *golden tal* (Golden Dale). It is located in the mountains that are guarded by abominable monsters. In this country, the inhabitants don't ever die unless they choose to, a motif reminiscent of the legends of the Hyperboreans.[72]

The otherworld, the land of the dead, what the Celts call the Land of the Ever Young (*Tír na nÓg*), the Land of the Living (*Tír na mBeo*), and the Delightful Plain (*Mag Mell*), and the ancient Scandinavians called *Valhöll*, is adorned with the features of a paradise beyond the grave. The Christians countered this with their earthly paradise, also located on a mountain.

While the Venerable Bede (673–735) says that this earthly paradise was to be found in the East beyond seas and mountains (that thus
serve as a frontier), Remigius of Auxerre stated that it was on top of a
mountain and for that reason had not been washed away by the Flood.[73]
In Aethicus Ister's *Cosmography* (eighth century), he indicates that it
is inaccessible: high mountains bar the land route and the heat of the
eastern seas forbids any approach by boat (note the relationship between
sea and mountain). Aethicus also believed that paradise was located in
the Caucasus and in the Indian mountains.[74] This is where the rest of
medieval cartography locates it as well. Angelomus of Luxeuil (died
855) says that four rivers flow out of paradise and by following them
back to their source one can reach this spot,[75] an idea that is developed
identically in the *Alexandri Magni iter ad paradisum* (Alexander the
Great's Journey to Paradise; first half of the twelfth century).[76] In his
De imagine mundi (The Vision of the World), written around 1123 and
revised around 1132–1133, Honorius of Autun says that a wall of fire
surrounds the earthly paradise.[77]

Other writers situate Eden in the Armenian mountains or on
Mount Atlas, which seems to be a recollection of the belief in classical
antiquity that the Hesperides were located at the foot of Mount Atlas.
The Grail temple was built in these mountains at the top of an onyx
mountain,[78] not far from the land of Prester John that was separated by
a crystal mountain from paradise.[79]

At the point where Christian and pagan notions of the *hortus deliciarum* meet is the site of Queen Sibylla and the home of Lady Venus in
the Tannhäuser legend. It is a demoniacal paradise and any who venture
there cannot be given forgiveness.

The mountain is the domain where all is possible. Only the sea
offers equal mythical richness—but isn't it frequently associated with
the mountain and just as ambiguous? A place of punishment and reconciliation, the abode of fairies and witches, hermits and demons, the
mountain is the frontier between the gods and men, between Christians
and the Antichrist,[80] and between good and evil. It is the place where
two diametrically opposed worlds confront each other by means of

heroes and chosen ones. I think, therefore, I am in a position to answer the twofold question raised earlier: monsters are the guardians of this frontier, this mythical bridge that connects our world with the next one and, as such, they prevent access to its riches and only submit before the one that has been chosen.*

---

*This can be compared to the theme of the *Gylfaginning*, chap. 26 (in Snorri's *Prose Edda*), which says the god Heimdall lives on Himinbjörg (Heaven's Mountain), near Bifrost (the rainbow bridge). He is the gods' watchman, and he sits there to guard the bridge (Bifrost) against the mountain giants. Here we find the bulk of the elements that we have unearthed in this analysis: the sacred mountain, the mountain as borderland and rampart, and the mountain as refuge.

PART IV

BORDERS AT THE MARGINS OF THE KNOWN WORLD

13

The Sea and Its Isles during the Middle Ages

A Journey into the Marvelous

Since the dawn of time, the sea has never failed to stir the human imagination. People viewed it as a mysterious and disturbing world whose secrets men strove to penetrate. Long before Jacques Cousteau, Alexander the Great had himself placed in a diving bell and lowered into the waters of the sea to see what its depths would reveal—and he saw monsters. The scholarly works of the Middle Ages provide splendid nomenclatures for these sea creatures with singular names that were interpreted literally by the miniature painters of manuscripts: "sea monk" (seal), "sea dog" (shark), "sea unicorn" (narwhale), "dragon," *serra* or *serta*, a mythical vision of the remora, eel, mermaid, tuna, swordfish.

The nave of the Church of St. Martin in Zillis, Switzerland (Grisons canton), has a ceiling of 158 panels that were painted in 1160; the entire perimeter depicts sea monsters. This arrangement displays the sea and its dangers well—all the more so as in medieval allegorical interpretation, life is seen as a voyage over an ocean full of dangers and diabolical temptations. For example, one who hears the siren's song—in other words, the song of the world—is lost. This is shown in the miniatures of the time that depict a siren pulling a passing sailor overboard to her. Around 1260, the Norwegian *King's Mirror* (*Konungs skuggsjá*), a

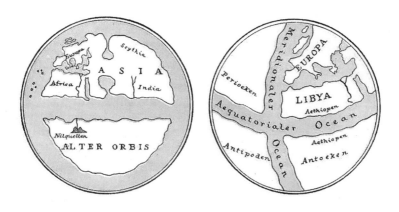

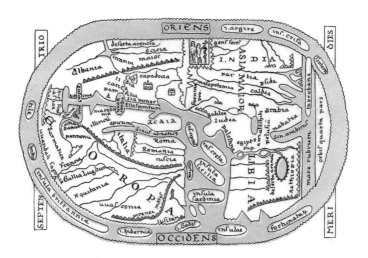

Three ancient maps: (top left) map of the world based on
Pomponious Mela; (top right) globe of the Earth based on Crates of Malus;
(below) Saint Sever's map of the world

book written in the form of a dialogue between a father and son, states (chap. XVI):

It is reported that the waters about Greenland are infested with monsters, though I do not believe that they have been seen very frequently. Still, people have stories to tell about them, so men must have seen or caught sight of them. It is reported that the monster called merman (*hafstrambi*)* is found in the seas of Greenland. This monster is tall and of great size and rises straight out of the water. It appears to have shoulders, neck and head, eyes and mouth, and nose and chin like those of a human being; but above the eyes and the eyebrows it looks more like a man with a peaked helmet on his head. It has shoulders like a man's but no hands. Its body apparently grows narrower from the shoulders down, so that the lower down it has been observed, the slenderer it has seemed to be. But no one has ever seen how the lower end is shaped, whether it terminates in a fin like a fish or is pointed like a pole. The form of this prodigy has, therefore, looked much like an icicle. No one has ever observed it closely enough to determine whether its body has scales like a fish or skin like a man. Whenever the monster has shown itself, men have always been sure that a storm would follow. . . .

Another prodigy called mermaid (*margygr*)† has also been seen there. This appears to have the form of a woman from the waist upward, for it has large nipples on its breast like a woman, long hands and heavy hair, and its neck and head are formed in every respect like those of a human being. The monster is said to have large hands and its fingers are not parted but bound together by a web like that which joins the toes of waterfowl. Below the waistline it has the shape of a fish with scales and tail and fins. It is said to have this in common with the one mentioned before, that it rarely appears except before violent storms.[1]

This extract already gives a sense of the way in which real creatures were perceived: they were interpreted in accordance with the legendary "funds" at one's disposal.

Dolphins were believed to be, in the time of Gervase of Tilbury (1209–1214), knights about whom the following legend was spread. One day, a sailor wounded a dolphin in the sea; immediately, an unprecedented storm struck the boat and a man resembling a knight came

---

*Perhaps the hooded seal.
†Literally "sea-giantess."

up on horseback. He asked the sailors to turn the guilty party over to him if they wished to be saved. By his own accord, the sailor climbed onto the knight's saddle who brought him in no time to a remote region where the wounded victim was resting on a luxurious, stately bed. The sailor was asked to remove the arrow that he had shot and to heal the wounded dolphin, which he did. He was then returned to his boat.[2]

The sea bottom sometimes resembles a forest, and the legend of Nicholas Pipe, also called Cola Pesce (Nicholas Fish), told around 1200, contributes an interesting detail. Nicholas, an experienced diver,

> used to claim that there was a wooded ravine under the water at Faro: and so he explained that it was the barriers of the trees on either side which caused the waves to surge against each other there, asserting that under the sea there were mountains and valleys, woods, plains, and acorn-bearing trees.[3]

But if waves are born this way, the whirlwinds that surround certain reefs, such as that of the Cyclades between Rhodes and Cyprus, have another cause: a young man had coupled with a dead woman who gave birth to a head with the gaze of the Gorgon. He tossed it into the sea but every seven years it turned toward the surface of the water, which placed sailors in peril.[4] The sea is therefore a place of perdition, for certain waters are extremely dangerous. Somewhere in the Indian Ocean, Hormus Island is surrounded by magnets that draw to them any ship carrying iron. It is also said that there is a magnetic mountain in the eastern seas that possesses the same property: a forest formed from the masts of trapped ships stands around said mountain.[5]

The sea is also a place of punishment: it is where Solomon, according to legend, sank the amphorae in which he had imprisoned the jinns. It is also a hiding place, and Christ's seamless robe was cast there and taken by a mermaid.[6] It sometimes has the value of revelation: after chaining up Gregorius on a small island, the key to his shackles was tossed into the sea while he was told that the day it was found it would be a sign that God had forgiven him.[7]

In short, the sea is the subject of a thousand beliefs and myths.

Some of these explain why it is salty, others why it ebbs and flows. It will not tolerate certain situations: anyone who sets sail with his legal wife and another woman will cause his vessel to shipwreck, and even in the nineteenth century, sailors still believed that a woman on board would bring bad luck. Nor should a woman give birth while at sea, "because the sea will not tolerate the soul that belongs to an injured person,"[8] anymore than it will tolerate that corpses be cast into it—it rejects them.[9]

A BIT OF GEOGRAPHY

On medieval maps of the world,[10] the seas are omnipresent and give the earth a "T" shape. The vertical bar of the "T" is our Mediterranean, the left side of the horizontal bar represents the Black Sea and/or the Don (Tanais). The right represents the Nile or the Atlantic. The Mediterranean and the Black Sea communicate with the ocean that surrounds the world, which permits travelers, like Duke Ernst, for example (ca. 1190), to go directly from one to the other. In the romance that bears his name (*Herzog Ernst*), Ernst leaves for the Holy Land and is driven off course by a storm that casts him into the area of the sea that congeals and the Magnetic Mountain.[11] Above the "T" we find Asia; in the lower left, Europe; and on the lower right, Africa. The ocean casts itself into the gulf of chaos as Adam of Bremen clearly says when recounting the voyage of Frisian sailors:

> And as they furrowed the seas from that place [Iceland] toward the farthest northern pole, . . . Of a sudden they fell into that numbing ocean's dark mist which could hardly be penetrated with the eyes. And, behold, the current of the fluctuating ocean whirled back to its mysterious fountainhead and with most furious impetuosity drew the unhappy sailors, who in their despair now thought only of death, on to chaos; this they say in the abysmal chasm (*dicunt esse voraginem abyssi*)—that deep in which report has it all the back flow of the sea, which appears to decrease, is absorbed and in turn revomited.[12]

A medieval map of the world with the major waters forming a "T," taken from a twelfth-century copy of Isidore of Seville's *Etymologiae*

This idea was already aired in the eighth century, in the *History of the Lombards* (I, 6) by Paul the Deacon (ca. 720–787).[13] As it happens, the oldest account is from Pytheas, who lived in the fourth century BCE. His narrative is lost, but the geographer Strabo cites the following extract from it: "It is not hard ice, it is not air, it is not water."[14]

The ocean that congeals, mentioned by Adam of Bremen, is the mythical vision of the ice pack. We find it to some extent on all the seas, and it carries a variety of names: *Oceans caligans* (dark sea), *mare concretum* (condensed sea); in the texts written in Old French, the *mer Betée*, which is to say the "frozen sea"; and the *mare coagulatum* (congealed sea).[15]

There is another interpretation, that of the Alexandrian Cosmas Indicopleustes (first half of the sixth century), the author of a Christian topography that strives to bring physical geography into accord with the Holy Scriptures, mainly Isaiah (40:20): the flat, nonspherical earth is surrounded by the ocean.

Around this extends the second continent on the eastern side where men dwelt following the Great Flood. During that time, people traveled over the ocean on our earth but since then the other continent is no longer accessible. The whole is bordered by high walls: on the top, the sky terminates in a vault parallel to the axis of the length. However,

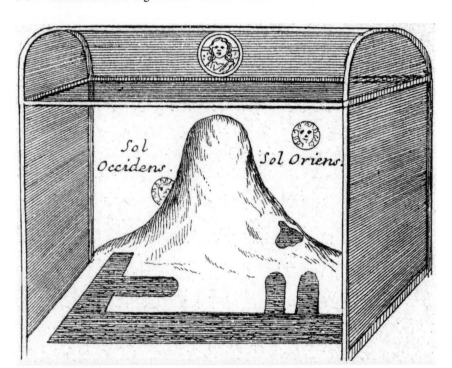

The construction of the world by Cosmas Indicopleustes

this no longer floats above the earth but is divided at mid-height by the firmament into two levels. The lower part of the sky resembles a cube with defined edges; the upper half is a giant upside-down bathtub. The lower part contains the earthly world: earth, water, and astral bodies; the upper part is the heavenly kingdom of Jesus Christ and the elect.[16]

In the work of Arabic geographers like Qatada (died 899) or Omara, a mountain stands at the world's edge. Its name is Qaf; a violent current causes the sea to enter at its feet and vanish.[17]

VOYAGES

All the seas on the globe are filled with islands. As navigators often do not know their position, they place their trust in providence, which as a good daughter, grants them extraordinary discoveries. In antiquity, the journey of the Egyptian pharaoh Necho II, the voyages of Pytheas of Massalia, or that of Hanno the Navigator from Carthage (fifth century BCE) brought back the perfect things to feed the imagination. Ulysses met the sirens and passed not far from Scylla and Charybdis, the monstrous sea maidens whose loins were girdled with the heads of baying dogs. In the Middle Ages, Irish literature had a specific genre dealing with sea voyages (*immrama*, singular *immram*); *The Voyage of Bran, Son of Febal*,[18] *The Voyage of Máel Dúin* (tenth century) and *The Voyage of Saint Brendan* are good examples. In the first of these, islands play a large role.

There is one supported by four gold pillars, and all there is wealth and pleasure: it is called the Land of Women. To get there, Bran sets sail with twenty-seven companions, with a first stop at the Isle of Joy, all of whose inhabitants laugh and shout nonstop. He then comes to the Land of Women (*Tír na mBan*) where all spend a year of good cheer and happiness. But gripped by homesickness, they return home and the first person to set foot on land turns to ashes.

In *The Voyage of Máel Dúin*, the protagonist sets off in a boat looking for his father's murderers and travels from island to island. He lands at the island of birds, where he is attacked by ants the size of horses, and where he sees a monstrous horse with dog paws. At the second island he finds a deserted castle; at the third trees that bear golden apples; a fourth that houses the frontier of the otherworld; and so on. The most fantastic island is likely the one surrounded by a revolving ring of fire, and one of the most noteworthy phenomena is the sea that is as clear as glass, a motif recycled in the legend of Saint Brendan, who says:

They found the sea so clear they could see everything all the way to the bottom. There were diverse kinds of fish lying on the seabed. The sea was so clear it even seemed they could touch them.[19]

As for Saint Brendan (died between 577 and 583), the abbot of Clonfert, he left Ireland in search of the earthly paradise that the Celts believed was on an island in the ocean to the west. This corresponds to the Isle of Apples (*Insula pomorum*) in the *Vita Merlini* (Life of Merlin) by Geoffrey of Monmouth (died 1155),[20] the land of fairies ruled by Morgana and where Arthur died.

This legend enjoyed considerable success, and on the maps of the early Middle Ages we see an island named *insula perdita* (the lost island), the one discovered by Brendan. Many of the islands on this voyage are the same as those visited by Máel Dúin, although Brendan encountered Jasconius, the Fish-Island, most likely a whale—a legend with which Arab geographers were also familiar. Brendan's story is exemplary because it permits us to see how very real phenomena are, out of ignorance, reinterpreted mythically. When the sailors passed within proximity of the Island of Smiths, which spits fires and is inhabited by demons who throw flaming blocks at the ship, the description is in fact that of the Icelandic volcano, Hekla.[21]

The reader can find convincing evidence of this with the help of this extract from *The Voyage*:

Now there appeared a misty land covered in smoke and stinking worse than carrion, enveloped in dark clouds and fog. . . . The abbot instructed them: "Know that you are being propelled toward Hell; never have you had such need of God!" Brendan made the sign of the cross over them: he was fully aware that Hell was near at hand, but the closer they approached, the less they saw and the darker the depths appeared to them. Sparks raced up from the bottom of the gulf, the wind hurled the fire, and never was thunder so loud. Flames and blazing rocks flew so high they hid the light of day.

When approaching the mountain, the monks saw a terrible devil emerging from Hell, huge and covered in flame. He held a hammer the size of a pillar in his fist. His blazing eyes caught sight of the stranger—he lingered to prepare a torment for them. Vomiting fire, he jumped into his forge and came out with a red hot mass in his tongs, which were so large they would need ten oxen to carry them. He lifted it skyward to fly above the brothers like a whirlwind, the bolt of a crossbow, or the shot from a sling. The higher he lifted it, the stronger and brighter grew its flames. But the slag did not reach them and fell harmlessly into the sea, burning like heather being cleared from the moor. It burned for a long while in the sea, spitting flames.

The wind carried the boat. The monks drew further away, pushed by the breeze. Often they looked back: the island was entirely in flames and covered in smoke. Thousands of devils were rushing about there; they could hear the cries and moans of the damned.[22]

And when Brendan and his companions saw what looked like a glass pillar standing in the middle of the sea, today we can recognize that it was an iceberg:

Quando uero cum celebrassent missas apparuit illis colunna in mare et non longe ab illis uidebatur sed non poterant ante tres dies appropinquare.[23]

When they were celebrating mass, a pillar appeared to them in the sea and was not far from them, but they could not approach it until three days later.

It is hard as marble and made of "clear crystal."

With these voyages, we have entered the domain of myths and legends. In the West, it is Ireland that is the isle with the greatest wealth of marvels,[24] in the words of Giraldus Cambrensis (1188), counselor to Henry II, king of England. Without a doubt, the island next richest in marvels would be Iceland, *ultima Thule*. But as all of this is well known. Let us turn instead to what was being said about the seas of the world in the tenth century.

THE SEAS AND THEIR ISLANDS

In the tenth century, a certain Ibrahim ibn Waçif Châh, a versatile Arab author, wrote his *Summary of Wonders* (*Muhtasar al-Agaib*) based on travelers' tales and geographical works. Two of his sources are *An Account of Voyages between India and China* by Abu Zayd, who preceded him by several centuries, and a curious narrative with the title *The Marvels of India*. Ibrahim's information matches that of Arabic geographers of the Middle Ages and even *The Voyages of Sinbad the Sailor* on certain points as well as those of Marco Polo, who notes: "There are one thousand and seven hundred islands in this Indian Ocean."[25] Ibrahim mentions a dozen "seas" with a wealth of fabled elements worthy of our attention. Marked by a certain disorganization that reveals they were compiled from various sources, the seas and their islands are the subject of several chapters. I will list this information to make it clearer:

1. The ocean that surrounds the earth is called the Outer Sea, the Green Sea. Here we find Solomon's castle, cities that float on the water and vanish when sailors appear—a theme that recurs several times in slightly different forms—and *telesmata*, such as the statue that seems to say "Whoever passes beyond the fire shall be shipwrecked." The islands here are many and quite extraordinary. We find:

   - The Isle of Slumber, in the middle of which stands a large pyramid of shiny black stone surrounded by bones on all sides. Whoever sets foot on this island will become lethargic, lose all strength, and succumb.
   - The Island of the Cynocephali, inhabited by people with dog heads, and another island inhabited by the acephalic (headless), androgynous creatures whose speech resembles the chirping of birds.
   - The Island of the Dragon where Alexander the Great defeated a voracious dragon by ruse, an adventure that can be read in the *Alexander* of Meister Babiloth, a fourteenth-century German author.[26]
   - The Island of Malkan, inhabited by a fish-eating people with animal heads and human bodies.
   - The Isle of the Roud, creatures with wings, fur, and sharp horns; they are said to be ancient Satans (jinns).
   - The Island of Gâmia (the Submerged Isle), an animal as

round as a ball that shows itself for six months of the year and remains invisible otherwise.

- The Island of the Crystal Castle, which is found in the Alexander the Great legend and, oddly enough, in a Czech chapbook rich with exotic elements—in it, the hero Bruncwig reaches Mount Karbunkulus (carbuncle) that shines like fire.[27]

2. The Black Sea of pitch meets the Outer Sea; it is fetid, and an island called the Silver Citadel is in it.

3. We then come to the Sea of China with its 12,800 islands, full of dangers and wonders. Here we find the whirlpool: when it catches a ship, the vessel spins around until it sinks. The Crystal Castle is illuminated by candelabras that never go out and beyond it is a nameless sea, whose width is unknown and where live fish with human faces. They have wings and fly to land during the night to eat grass on the shore.

The Sea of China is inhabited by people living in the water. These folk come on board when the seas are rough, a legend about which Ibrahim provides more details in another place.

There is a spot in this sea called Sandji. This is where there are more winds, storms, perils, and things that cause fear. Children measuring five spans come out of the water and leap aboard boats, run around them in every direction without causing harm to anyone, and then dive back into the waves. When the sailors see them, they know that the winds are going to turn into a storm.

On the Island of Er-Râmini there live dwarfs that are four spans in size; they climb trees without the help of their hands and pursue ships by swimming at the speed of the wind. There is also the Isle of Baratâ'îl, which some claim is the home of the Antichrist, Deddjâl. Let us note that Ibrahim also locates this in the aforementioned Sea of China. Incidentally, we should also note that demons and other devils were often banished to islands that are sometimes quite similar to hell, according to legend. In the chanson de gest *Huon de Bordeaux*, written around 1220, when the sprite Malabron asks Auberon where Huon is, he replies: *ens l'ille Moysant*; / *a III. Lieues est enfer li puant* ("On the island Moysant, three leagues away from the reeking hell").[28] And in the Venice version of the Old French *Roman d'Alexandre* (Romance of Alexander), the magicians who contend with Moses are banished to the Isle of Orion.[29]

Located at the borders of the Sea of China, the Island of Women is only inhabited by women who are impregnated by the wind and only give birth to daughters; it is said that gold grows there like bamboo, and they feed on it.

4. We then come to the Sea of Herkend, east of India. There a fish lives, which plants and shellfish grow upon, and in such profusion that it is often mistaken for an island (see my comments above about Jasconius); this is a very widespread legend. There are also large snakes there who go into the desert and swallow elephants. It is claimed that one thousand and seven hundred islands can be found there, all governed by women and rich in amber.

5. Separated from the previous sea by one thousand and nine hundred leagues, the Sea of Dâwendjid contains Ceylon where one can see Adam's footprint at the top of a mountain.

6. In the Sea of Senf (= the Gulf of Siam) it is possible to see a white castle that walks on the waters and sometimes reveals itself to sailors before dawn. This is a sign of salvation, gain, and good fortune. This sea has the Island of Baratâ'îl, home of Deddjâl the Antichrist; el-Berrâkah, "the Shining One" with its invisible inhabitants; and another, nameless island with gleaming white homes and domes that draws away and vanishes when approached. This sea connects to the Wâk (most likely Japan) and its end is marked by a mountain where a blazing fire burns night and day.

7. The Sea of Oman and of Yemen: what stands out here is Salatâ, an island inhabited by people whose conversation, cries, and movements are all audible, and to whom people can speak and

receive answers from, but who cannot be seen. This island has an abundance of delights. The Island of Farch is named after a tree whose bark is a remedy for all ills. Whoever eats it never falls ill until they die and they never age. If their hair is white, it turns black again. Es-Sarîf is an island that appears to sailors, but they are never able to make landfall there: when they think they are right next to it, it moves away. This legend recurs about the Mediterranean and the islands of the Occident, with this specification: "When you reach the point from which you started, it can be seen again as before." It is certain that a number of these islands are only mirages.

With these extracts from the *Summary of Marvels*, which needs to be supplemented with other narratives,[30] we have a good overview of the way the seas have fueled the imagination. If there is the fear in the face of unknown spaces and dangerous waters,[31] there are also many dreams—in particular, of wealth. All the islands of the Oriental seas are quite rich, and travelers and geographers have drawn up lists of their products and natural resources. The taste for the marvelous underlies the travelers' tales, reminding us of Sinbad's voyages, or else those of Europeans like Marco Polo or Bernhard von Breydenbach: the mental perspective is the same. The astonishment, stupefaction, or horror when confronted by the scandalous mores on some islands (coprophagia, cannibalism, nudity, and so forth) are a continual source of legends. When speaking of the Nicobar Islands, Marco Polo is scandalized by the sexual freedom of the inhabitants, who couple "like dogs in the street wherever they may be, with no shame, and the father respects not his daughter nor the son his mother, because everyone does what he wishes and what he can."[32]

The seas are the domain of all possibilities and, if the navigator is attentive, he will be able to make port with his fortune assured. In fact, signs have been placed almost everywhere as a warning. Earlier I mentioned the *telesmata*; let us take them as an etiology. The satans, for example, have made castles in the sea for different individuals. This was the case for Misrâm, the third king of Egypt:

There [in the sea] they built for him the white fortress, and they placed above an idol of the Sun on which they wrote his name and the history of his reign. They also erected a copper idol on which they wrote: . . . I have established the sure talismans, the talking images, the boundary markers in the sea that stop the navigators.[33]

The gaze trained upon the world is wondrous in itself: all that is unknown and unique is transfigured and becomes a miracle; this immediately triggers a mythic explanation. We have a good contemporary example. On November 14, 1963, some Icelandic fishermen witnessed an island emerge from the sea some twenty kilometers from Heimaey. This island eventually grew to a size of two square kilometers. Because there is a fire giant named Surtr in Norse mythology, the Icelanders named this island Surtsey, "Surtr's Isle."

The medieval navigator is an interpreter of nature. We could compare him to a photographer who provides us snapshots without telling us because he is unaware that he does so, and that his images are going through filters, if not even distorting prisms. For the sailor of the Middle Ages, these filters are his native civilization his culture, which includes myths and legends, and his knowledge along with that of his time, his religion, and his value system. So, there is no objectivity here, and this subjectivity is bound the narrative techniques and particular descriptive elements that embellish the world and make it fantastical.[34]

14

The Backdrop of the Adventure Sites in Medieval Romances

In the romances of the Middle Ages, the plot unfurls in places that are always the same and where nature and culture, adventures and interludes are in constant opposition. The landscape is stereotyped; *locus amoenus* and *locus terribilis* are encountered by turn, and, in each case, the narrators use identical elements for describing them. Let us look at two Arthurian romances by Ulrich Füetrer (fifteenth century), *Persibein* and *Poytislier*, to illustrate this point; the number of times the term occurs is indicated in parentheses.

In *Persibein*,[1] the civilized space is characterized by *stat* (town, 12), *burg* (castle, 12), *klawse* (hermitage, 6), *closter* (cloister, 2), *veste* (fortress, 1), *hof* (court, 5), *haws* (house, 1), and *palas* (palace, 1); the movable habitat is represented by *pavilûn* (pavilion, 2). Cultivated land is designated by *acker* (crop field, 1), the grassland by *gruen* (green, 10) and *plan* (meadow, 3). These places are the starting or arrival points of the plot that takes place primarily in the "savage space," *diu wilde* (1), whose descriptive elements are, in order of importance: "forest," *wald* (28; with the variant *vorecht* [2]); "mountain," *berg* (12), also reprised as "stone," *stain* (12), or "cliff," *stainwand* (4), and "crag," *vells* (1), whereas "cavern," *höl* (5), implicitly refers to it; "field," *veld* (14), in the sense of

185

the *veld afrikaans*; "swamp," *mos* (4); "moor," *hade* (3); "water," *wag* (3); and "island," *insel* (1). Roads are simply designated by "route," *strasse* (8), and "path," *weg* (5). Situated between wild and civilized spaces are the elements of faery sites: "linden," *linde* (4); "spring or fountain," *brunn* (4); "meadow," *awe* (6) and *anger* (10).

In *Poytislier*,[2] things are similar. The human habitat is represented by *burg* (14), *haws* (11), *stat* (6), *hof* (6), *palas* (6), *turn* (tower, 4), *vestie* (fortress, 2), *schloss* (castle, 1), *klawse* (2), *kapell* (chapel, 1), and *garten* (garden, orchard, 2). The movable habitat includes the *pavilûn* (2) and *gezellt* (tent, 2). Nature is divided between: fertile land, the *wiese* (meadow, 3), *plan* (8), *anger* (grassland, 7), and *aue* (wetland, 7); sterile land, the *haide* (moor, 1); vast spaces such as the field (*velld*, 4), forest (*wald*, 11), *tan* (pine forest, 1), mountain (*perc*, 7), *stainwand* (2), *stainhaufen* (pile of stones, 1), *hol* (cave, 4); and water in the form of *mer* (sea, 4), *wag* (running water, 4), *see* (lake, 2), *brunnen* (fountain, spring, 3), *pûchlein* (brook, 1), *wasser* (water, 1), and indirectly by *stade* (riverbank, 3). Absent in *Persibein* and mentioned in the work are *brücke* (bridge, 3) and *gras* (grass, st. 243), in the sense of "earth, ground." Furthermore, routes of contact, going from the most to the least passable, are: *strass* (route, 1), *weg* (large path, 4), *weglein* (footpath, 1), and *steig* (little path, 1).

We should not be misled into thinking that all these elements are used at random: they interlock to form the sites and serve as so many signals for the listeners/readers. In *Persibein*, the forest-covered mountain provides the context for the first adventure (st. 9–31); further on (st. 232ff.), we have the meaningful sequence of *closter* (cloister) > *gepirge* (mountain) > *klawsen* (cell, hermitage) + giants, and in stanzas 243–49: forest > cell > fortress > linden > palace + giant (*wallt* > *klaws* > *veste* > *linde* > *palas*). Füetrer marks out the hero's journey this way and the wording is a kind of anticipation for what is going to happen. The crossing of the *no man's land* between nature and culture is expressed by *geuillde*, *haide*, and sometimes *velld*, and immediately leads into the adventure. Gaban and three other knights leave the court, *riten pirg und mannagen walld* (crossing over mountains and through many forests), *oder wo si sunst et awentewere funnden* (9, 6–7). To see if they find adventure, we see them *zue velld reiten* (10, 4), *in das vorecht Precilian* (10, 6), crossing *pirg, geuillde* (12, 1), and then seeing *ain perg uil Koch* (12, 6). Their reaction is enlightening: *sy wolten ye pefinden / ob auf dem perg icht wär von awentewr* (they wanted to know if there was adventure to be had on the mountain). They scaled it and found a *locus amoenus* (14) in the form of a stone standing in a field: *zue mitten annger sehen / thetten si ainen stain* (15, 1–2). They could not approach this stone, which is a "test of virtue" (German *Tugendprobe*). They return to Nantis to relay what they have seen, and the adventure is set off. The reader will recall that the progression of the heroes to the adventurous site is accompanied by growing tension that reflects or causes the elements of the landscape.

On another occasion, Persibein "crosses through a green forest on horseback" (*rait durch ainen gruenen walld*; 129, 2) and meets a maiden whose father was captured by a giant who wishes to burn him. In the fifteenth adventure, the plot is set in motion this way (st. 216–33): Persibein is a guest at a castle where his host tells him:

> *zw Isaual dy strassen*
> *ist so recht vngehewr*
> *das ir dy rais sont lassen:*
> *ain mos so schreit von willder awentewr* (219, 1ff.).

> The Isaval road
> is so disturbing
> that it would be better not to take it;
> there is a screaming swamp, wild adventure.

The hero leaves and enters the forest, where he is welcomed by a hermit. He succeeds in passing the test of the *fier baiser* ("daring kiss") and leads the woman he freed to a monastery (st. 232). Hermitages and monasteries are enclaves in a savage world that allow tension to be relaxed, and this is used to relaunch the plot.

Another example: Poytislier has set off to hunt the white stag in the forest (*zu wallde*; 96, 7). His hunting dog races off in pursuit of the animal followed by the hero "through a pine forest" (*all twerches durch ein tan*; 98, 2), who gets lost. He makes camp in a meadow (*auf einer wis*; 99, 1), spots the stag "on a moor" (*auf einer haide*; 99, 5), gets lost again, and "he sees a delightful house in a meadow" (*er sach ain wunikliches haws auf ainem plan*; 101, 6–7), where he is welcomed by two maidens. The route he has followed is designated as "unknown way" (*vnkunnde straß*; 102, 2). The text inspires no alarm because, after having crossed the forest-frontier, the hero has entered a land of faery guided by the stag.

Before his meeting with the beautiful Floraklar, who shall give him her love, we have the sequence: *plan* > *awe* > *haws*, and thus we know he is not risking any danger. After losing Floraklar, a rationalized fairy, he searches for her everywhere: he traveled "through many lands, mountains, and broad meadows" (*durch straich er manig lanndt / pirg, walld vnd weyte awen* (198, 2–3), until a dream frees him from his torment, something that takes place at a specific site: a stone close to a linden tree (st. 199). We know that the wild space is a domain forbidden to knights because of the giant's question to Poytislier: "What brings you into the wild?" (*was pringt dich in dy willde*; 279, 3).

It is easy to find a multitude of such examples, but I will single out only two. In *Daniel von dem blühenden Tal* (Daniel of the Flowering Valley) by Der Stricker, the adventure *Von der grüenen Ouwe* ("Of the green meadow"; v. 4109ff.) opens with these words: *Er folgte der strâze in den berc* ("He [Daniel] followed the road into the mountain"; v. 4110).

In *Iwein* by Hartmann von Aue, Kâlogrenant makes his way to the wild space (*diu wilde*), enters the forest (*wald*), discovers some cleared land (*ein breitez geriute*) where some aurochs and bison are fighting and spots a man quite wild in appearance (*harte wilde*), who is large and terrifying (*michel, eislîch*). The wild man reassures him by saying: "He who doesn't do anything to me shall have me for their friend" (*swer mir niene tuot, / der sol ouch mich ze vriunde hân*). This figure has long been recognized as a guardian of the otherworld and a "master of animals," a point I will return to later.

Forging a close bond between landscape and plot is therefore a constant in the medieval romance, and even the epic. This is true in the *Song of Roland*, and as a reminder I also want to mention the role played by the Ardennes forest in *Partonopier und Meliur* by Konrad von Würzburg; that of the Vosges in the *Waltharius* and the Odenwald in the *Nibelungenlied*; and the role of the mountain in the romance-like epics of *Dietrich von Bern* and *Seifrid de Ardemont* (attributed to Albrecht von Scharfenberg). In addition to the landscapes mentioned, several places reappear frequently. A glance at the *Prose Lancelot* and the Matter of Britain gives us specific sites: the passes (fords and bridges); the graveyards with their multitude of enchanted, fiery, bloody, healing tombs; and the fountains, springs, and lakes. It is rare for an adventure not to have a connection to one of these places. The revelation of an identity or the future, for example, is made by lifting the lid of a grave; that of legitimacy and/or courage, by defeating the defender of a pass, and so on. All of this begs the question: Why are these places the privileged sites of the adventure?

If we extend our research in every direction, we can observe that these places are also those around which beliefs revolve and live: the *Handwörterbuch des deutschen Aberglaubens*[3] and the *Atlas der deutschen Volkskunde*[4] reveal it for Germany;* in France we need only refer to the works of Paul Sébillot[5] and Anatole Le Braz;[6] and for Iceland, the traditions collected by Jón Árnason.[7] Whether the stories are the work of clerics or collected from rural folklore, the fundamental information remains the same: man lives in a haunted world. Let us briefly examine this point.

Man has always been aware that he is not the world's first inhabitant, and every civilization has crafted its cosmogony accordingly. The Greeks saw themselves as the successors of the gods, and the races of gold, silver, and bronze. The Celts considered the settlement of Ireland as a succession of invasions. According to Geoffrey of Monmouth, when Brutus and the Trojans disembarked on Albion, the island was only populated by giants. The ancient Scandinavians situated a giant (Ymir) at the origin of the world, then dwarfs—we know nothing of their

---

*[These reference works are the *Dictionary of German Superstitions* and the *Atlas of German Folklore*, respectively. —*Ed.*]

origin, but we do know that four of them occupied from the first the four cardinal points—and then mankind. The prose preface of the late medieval German *Heldenbuch* (Book of Heroes), printed around 1483, gives the following order: dwarfs, giants, heroes/men.[8] The earlier races hardly ever disappear completely. They retreat before humans or keep their distance from them. The giants of the North live in Utgard, and the dwarfs live in hollow mountains and stones. In Ireland, the Tuatha Dé Danann retreated into the mounds and their underground palaces. In the areas east of the Rhine, giants and spirits of all races (*nichus, scrat,* and so on) reside in *diu wilde*. These are the first assumptions, before any Christianization. In the early Middle Ages, they are revealed by the rites and forms of worship—dedicated to stones, trees, springs, and crossroads—which the homilies and penitentials condemn.[9] These and other places are at the center of what the clerics first called "paganism," and later "superstitions." Mountains were deified, as is attested by the place names that remain evidence of the highest value for these remote eras about which information is quite scarce. However, in addition to place names like *Heilighberc* ("Holy Mountain," anno 816),* *Heiligbrunno* ("Holy Spring," anno 823), *Heiligenforst* ("Holy Forest," anno 1065), or *sacrum nemus* ("sacred grove," eleventh century, near Haguenau), *Heiligenholtz* ("Holy Wood," anno 1180), and those coined from the names of Gods, we also find *Scratinpach* (eighth century), *Scrateinberge* (anno 1120), *Tursinruth* (*anno* 1143), and *Wihtungen* (anno 825), which are place names coined from *schrat, durs/thurs,* and *wicht,* which are terms for land spirits.[10] In England, for example, we can find *Pokerich* (anno 1314), *Pokin tuna* (anno 1201), and *Puclan cyrce* (anno 946), meaning, respectively: "Puck's Stream," "Puck's Enclosure," and "Little Puck's Church" (Old English *puca*; cf. Old Norse *púki,* German *puk*). The devotion shown to stones and boundary markers is reflected in the place name *Wihestaine* ("Holy Stones," twelfth century); that which is focused on forests would be *Wihinloh* ("Holy Forest," anno 901); on rivers, *Wigbeke* ("Holy Stream," anno 1007); and on mountains, *Wihenberc*

---

*[Latin *anno*, "in the year," refers here to the date of the document containing the place name. —*Ed.*]

("Holy Mountain," anno 1145). We can infer from a place name like *Wichtlisperc* ("Little Wight's Mountain," anno 1111), that the mountain in question was reputedly inhabited by individuals from a family of dwarfs.[11]

A thousand details inform us that these places are the residence of tutelary spirits: it is not the stone, tree, or fountain that is worshipped but the being who occupies it. If, at the beginning of Common Era and according to the testimonies of Tacitus and other Roman historians, the *fana* (sanctuaries) and *nemora* (groves) were the refuges of the gods, a normal process allowed them to return to their pantheon, leaving behind their hypostases and subsidiaries. For example, epigraphy teaches us that the local place spirits are, in acts of devotions, associated with the mother goddesses, which probably implies the coexistence of the high gods and the place spirits, and that perhaps—although this remains no more than a hypothesis—the latter may have existed anterior to the former. A stone found near Xanten (Germany) says that Septimus Flavius established a temple for the *Matres Quadriburgenses* and the *genius loci*.[12] On another stone we read that Caius Tauricius Verus fulfilled his vow to the *Deae Vapthiae* and to the *genius loci*.[13]

The Church had to juggle with these ancestral beliefs the better to extirpate them and it created legends that are more or less Christian mythology, and which contain many reminiscences of classical antiquity, mainly from Ovid. Because woods, mountains, springs, and so forth housed spirits—a common and pre-Christian belief—the Church had to explain their presence in these sites in its own way. In order to be credible, it was not enough to simply demonize them; the Church had to provide an explanation for why the spirits remained in these places. Let us take a look at how this was done.

Whether it is Martin of Braga (died 580) or Pirmin of Reichenau (died 753) speaking, the words remain the same: the inhabitants of these sites are fallen angels. Martin said of them: "Many are those who remain in the sea, rivers, springs, or forests; ignorant men honor them like gods and give them sacrifices."[14] For Pirmin all of these practices were a form of "demonic worship."[15]

Things were defined a little more explicitly by Gerald of Wales, or

Giraldus Cambrensis, in his *Itinerarium Cambriae* (I, 12), where he reports about such a spirit that, when interogated, explained:

> Before Christ assumed human form, demons held great power over mankind, but this was much diminished at His coming. They dispersed in every direction and scattered to flee His presence. Some hastened into the sea, others into the hollows of trees or the clefts of rocks, and I myself leapt into a well.

Walter Map (1135–1209) reports almost the same thing in his *De nugis curialium* (Courtiers' Trifles) while showing off his erudition: the rebel angels had been cast down to earth "sometimes in vast deserts, and sometimes inhabited areas, depending on their sin." Deceived by the devil, our ancestors believed that they were demigods and demigoddesses (*semideos aut semideas*) and, depending on where they lived, "they were called Hill-creatures, Sylvans, Dryads, Oreads, Fauns, Satyrs, and Naiads" (IV, 6). The beginning of this list is reminiscent of Ovid (*Metamorphoses*, I, 190ff.). The texts state unanimously that "demons"—a convenient term for the clerics to use, but one that is often obscure to us—therefore remain *in locis desertis et inviis* (in deserted and impassable places), which also includes the *locus silvosus* (wooded location). Gervase of Tilbury (1152–1218), who was in the service of the emperor Otto IV of Brunswick, says of spirits that he calls *follets*: "They slip into stones and woods" (*Otia imperialia*, I, 18); This is an important detail, since in the Germanic-speaking areas a spirit often enters a house and becomes its household spirit via the wood used to build the home.[16]

I would like to remind the reader that in Old Norse, *dvergr*, "dwarf," is also the name for a crossbeam, and the term *ans/áss* can refer both to a main beam and a god of the Æsir pantheon.*[17] The "capstone" brought

---

*In my view, terms such as Gothic *ans*, "beam," and the Proto-Germanic *ansuz, "god," need not be seen in opposition; we can easily accept a metonymy. The Germanic gods are binders (see p. 43 in the article by Polomé cited in note 17), and it so happens that the main beam ensures the cohesion of the roof and therefore the entire house. We also know that beams were revered in the Germanic countries, a custom that survived in Norway until the nineteenth century (cf. *Handwörterbuch des deutschen Aberglaubens*, 1:856).

by the Church to their construction of an explanation for land spirits is the legend of the neutral angels: the angels who sided with neither God nor Lucifer. They were punished and exiled to earth, where some fell into the waters and other into the rocks. This legend appears in Wolfram von Eschenbach's *Parzival* (471, 15–25), in the *Chanson d' Esclarmonde* (v. 2748–76), and the *South English Legendaries*. Dante was also familiar with it.[18] An echo of the legend can be found in the anonymous Middle High German versified paraphrase of the *Magnificat*:

> *Dhe tiuvile hat got zu sprengit,*
> *ovir al die werlt gemengit,*
> *in wazzer und in berge*
> *daz sin nickere unde twerge,*
> *in walde unde bruche,*
> *got hat ur cleine ruche,*
> *daz sin elve, dhorse und wichte,*
> *de der werlde tugin ze nihte.*

> God has let the devils tumble,
> across all the world a-jumbled—
> in lake and in mountain,
> there are nixes and dwarfs;
> in woods and on moorland,
> —God has slight concern for them—
> there are elves, thurses, and wights,
> who in this world are good for naught.[19]

These Christianized elements of antiquity were then employed by the writers of medieval romances, who took an additional step: some *genii loci* were anthropomorphized; others were retained intact or given a monstrous form. In the first case, we have the many "ladies of the lake" and "fairies of the fountain," who are often Christianized. But other waters still held the theriomorphic spirits: dragons, snakes, and sometimes a cat—as in the tale of King Arthur's encounter with the Chapalu, the monster of the lake of Lausanne.[20] A clear allusion to this phenomenon appears in the Anglo-Latin *Liber monstrorum* (Book of Monsters): "It is said that in the swamps there are monsters with three human heads, and the fable is told that they live in the depths of the ponds, like nymphs" (I, 34). Grendel from *Beowulf* immediately springs to mind.

In the hagiographies, these demonized spirits appear in the legend of Saint Martha, who overcame the monster called the Tarrasque; Saint Marcel, who tamed the water spirit of the Bièvre; and so on. In the foundation legends of cities, it is not uncommon to see the founding hero slay a dragon before being able to establish a settlement, for example the dragon of Wawel, Poland.[21] Sometimes the dragon has its lair at the outskirts of the town and receives sacrifices every year (as with the Graoully of Metz) until a holy man puts a stop to it. This type of legend includes the victories of Saint Véran over the Coulobre (cf. Latin *coluber*, "serpent"), Saint Romain over the dreadful dragon known as La Gargouille, Saint Quiriace over the Lizard, and Saint Loup over the Cockatrice. Even if the prototype for these tales seems to be that of Saint George, a careful examination of the facts reveals that the victory of the saint over the devil/dragon is in fact based that of the human over the theriomorphic *genius loci*. This is also evident from the habitats of these monsters: the Cockatrice has its lair on Mount Don, the Tarrasque hides in the woods along the Rhône, and so forth. With great acuity, Jacques le Goff has shown that Saint Marcel's victory over the dragon was the Christian form of man's victory over a *genius loci*.[22] With no great risk of error, we can explain a passage from *The Book of Verona* (*Das Buch von Bern*, v. 1533ff.) in just this way. A storm drives Dietwart and his companions onto an island. A dragon emerges that kills Tibalt and thirty men before Dietwart takes care of him so he can no longer harm anyone.

In the romances, the *genius loci*, wicked or not, takes the form of a giant or dwarf, and these figures are always pagans if the writer takes the trouble to inform us. In *Dietrich's First Quest* (*Dietrichs I. Ausfahrt*) as in Hartmann von Aue's *Iwein*, the giant and the *waltman* (forest man) should be considered as the fictionalized form of place spirits whose prey are the herds.[23] When Dietrich kills a wild boar in the Tyrolean mountains, he provokes the sudden entrance of a giant mad with rage who demands compensation from him; the churl of *Iwein* guards wild animals and knows how to make them obey him: they would kill anyone else. Another figure that comes to mind is the ogre present in *Virginal* and in the *Wunderer*.[24] For dwarfs, we can look to Laurin and his wondrous rose garden fenced in by a silken thread. If the proposed interpretation seems dubious, all one needs to be persuaded is to study the texts from before the year 1000. *The Life of Saint Gall*, written by Walafrid Strabo (died 849) provides us with the stage of the belief before the romances: Gall, accompanied by his deacon Hiltibodus, set up his hermitage on a solitary spot on the banks of the Petrosa, a river teeming with fish that flows into Lake Constance near Rorschach. One day while fishing, Hiltibodus spotted two female "demons" that threw stones at him and bemoaned the death of the fish, adding: "What should we do? Because of this stranger we cannot remain among people or in solitude."

A little later, Hiltibodus was hunting and overheard the spirits of Mount Himilinberc expressing their sorrow over the death of those around them.

Moreover, Walafrid notes that "pagans falsely accused Saint Gall to Duke Gunzo, saying that, since the arrival of strangers, the hunts were reduced in quarry (*propter illos advenas venationes publicis in locis fuisse desolatas*)."

In his commentary on this *Vita*, L. Knappert notes that there was a close connection between the place spirits—in this case, demons of the mountains and waters—and animals, who were in fact their protected creatures or their "herd."[25] By settling in these wild places, Saint Gall drove the spirits away and thus caused a reduction in the number of game animals. We should recall that the *piscatus conductores* made vows to Hludana,[26] as shown by the Beetgum Stone (Frisia); she is a goddess of the third function* who is comparable if not identical to Hlóðyn (= Jörð), the mother of Thor. This collusion between *genius loci* and game animals, such as can be glimpsed in the text of the *Vita*,

---

*[In Georges Dumézil's tripartite theory, the third function refers to that of fertility. —*Ed.*]

enables us to broaden our interpretation of the hunters' tales found in medieval literature that led to an encounter with a fairy: the beast being hunted is the fairy's animal double. It so happens that fairies are not only the medieval "ecoform" of the Norns and Parcae, but also an avatar of rustic goddesses. More extensive research is called for to understand how the conflation between place spirits and fairies was made. More recent Alpine legends shed some clarifying light on these problems. I will only mention that of the inveterate hunter who depopulates a region. The place spirit, the master of the game animals, makes a contract with him, promising to furnish him the game he needs if he stops hunting. One day the hunter yields to his synergetic demon and death takes him immediately.

If we accept that every place has its spirit, it is easy to grasp the reason that compelled the storytellers to situate the adventure in sites laden with religiosity. This would shed light on tales that, at a hurried glance, appear to be nothing more than marvelous fabulations like the story of the tower that expels watchmen and that of the ladies who appear in holes in the cliffs, both recounted by Gervase of Tilbury (*Otia imperialia*, III, 20 and 43).

Let us shift to another horizon. When Saxo Grammaticus, the twelfth-century author of the *Gesta Danorum* (Deeds of the Danes), recounts the journey of Thorkillus to the hall of Geruthus—a voyage into the otherworld—this is the story he tells. Dying of hunger because of bad winds and currents, Thorkillus and his companions spied an island with steep sides on which it was difficult to make landfall. Thorkillus then advised them to kill no more cattle than they needed, "otherwise the local guardian deity (*deus loci praeses*)* will not allow us to leave again." The sailors went over their limit and each ship had to sacrifice one man in order to be able to continue their voyage.[27]

The adventure sites therefore need to be analyzed on several levels, as they appear to represent the stratification of both ancient and more recent elements; these are places where beliefs and literature intersect. The backdrop of these sites is charged with meanings, which the

---

*The Latin phrase perfectly matches the sense of the Norse term *landvættr*, "land spirit."

romances reemploy in service of the overriding theme of the quest. The quest is primarily that of a search for one's own identity, and this is only revealed after many adventures that place the hero in contact with representatives of the otherworld. While the goal of the adventure is the accession to sovereignty, it is surprising to see that this encompasses the visible and the invisible; hence the necessity to defeat or tame the place spirits. I believe that what we have here are the last vestiges of the ancient concept of the sacrality of the ruler, who can have no hope of seeing his subjects prosper unless he masters every aspect of sovereignty—the first Dumézilian function, which is a dual function since the king is also a priest. We can see these ideas reappear behind the figure of the *wounded* Fisher King in the cycle of Grail legends. The wound to his virility creates the *terre gaste* (wasteland). In the anonymous Old French poem *Elucidation* (early thirteenth century), the belief in place spirits is still evident behind the beautiful women that offer food and drink to errant knights. Abducted and raped by King Amangons and his men, these fairy women vanish and the entire land is stricken by drought and sterility.[28]

The last link that allows us to connect these entitities—the dwarfs, giants, and fairies that surface throughout the adventure—with place spirits, is, in my opinion, the landscape itself, which should not be separated from the function of said wondrous beings if we are trying to see whether the narrator is referring to folk beliefs or simply writing fiction. We should always keep in mind that the romance feeds on *realia*—rethought and recast in writing—but barely strays from the mental world of its audience; otherwise, how would it enjoy success? Medieval literature is therefore a primary source for historians of the *mentalités* of that time, provided they have the right interpretive tools at their disposal. These tools will permit a stratigraphic study.[29]

15

The Taming of the Land

*Reflections on Human Beings
and Their Environment*

Whether we are reading a medieval romance or a more recent legend, a chronicle, or a saga; or studying the rites and practices of the Germanic world; or consulting the *Atlas of German Folklore*,[1] or Bächtold-Stäubli's *Dictionary of Superstitions*,[2] we are struck by one fact whose recurrence cannot be the work of chance: all the phenomena that are *a priori* marvelous, paranormal, or strange share one thing in common. They take place in a small number of places, passages, or borderlands on the margins of the known world. Moreover, certain types of these sites— mountain, forest,[3] moor, sea—undeniably straddle this world and the beyond, forming a line of demarcation between civilization and wild space, a no man's land between the world of humans and the world of spirits. The crossing of these "passes" often occurs accidentally—in pursuit of a white stag, a wild boar, or another animal*—or intentionally, for example by running off to pursue an adventure about which one has heard tell. This is when we encounter supernatural beings.

The continual coexistence of humans and spirits can come as a surprise, particularly due to the fact that both cohabited quite often before the world was divided into two parts, with each being ascribed a defined

---

*This theme or motif is that of the animal guide.

territory, and we may wonder about the persistence of these beliefs, which, under concealed forms, fuel tales, legends, and romances, as well as—from an ethnological perspective—holidays and associated rituals. Many things become clear when, by carefully conducting a kind of "mental archaeology," one goes to the trouble to scrutinize the old texts and cross-reference the information they contain. You will then discover that, consciously or not, man felt himself to be an intruder in the natural space that received him—and which was already inhabited by spirits, the true owners of the land and sole bestowers of the fertility that was indispensable for human survival. We no longer encounter the ancient cult of the earth mother but its dissolution, degradation, or perhaps what might be just another of its forms conditioned by the "law of ecotypes."

The old Germanic texts enable us to clarify these assertions and see how man tamed his environment and took possession of the land. The constraints this caused led to the creation of rites, within which shifts occurred that changed the nature of the venerated beings, leaving them with only their tutelary function. From the Earth Mother we go to the *Matronae*, and from them to the fairies, especially in the context of what I have elsewhere called "the fairies' repast," a propitiatory rite intended to bring prosperity to the *domus*, and obligatorily renewed during the cycle of the Twelve Days [of Christmas] or during the Calends of February. In this way we pass from the undifferentiated local place spirits to elves and dwarfs, with whom the dead ancestors were commingled.[4] Despite the prevailing disorder of low mythology, still called "folk mythology," it is possible to see the rapports between man and the land. They can be described in two words: *expropriation* and *propitiation*.

Primeval land is inhabited by spirits. When Harald Gormsson, king of Denmark, consulted a sorcerer to learn more about Iceland, the latter sent his double there in the form of a whale. It swam around the island and "saw that the mountains and all the cracks were filled with spirits."[5] Before it was settled, the island of Gotland in Sweden belonged to the spirits and had the unique feature of sinking beneath the water during the day and emerging at night. The elven "evil spells" ceased once the settlers began to fight or negotiate with the place spirits.[6]

To settle new land, it was therefore necessary to take into consideration the invisible inhabitants whose land was being taken. They were dispossessed in a variety of ways.[7] People would intimidate them with fire or with other magical rites. We often see the ancient rite of *circumambulatio*: a domain would be delineated by walking all around it with an ox, a heifer, or a horse between sunrise and sunset. Another method was lighting fires, each visible from the next and allowed to burn into the night. The sacred nature of such rites—there are quite a few more—is obvious, and the texts say that the settler was "hallowing the land" (the Old Norse verb *helga*). One hallowed thing is therefore replacing another, which is evident when we consider that people often resorted to the gods for the choice of a site. The new landowners also propitiated the spirits, if they had not been able to scare them away, by sending them regular offerings in the form of porridge or buttered pancakes.[8] These offerings are comparable to a tacit contract: one buys the neutrality or benevolence of the *genius loci* with whom one must live in symbiosis; this is the only means for ensuring that the farm or other enterprise on the land would prosper. Sometimes a dead ancestor was entrusted with the job of choosing the settlement site.[9] The deceased could, thanks to his new status, enter into contact with the spirits and the gods, and he will know what is beneficial for his kin.

One detail I will mention in passing: the purpose of the grimacing figureheads on Scandinavian boats was to frighten the land spirits of the country being attacked and therefore obtain victory more easily (cf. Úlfljótr's Law).[10] In the saga that bears his name, Egill, son of Grímr the Bald, casts a spell over the spirits of Erik Bloodaxe's kingdom: they would have no rest until they expelled the king and his mother from the land.[11]

Once the area had been delimited, the house and various enclosures were built. The organization of the space went hand in hand with its consecration and it can be made concrete by a series of circles centered on the main dwelling house, which, as certain clues allow us to confirm, had a sacred aspect. Perhaps this is because it was where the good dead were buried, who gradually transformed into tutelary ancestors that looked after the family's affairs. The enclosed space in front of the house (*tún*) is a consecrated space: here they raised an animal that was intended for sacrifice at the winter solstice, the feast of the dead and of the elves. In this same space stood a tree (*bótré* or *túntré*) in which the spirit of the place lived.[12] A rock was sometimes his home.[13] The cult site was in an enclosed space. Around this enclosure stood the *garðr*, a hedge or small wall of dry stones, or even wooden stakes connected by clumps of earth and stones, a protection against men and spirits. A spirit similar to the Roman Sylvanus orientalis presided here.

Taking possession of the land was not only done for farming or raising animals. Political, legal, and religious procedures—the latter two being practically inseparable—always took place within an enclosed space. Hazel posts connected by a rope were used to mark off the boundaries of the assembly (*Thing*). This was called the *vébönd*—a compound of *vé*, meaning "sacred place, sanctuary," and *bönd*, "bonds, fetters," but also meaning "gods" for the Germanic gods are "binders."[14] The space enclosed is this way is called "judgment ring" (*domhringr*) and designated a "very sacred space." The same was true in ninth-century Germany: the placement of the tribunal (*mahalstat*) was marked off (*kimarchot*), and the Ripuarian laws refer to the oaths made in the hazel enclosure (*in haraho iurare*). For their part, the ancient Anglo-Saxon laws indicate that places of worship were enclosed: a fence would be erected around stones, trees, a spring, or a meadow, and the delimited space was called *friþgeard* or *friþsplott*.

I would also like to point out that duels (*holmganga*, meaning "going [with weapons] to an island") takes place in a space marked off by hazel posts, and the combat would be preceded or followed by the sacrifice of an animal to the gods.

The human thus appropriates the land and tames his space in successive waves, reminiscent of the rings made by a rock falling into the water, and the thematics of the circle, evident in enclosure procedures, are predominant in the relationship human beings maintain with their space. But in the early Middle Ages, human habitation was sparse, and while a person was protected on his lands—there he enjoyed his sacred inviolability—as soon as he left them, he was again confronted with the problem of spirits. This is something that is clearly visible in the charms and spells intended to guarantee a peaceful journey. He therefore must conquer a new space.

This can be seen through the organization of space based on naming places: the place names demarcating roads, setting the boundaries of estates, districts, and so forth served as a support to these landmarks. Space lost its anxiety-causing immensity and the "wild" gradually receded. As it happens, the choices of place names—when they are not simply representing a physical feature of the land—are not made randomly. Mythic and religious elements also play a role and thus we find names like "Freyr's Field" and "Thor's Mountain." That is to say, these sites were placed under the patronage of known entities whose power would counter that of the unknown and terrifying spirits, or limit it. The remaining *terrae incognitae* formed spaces encircled by the civilized world, thus clearly demarcated and synonymous with danger. Such places were natural reservoirs for the beings of low mythology that were gradually repressed. They were not confined to these areas permanently but could come out on certain dates or in certain circumstances.

I cannot develop all the points adumbrated here, but I would like to emphasize one in particular that I feel is fundamental. Everything I have said about human beings and their natural environment can also be said about humans and time because, in mythical thought, time and space are the same thing. This is perfectly reflected in the preposition system of the older Germanic languages, and an examination of calendrical feast days testifies to the "taming" of time. But because of the discrepancy between the solar and lunar calendars, twelve days have been given a particular status. They are a *no man's time* that belongs to the spirits, hence their open character that allows revenants, elves, and household or land spirits to come out and hasten to look for the offering they are due.

What the wild, primeval areas of land represent in space, the Twelve Days—among other well-known dates—represent in the domain of time. In short, taming one's environment—whether in space or time—primarily passes through the repression of the spirits into another world, which continues to overlap with that of human beings and was closed off bit by bit as Christianity advanced.

16

Borderlands of the Otherworld

For some time now, it has been impossible to overlook the fact that the medieval space was divided, *grosso modo*, into two. On the one hand, we have nature, and on the other, we have culture or civilization: thus, the *locus terribilis* and the *locus amoenus*, which are generally well expressed in toponyms.* If this division reflects the obvious and structures our world, it erroneously suggests a clear separation between two distinct domains and the presence of one or more obvious borders. It would be appropriate to add some nuance to this view, because things are not so clear-cut. There are, in fact, a multitude of demarcation lines, whose names vary accordance to the land: Latin *confinium, fines, termini, limes*; Germanic *marka, gemarkung, garðr, Grenze* (from the Slavic *granica*); and they are not all redolent of written law or custom but of the history of mindsets and beliefs. They can be natural: forest, Myrkviðr in Norse texts, Nemus Boemicum, which, to the south, joins with the forest of Bavaria and the Austrian Nordwald, and to the north, the Hvozd Silva,[1] the forest of *Gui de Warewic* (v. 12223ff.); water in all its forms;[2] moors (*Lai de Désiré*); and crossroads (*bivium et trivium, compitalia*). They can be artificial: hedges, fenced-in areas, boundary markers (see that of Galvoie in *Le Conte du Graal* [Perceval, the Story of the Grail], v. 6602), pillars (as in the Second Continuation of the *Conte du Graal*, v. 31583ff.), string (as in the Middle High German romance of *Laurin*),

---

*See chapter 14, "The Backdrop of the Adventure Sites in Medieval Romances," in the present collection.

stake, and a marked tree.* We have magical frontiers—for example, bridges[3] or the air (*Erec et Enide*). In 1283, the posts holding up a string to mark out the space of a judicial duel were called *septa iudicalia*.[4] The purpose and function of these borders was to assign a territory to serve as a basis for social, family, and clan matters, and they support the identity of a human group. In the Middle Ages a person did not exist unless connected to a defined area of land, and there was no fate worse than to be "without hearth or home." Given all that the foregoing comments imply, we will concern ourselves here with the stairs into the beyond, the otherworld. We should not view this solely as the world of the dead but also the dwelling place of supernatural beings—both visible and invisible—who are able to involves themselves on the affairs of human beings and are alternately dreaded or loved.[5]

We need to acknowledge that man is not the earth's sole inhabitant but that he has neighbors, his world is haunted, and their presence forces him to take certain precautions and compels him to respect taboos—in short, it shapes his life similarly to how it is structured by territorial boundaries and domains, bailiwicks, advocateships (*avoueries*; Swiss *Vogteien*), and so forth. Until the present, this point has remained obscure because outside the Germanic and Scandinavian texts, we only have scant bits of information scattered throughout the literature. The situation of having neighbors that are nonhuman or, if you prefer, superhuman—the dead, spirits, genies, demons—compels men to be cautious: they must propitiate these entities and earn their neutrality or else expel them, and to do this, they must distinguish themselves from them, in other words, draw a borderline between the nonhuman and the human.[6]

This border is present once the rites of taking ownership of a piece of land have been performed. Such rites essentially seek, in the Germanic world, to expel the spirits of place in order to appropriate their territory. In the lands of the medieval West, this is a religious operation. I will not go into it in depth as I have already written an

---

*These categories correspond to Germanic terms like *hag, garðr, rá, vaden, stak,* and *lah,* respectively.

extensive study of the topic.* I would simply like to remind the reader that the result of these rites is to establish a border between the human world and the world of the spirits. This border can take material form in a variety of ways: through a furrow, a hedge, a small temple located on the edge of the property, a low stone wall, boundary markers (*marcstein, limetanus, mutulus*), stakes (*rå* in Sweden), or trees marked with a sign like the cross or even—as in Rhaetia—a crescent moon. It can also follow the contours of the land, the network of waterways, and rest upon the landscape's most striking features. Most of the time, the border is established by means of a circumambulation, designated in Latin by the verbs *cavallicare, peragrare,* and *circumducere,* and by the Old German *pireisa, lantleita, underganc, umbeganc*—rites that still survive today in certain folklore festivals such as the Flemish Omegang and the Breton Troménie, although their original meaning has been lost. The *amburbium* in Rome also likely had the purpose of renewing the physical and spiritual frontier that made the city a sacred space.

The frontier of the domain is itself placed under that protection of a minor deity equivalent to the Romans' Sylvanus orientalis, the god Ezagulis of the Lithuanians, and Dusios of the Gaulish world.[7] It is therefore sacred, something that clearly reflects a recurring legend, that of the dishonest surveyor condemned to become a revenant for having moved boundary markers. The same mindset can be seen in the legend of the peasant who claimed ownership of his neighbor's land by making furrows in a field that did not belong to him. He too was unable to find rest after death. The border marks off a space that can be considered enclosed because it was delineated, and inside of which the human being enjoys a particular status. According to the ancient Scandinavian texts, he has a sacredness there (*manhelgi*) that only proscription can take from him. This space is organized concentrically around a center denoted by the dwelling place, which is itself placed under the protection of a household spirit of the first inhabitant of the site who was, in earlier times, often buried beneath the house or in proximity to it. When

---

*Demons and Spirits of the Land: Ancestral Lore and Practices (Rochester, VT: Inner Traditions, 2015).

the dwelling is enclosed, it too is sacred and the ancient Germanic laws inform us that this sacredness vanishes once the roof has been removed from the house in the event its owner has been condemned,[8] an act that transforms it into an open space. We can never overemphasize the importance of the opposition of closed/open. This opposition underlies the structure of many romances that follow the schema of the quest: the key ordeals and the crowning of the hero take place within enclosed spaces, whereas the adventures that take place in the wild, open spaces form the preliminaries to the achievement of the quest.

The presence of a border is revealed thanks to a recurring theme, that of the monster.[9] In the romances, it is quite often the material expression of the place spirits, a point studied extensively by Francis Dubost,[10] and the victory of the knight or saint over the monster has the result of expanding the civilized space a little further, of opening new lands to men. Indeed, wild spaces have been regarded as where spirits live since time immemorial: it is where they are banished by exorcisms.*[11] Witches are also banished here, and the legend of the origins of the Huns illustrates this point: King Filimer banished the witches known as Haliurunae to the solitary wastes of the East. There they met spirits with whom they copulated carnally and gave birth to the Huns.[12]

The proximity of dangerous monsters, representing the earlier powers dangerous to Christianity, were often mentioned in the texts and called for certain rites. The regular sacrifice of a human being or animal[13] is a motif that appears in the legend of Saint George as well as in that of the Graoully of Metz; Gottfried von Strassburg's *Tristan*; *Virginal* (thirteenth century); and the romance by Heinrich von dem Türlin, *Diu Crône*, as well as in the legend of the founding of Kraków. Through the payment of a tribute, the neutrality of a malicious neighbor can be acquired if there is no other way to get rid of it.

In the case of fairies, we may note two important points: that of

---

*The reciter addresses, for example, *grando, procella, diabolus, satanas, angeli satane, angeli tartarei*; conjures it (them); and commands it (them) to go to dry and deserted places (*loca arida et deserta*).

leaving plates and pots uncovered, and that of setting the table.[14] In the first case, in order to attract to oneself and one's dwelling the benevolence of the *bona res* and of those neighbors toward whom it was best to be wary and whose wrath was to be dreaded, not a plate would be covered, no pot sealed, and no barrel corked. People knew that if those things were done, it would provoke the ire of the fairies who visited homes at night in the retinue of Abundia or Satia. Citing the Bible, the Church condemned this rite, which it viewed as unclean. In the second case, a table would be set for the *dominae nocturnae* during the Ember days, the Spring and Autumn equinoxes, and the cycle of the Twelve Days. This propitiatory act is the medieval variant of the Roman table of the dead and smacks of rites of commencement: it is a good omen to proceed in this way. This spirit meal has a variant that is well attested in French medieval literature and more recent folk traditions in France, Romania, and Greece. At the birth of a child, a table is set for the fairies—understood here to be the goddesses of fate, the Parcae or Moirai—to ensure they are satisfied and bless the newborn with good fortune. We know what happens: a knife is missing from the table, a fairy gets upset and casts a curse that her companions cannot lift even if they succeed in lessening the outcome. This is the theme of Sleeping Beauty that emerges in *Perceforest*.

The spirits grouped together under the generic name of "dwarfs" are also given offerings. *Kormák's Saga* speaks of a sacrifice at the elf mound;[15] the *Saga of Christianity* (*Kristni saga*, chap. 2) mentions offerings made to a stone, the residence of the family's tutelary spirit;[16] and the *Book of the Settlement of Iceland* (*Landnámabók*) refers to offerings made to the spirit of a waterfall.[17] In every case it is a sign of respect for the other, the neighbor (visible or invisible), on whom one depends, *volens nolens*, with respect to one's means of existence.

The essential purpose of the border is likely to protect humans from their supernatural neighbors, whatever form they take: giants or dragons, dwarfs or *bestiae*, spirits of all kinds—those that the Latin texts call *faunus, pilosus, sylvanus, satyrus*, and *dusius*, and the Germanic texts call *alp, zwerc, vættr* (elf, dwarf, spirit), and *óhreinn andi* (unclean spirit)[18]—who will not tolerate any incursion into their domains. If a man or even an animal ventures into it, these neighbors will attack. The most common form is the illness that results from being struck by an invisible projectile.[19] Moreover, in ancient times, illnesses were understood to be active entities, and people sought protection from them in a thousand different ways. These include drawing a demarcation line around you with an iron object. Frequently, a magical border can also be created by wearing phylacteries, ligatures, and relics, as well as the sign of the cross—a veritable *lorica*—or the incantation of a charm or prayer, the use of an iron object or holy water, or even with a track or a circle,[20] the latter form perhaps being the most common and repeating in miniature what the human being achieved by delineating his domain. A good example of this can be found in the work of Cesarius of Heisterbach, in his story of the priest's concubine,[21] and in the anonymous stories of the revenants in Byland (Yorkshire).[22] When it concerns a village or dwelling, a furrow is dug, a rite to which the *Indiculus superstitionum* (eighth century) alludes. A similar rite, which until recently was still attested in Romania, specifies that this furrow holds in the spirits of illnesses, especially that of the plague.[23]

Here we need to discuss bells again. As mentioned earlier, it was once believed they drove away evil spirits, so they would be rung whenever storms were threatening in order to dispel the demon that was bringing them.* The sound of bells likewise marks a specific borderline: any demons within earshot of their pealing will be rendered powerless. In Denmark, a bell in Roskilde bears a Latin inscription that says: "My voice is a terror for all evil spirits,"[24] and everyone knows how legends have made use of this belief, recounting how the spirits of paganism or dwarfs left when a church was built and its "voice" began to be heard. If we take into consideration the acoustic spread of noise, the image of a circular zone emerges. This is sanctified in two ways.

The first method is Christian: the virtues of the bell and its voice are amplified by engraving on it the Greek letters *alpha* and *omega*, symbols of God; or else crosses; medallions bearing the image of Jesus, Mary, or

---

*See chapter 11, "The Masters of Weather: Tempestarii, Coercers, Defenders, and Others," in the present volume.

the saints; the symbols of the Evangelists; the blessing of Saint Agatha;[25] or even sacred names like Agla, Adonai, and Tetragrammaton. The second reflects a Christianized paganism: the alphabet either complete or incomplete, in order or not, is carved on the bell, and it can appear in isolation or accompanied by a spell. Sometimes the letters are identical or different, and sometimes they are even reversed. Sometimes the alphabet would even be repeated three times and inscribed inside a cross. Forty-two bells from the Middle Ages have been discovered that bear the alphabet. Here are three examples.

In Saint-Léger-de-Montbrun (Deux-Sèvres, France) we can read this inscription on a thirteenth-century bell: † ABCDEFG.J. KLMNOPQ; in Ennetach (Baden-Wurtemberg, Germany), an alphabet of twenty letters (from a to v) is augmented with: † Lucas * Marcus * Mahtevus * Iohannes † and accompanied by a dragon and an eagle in a medallion; the bells of Älgarås and Färed (Sweden, thirteenth century) bear, written in runes, FUÞARK, which is the beginning of the runic alphabet—followed by hniAstRmL, with A, R and L in uppercase letters.[26]

Spirits are not the only ones to possess a territory, and humans maintain other close relations with the dead. Even though the dead are often confused with the spirits that the literature calls dwarfs, elves, nightmares, nymphs, or fairies[27]—in other words, the dead are conflated with the supernatural beings surrounding us—when the memory of their name and their remembrance fades, they remain our neighbors for a certain time. In Germanic paganism, the dead are not the departed—they are living beings possessing a new status and a new dwelling, and their grave, I might emphasize, is an enclosed space.[28] Thus, any violation of a tumulus or burial mound is comparable to crossing a border; it is an impious act that justifies the dead person's entry onto the stage.

With Christianity spread the custom of burying the dead in a cemetery and no longer on the person's land or in their house, the necropolis became the dwelling place and domain of the dead—a consecrated space not only because it is blessed, but also because it is enclosed, even if often only symbolically. A wall or small wall, called a *kirkestile* in medieval England,[29] equipped with a door, girds the cemetery,[30] often flanked by a chapel where the dead celebrate their own divine services on certain dates.[31] This legend appears as early as the sixth century in the work of Gregory of Tours (*De Gloria confessorum*), then in the eleventh century in that of Thietmar von Merseburg, and lastly in the *exempla*. It is known under the name of "mass of the dead" or even "divine service of ghosts" (*Geistergottesdienst*).[32] While, from a Christian perspective, the wall forms the boundary between the living and the dead, it also aims—in combination with the blessing of the land—to prevent the intrusion of demons who, as everyone knows, have a habit of slipping into corpses in order to animate them and then spend their nights causing harm and mischief to humans.[33]

The demarcation and enclosing of the *dormitorium* are therefore in fact a dual protective measure: they fasten the dead to one place, and they prevent attacks by demons. Moreover, each grave of the necropolis is a dwelling protected by funeral rites: during the burial, the site was blessed and sometimes even with incense as the fragrance puts evil spirits to flight. We should note that the sacred nature of cemeteries also emerges from the fact that in Germanic regions, even in 1266, legal decisions were made there.[34] Nor should we forget that the cemetery is both a border and a point of passage to the adventure or to an otherworld.[35] This is something shown again and again by the *Prose Lancelot* and the Arthurian cycle in general.

But danger comes above all from the dead that are not found in the cemetery. Usually, these are individuals whose lives were considered as a plague on the community of that time: criminals, suicides, and women who died in labor. Christianity added to this group certain sinners who did not receive last rites or who had died without repenting. We should not forget that in medieval mentalities, the dead man is the legitimate owner of the place where he is buried. This means that he has rights over a space that is admittedly reduced, but which still exists. People may recall the many curse tablets found in Roman graves that promise punishment to any who violate the sepulcher.[36]

When the dead man's neighbors, the living, know the location of the tomb, they can avoid it, but sometimes out of ignorance they will linger in this spot or walk on the grave. This amounts to a violation of domicile or a profanation, an impious or disrespectful action, and punishment will not be long in coming: an illness will strike the care-less person and people will say he has ventured into the *loca incerta* (Middle High German *unstæte*).[37] We know that suicides would be bur-ied where they had killed themselves, and the place was indicated as such in one way or another. To protect oneself from any possible attack by the deceased, every person passing nearby this place would cast a stone or branch on the grave as a propitiatory offering or as a protec-tive measure, a custom that persisted into the nineteenth century. The accumulation of stones was intended to prevent the dead person from leaving the grave. When passing through a crossroads, a place where certain kinds of criminals were buried, people would behave in the same way. Everything people did amounted to demarcating a magical and religious border between oneself and the dead, for these neighbors had never truly departed; they remained stuck between two worlds and continued to live. This was a belief that Christianity never succeeded in eradicating completely.

Let us return to the cemetery.[38] It would be interesting to chart its topography as the emplacement of each grave is meaningful. This study remains to be done, but we already know that the cardinal points play an important role there. The north wall was reserved for those dead who inspired mistrust and it is no secret that some dead individuals did not accept the neighborhood that one attempted to impose on them. Several *exempla* tell the story of this or that dead individual who is found outside of the grave or cemetery the day after his or her burial and how people were obliged to bury them somewhere else. We also know that some dead individuals were placed beneath the gargoyle or rain gutter of the church, which can be interpreted two different ways: this could either involve a form of lustration or a protective measure, as water is one of the most effective means for preventing the return of the dead. We should also discuss the problem of tombstones, which plays an important role in Arthurian literature. For example, they pose no obsta-cle for the dead to leave (cf. *L'âtre périlleux* [The Perilous Cemetery]),[39] especially when, apparently, they do not bear any symbols reinforcing their status as a border.

We should also mention the borders of the beyond as an empire of the dead. In medieval romances in which the land of shades has been extremely rationalized while at the same time transposed into the sphere of the marvelous and of faery, this border regularly assumes the form of a waterway, a forest, or a mountain. These three sites can sometimes be combined, and this is why we encounter, for example, forested mountain islands. Sometimes the border is marked by a boundary marker, and whoever steps past it, never returns. In the romances about Alexander the Great, the Land of the Blessed is sometimes separated from the land of men by a mountain and deserts, and sometimes by clouds, like those of the Land of Darkness.* As for the earthly paradise that is suggested in the legend of the magnet of men, it sits on the other side of a mountain. Whoever crosses into it bursts out laughing and disappears forever.[40] In the Arabian legends of the Middle Ages, the City of Copper or the City of Brass—it is not entirely clear which world they belong to—are separated from our world by a desert of sand and cannot be found by those who seek them.[41] It is evident that each civilization has conceived the borders of the beyond in terms of its own culture and geographical environment.

In Germanic-Scandinavian mythology, the border is one or more rivers spanned by a bridge.[42] In the *Gesta Danorum* (Deeds of the Danes), Saxo Grammaticus describes a passage of this kind in the voyages of Thorkillus, and a revealing detail shows that only the dead can use the bridge. When Thorkillus and his companions reach the border of the beyond, a river spanned by a bridge, they cannot go over this bridge and must cross the river in Guthmund's boat.[43] In the mythological tales, the underworld is surrounded by a rampart or a metal grate. Even the topography of the underworld reflects and knows the notion of a border. In the *Eneas* by Heinrich von Veldeke,[44] the places are clearly separated: the fields of tears, a veritable antechamber in which the *immaturi* wait for the hour of their death to toll; the Elysian Fields, where the hero meets his father; and, in the distance, the deep pit of Tartarus.

---

*See chapter 10, "The Raft of the Winds: Toward a Mythology of Clouds in the Middle Ages," in the present volume.

Having reached the end of this quick presentation, I believe we should retain one essential point: every border functions on two planes and has two meanings. The demarcation encircles and marks off a territory with regard to the Other, but this Other is not exclusively a human being; it is often a supernatural being. This is the reason why so many religious rites accompany this demarcation, reaffirming it at fixed dates—for example, at the change of a sovereign—and reactivating its sacredness. This is something that continued into the twentieth century with the Breton *troménies.*[45] The second point I wish to emphasize is the following: even if the border is purely symbolic, it forms an enclosed and sacred place, dedicated to a god or to a saint in older times—in other words, the area is placed under their protection, as the place names clearly indicate. People rely on them to ensure its defense against all potential enemies. This aspect of the frontier has been secularized and sometimes replaced by magical measures and talismans like those that the magician Virgil used to protect Rome against reptiles or vermin, or those that protected Arabian cities, especially against foreigners, as they immediately signaled the arrival of every stranger.

17

The Spirits of Nature and of Humans in the Middle Ages

Aspects of Their Relationship

A careful reading of the medieval documents of western and northern Europe reveals that the earth is inhabited by spirits of all sorts that coexist with human beings peacefully, neutrally, or hostilely.

Over time, a bipartite world was established in which both man and spirit were ascribed a well-defined territory: the civilized world stood in opposition to the wild and uncharted land, a terrible and threatening place because it was inhabited by fantastic and unknown beings. We may wonder about the persistence of these beliefs, which, in disguised or debased forms, fueled tales, legends, romances, and—from an ethnological perspective—holidays and associated rituals. Many things become clear when, through a careful "mental archaeology," we take the trouble to scrutinize the old texts and cross-reference their information. We then discover that human beings, consciously or not, consider themselves to be intruders in the natural space that receives them and is already inhabited by spirits—the true owners of the land and the sole bestowers of the fertility necessary for survival.

I will begin here by revealing the traces of the presence of the spirits of nature from the period of classical antiquity, then I will discuss the rites for taking possession of a piece of land, and, lastly, I will take a look at how humans settle and tame their environment.

If, at the beginning of the Common Era and based on the testimony of Tacitus and other Roman historians, the *fana* and *nemora* were the refuges of the gods,* a normal process allowed them to return to their pantheon, leaving behind their hypostases or their subsidiaries. For example, epigraphy teaches us that the local place spirits are, in acts of devotions, associated with the mother goddesses, which probably implies the coexistence of the high gods and the place spirits, and that perhaps—although this remains no more than a hypothesis—the latter may have existed anterior to the former. A stone found near Xanten on the Rhine says that Septimus Flavius Severius established a temple for the *Matres Quadriburgenses* and the *genius loci*; on another stone we read that Caius Tauricius Verus fulfilled his vow to the *Deae Vapthiae* and to the *genuis loci*.[1]

When Harald Gormsson, king of Denmark, consulted a sorcerer to learn more about Iceland, the latter sent his double (*alter ego*) there in the form of a whale. It swam around the island and "saw that the mountains and all the cracks were filled with spirits."[2] Before it was settled, the island of Gotland belonged to the spirits and had the unique feature of sinking beneath the water during the day and emerging at night. The elven "evil spells" ceased once the settlers began to fight or negotiate with the place spirits.[3] We may also note that the purpose of the grimacing figureheads on Scandinavian boats was to frighten the land spirits of the country being attacked and therefore obtain victory more easily (cf. Úlfljótr's Law).[4]

Alongside place names like "Holy Mountain" (*Heilighberc*, anno 816)[†] and those that are coined from the names of deities, we find the "Schrat's Stream" (*Scratinpach*, eighth century), "Schrat's Mountain" (*Scrateinberg*, anno 1120), "Thurse's Clearing" (*Tursinruth*, anno 1143), and "Wights' Clearing" (*Wihtungen*, anno 825)—place names coined from *Schrat*, *Durs/Thurs*, and *Wicht*, which are various names for nature spirits or wights.[5] For England we should note, for

---

*[Latin *fanum* (pl. *fana*) "shrine"; *nemus* (pl. *nemora*) "(sacrificial) grove." —*Ed.*]

†[Latin *anno*, "in the year," refers here to the date of the document containing the place name. —*Ed.*]

example, *Puclan cyrce* (anno 946), *Pokin tuna* (anno 1201), and *Pokerich* (anno 1314), which denote "Little Puck's Church," "Puck's Yard," and "Puck's Stream," respectively (from Old English *puca*; cf. Old Norse *púki*, German *puk*). The worship of stones and boundary markers is evident from the place name "Holy Stones" (*Wihestaine*, twelfth century); and likewise the worship of forests in *Wihinloh*, meaning "Holy Grove" (anno 901); rivers in *Wigbeke*, "Holy Stream" (anno 1007); and mountains in *Wihenberc*, "Holy Mountain" (attested in 1145). From a place name like "Little Wight's Mountain" (*Wichtlisperc*, anno 1111), we can infer that the mountain in question was reputedly inhabited by the members of a dwarf family.[6] Thousands of details tell us that these places are the residence of spirits and wights: it is not the stone, tree, or fountain that is worshipped but the being who occupies it.

SETTLEMENT

To settle new land, it was therefore necessary to take into consideration the invisible inhabitants whose land was being taken. They were dispossessed in a variety of ways.[7] People would intimidate them with fire or with other magical rites. We often see the ancient rite of *circumambulatio*: a domain would be delineated by walking all around it with an ox, a heifer, or a horse between sunrise and sunset. Another method was lighting fires, each visible from the next and allowed to burn into the night. The sacred nature of such rites—there are quite a few more—is obvious, and the texts say that the settler was "hallowing the land" (the Old Norse verb *helga*). One hallowed thing is therefore replacing another, which is evident when we consider that people often resorted to the gods for the choice of a site. The new landowners also propitiated the spirits, if they had not been able to scare them away, by sending them regular offerings in the form of porridge or buttered pancakes.[8] These offering are comparable to a tacit contract: one buys the neutrality or benevolence of the *genius loci* with whom one must live in symbiosis; this is the only means for ensuring that the farm or other enterprise on the land would prosper. Sometimes a dead ancestor was entrusted with the job of choosing the settlement site.[9] The deceased could, thanks to his new status, enter into contact with the spirits and the gods, and he will know what is beneficial for his kin.

In 496, Clovis granted John, abbot of Reomay (Burgundy) as much land as he could cover perched on his donkey while the king was taking a nap. Incidentally, Flodoard of Reims tells the same story about Saint Remigius (*Hist. Rem.*, I, 14). Jakob Twinger von Königshofen's *Chronicle* (fifteenth century) says concerning the history of Alsace that King Dagobert II made a gift to Saint Florentius of the land he could cover on a jennet while he was finishing his bath and getting dressed.

In the *Life of Saint Malo*, written at the end of the ninth century by the deacon Bili, Malo commands Domnech to do this: "In the name of Christ, Son of God, take two young, untrained oxen and put them in a single yoke, followed by a plow, and I will give you all the land they can walk around between the rising and the setting of the sun (*du ortu solis ad occasum*) as your own, for eternal life, and in perpetual possession and whoever shall change anything despite you and your authorization, may he be cursed by your prayer" (chap. 34). The end of the paragraph strongly resembles a curse spell.

Louis the Pious granted Henry the Guelph the land he could mark off with a plow during the time the king slept at noon. During the expansion of Zittau by Ottakar II of Bohemia, in 1255, a furrow was dug while the king and the noblemen of the realm followed on horseback. Charlemagne's capitulary *De villis* (§27) says the land belongs to him who can travel around it in one day (*in unum die circumire*).

DEMONIZATION

All of these nature spirits become demons after the Christianization of the West.

Whether it is Martin of Braga (died 580) or Pirmin of Reichenau (died 753) speaking, the words are the same: the inhabitants of these sites are fallen angels.* Martin said of them: "Many are those who

---

*See chapters 11 and 14, and their respective endnotes, for further discussion of the legend of the neutral angels.

remain in the sea, rivers, springs, or forests; ignorant men honor them like gods and give them sacrifices."[10] The Church constructed an explanation for spirits and demons of the land: the legend of the neutral angels—certain angels who sided neither with God nor Lucifer. They were punished with exile on earth; some fell into the waters, others into the stones, and others into the woods.

In the work of Gerald of Wales (Giraldus Cambrensis), who wrote at the end of the twelfth century, one interrogated spirit replied:

> Before Christ assumed human form, demons held great power over mankind, but this was much diminished at His coming. They dispersed in every direction and scattered to flee His presence. Some hastened into the sea, others into the hollows of trees or the clefts of rocks, and I myself leapt into a well.[11]

Walter Map (1135–1209) reports almost the same thing in his *De nugis curialium* (Courtiers' Trifles) while showing off his erudition: the rebel angels had been cast down to earth "sometimes in vast deserts, and sometimes inhabited areas, depending on their sin." Deceived by the devil, our ancestors believed that they were demigods and demigoddesses (*semideos aut semideas*) and, depending on where they lived, "they were called Hill-creatures, Sylvans, Dryads, Oreads, Fauns, Satyrs, and Naiads" (IV, 6).[12] The texts state unanimously that "demons"—a convenient word for the clerics to use, but one that is often obscure to us—therefore remain *in locis desertis et inviis* (in deserted and impassable places), which also includes the *locus silvosus* (wooded location). Gervase of Tilbury (1152–1218), who was in the service of the emperor Otto IV of Brunswick, says of spirits that he calls *follets*: "They slip into stones and woods."[13] This is an important detail, since in the Germanic-speaking areas a spirit often enters a house and becomes its household spirit by means of the wood used to build the home.[14]

Christianized in this way, the ancient entities evolved: some nature spirits were anthropomorphized, while others were retained or given a monstrous form. In the first case, we have the many "ladies of the lake" and "fairies of the fountain," who are often Christianized. But other waters still held the theriomorphic spirits: dragons, snakes, and sometimes a cat—as in the tale of King Arthur's encounter with the Chapalu, the monster of the lake of Lausanne.[15] A clear allusion to this phenomenon appears in the Anglo-Latin *Liber monstrorum* (Book of Monsters): "It is said that in the swamps there are monsters with three human heads, and the fable is told that they live in the depths of the ponds, like nymphs" (I, 34). Grendel from *Beowulf* immediately springs to mind.

In the hagiographies, these demonized spirits appear in the legend of Saint Martha, who overcame the monster called the Tarrasque; Saint Marcel, who tamed the water spirit of the Bièvre; and so on. In the foundation legends of cities, it is not uncommon to see the founding hero slay a dragon before being able to establish a settlement, for example the dragon of Wawel in Poland, and the Graoully of Metz.[16] Sometimes the dragon has its lair at the outskirts of the town and receives sacrifices every year until a holy man puts a stop to it. This type of legend includes the victories of Saint Veranus over the Coulobre (cf. Latin *coluber*, "serpent"), Saint Romain over the dreadful dragon known as La Gargouille, Saint Quiriace over the Lizard, and Saint Loup over the Cockatrice. Even if the prototype for these tales seems to be that of Saint George, a careful examination of the facts reveals that the victory of the saint over the devil/dragon is in fact based on that of the human over the theriomorphic *genius loci*. This is also evident from the habitats of these monsters: the Cockatrice has its lair on Mount Don, the Tarrasque hides in the woods along the Rhône, and so forth. With great acuity, Jacques le Goff has shown that Saint Marcel's victory over the dragon was the Christian form of man's victory over a place spirit.[17]

The *Life of Saint Gall*, written by Walafrid Strabo (died 849), provides us with the ancient stage of the belief. Gall, accompanied by his deacon Hiltibodus, established his hermitage in a lonely place on the banks of the Petrosa, a river teeming with fish that spilled into Lake Constance near Rorschach. One day while fishing Hiltibodus saw two female "demons" who threw stones at him while lamenting the death of the fish. They went on to say: "What should we do? Because of this stranger, we cannot remain among people or in solitude."[18]

In the northern Germanic-speaking lands, several clues provide us with a glimpse into other kinds of contracts, which are confirmed by folk traditions that were still alive in the nineteenth century. It seems that a place was reserved for the spirits in close proximity to the house— in other words, an alliance had been made with them. This most often involves a stone or tree to which offerings are made. In the *Kristni saga* (Saga of Christianity) we read:

> At Giljá there stood a stone to which he and his kinsmen used to sacrifice, and they claimed that their guardian spirit lived in it. Koðrán said that he would not have himself baptised until he knew who was more powerful, the bishop or the spirit in the stone. After that, the bishop went to the stone and chanted over it until the stone broke apart. Then Koðrán thought he understood that the spirit had been overcome. Koðrán then had himself and his whole household baptised, except that his son Ormr did not wish to accept the faith.[19]

The text needs no commentary as it clearly shows that Koðrán feared the wrath of the spirit who protected his farm and wanted to be certain that God would protect him if he converted.

Numerous more recent testimonies confirm that offerings were made to nature spirits who lived under stones. A peasant of Sönderstrup in Denmark owned a spirit and gave him porridge near a stone. His son saw him and asked what he was doing. "It's for the *gaardbo*," his father replied. The son overturned the stone and found congealed blood beneath it. The next morning, the farmer's best cow was found strangled in the barn. Near Omland farm in the parish of Fjotland, Norway, there was a stone with a crack into which the local people deposited food and drink on Christmas night.

Waldemar Liungman, who carefully studied the numina connected to places, noted that in two manuscripts written in Old Swedish, the phrase *tomta gudhane*, the "gods of the building place," occurred. In the first manuscript, *Själinna thröst* (The Consolation of the Soul), there is a woman who, after the meal, sets the table for these creatures and says that if they come to eat, her livestock will do well and everything will prosper. In the second manuscript, which contains the text *Birgittas uppenbarelser* (Revelations of Saint Bridget), priests forbid this kind of worship of the *tompta gudhi* as it seemed to threaten their right to tithes in livestock, bread, wine, and other natural goods.

These place spirits are guarantors of the prosperity of the estate and already stand in close proximity to household spirits: when they are adopted by the inhabitants, or vice versa, the nature spirits become the protectors of the hearth, though it would be inaccurate to claim that this is always the case because the tutelary spirit can also be the former owner of the house, who, once deceased, was buried beneath the threshold or the hearth. However, I believe that it is necessary to be very attentive to the placement of the spirit within the defined space: the household spirit lives within the house, often near the hearth; the nature spirit is found outside. Be that as it may, we can also propose as a hypothesis that the adoption of a spirit and his introduction into the house is a counter-measure intended to thwart the conduct of the *genius loci*.

At the end of the sixteenth century, in his essay on the gods of the Samogitians (chap. 47), the Polish historian and theologian Johannis Lasicius (Jan Łasicki) speaks about the *Barstucci* (*Barstukai*), which he compares to dwarfs and whom he presents as servants of the god Piutscetum, patron of trees and sacred groves. The priest and historian Matthäus Prätorius (sixteenth century) gives us a glimpse of how special-ists, the pagan priests called *Kaukuczones* or *Barztukkones*, were capable of enchanting the cthonic *Barstucci*, or *erdmenlin* ("little earth-men"), so that they would make their home in this or that place. This is a good example of the taming of the land spirits and their transformation into household spirits.

In the Scandinavian lands, a tree, often a birch, generally stood next to the main house, and it was reputed to be the home of the place spirit, the spirit of the estate. The most common name for this spirit is *gardvord* (a compound of *gard*, "wall, boundary," and by extension meaning "estate," + *vord*, "ward, guardian"). The tree in question has several names.*

---

*For example, *boträ*, *boströd*, *vårdäd* (in which we can see the term *vard*), *tomteträd*, and *tuntré*.

It is an oak, a birch, an elder, or an elm, considered to be the tutelary tree on which the household's happiness depended (Sweden) and the dwelling of the *tomtegubbe*, another name for the place spirit. Offerings of food would be placed at the base of the tree and sometimes its roots would be watered with milk.

In Bö (Norway), there stood a tree at the foot of which propitiatory offerings were made to the *haugbonde* (mound- or hill-dweller) at Jul (Yule) in the form of broth. If the plate was empty the next day, then good fortune was assured for their cows and horses. We may note, incidentally, that similar offerings are found all over. In the Upper Telemark region of Norway, offerings were made to the *vätter* (wights) on the hills called *vättehauge* ("wight-hills"). In Västerbotten (Westrobothnia, northern Sweden), coins were offered to the *vitra*, in Funen (Denmark), fishermen did the same thing for the water spirit (*sjörå*) and, when crossing a ford, a coin would be tossed to the *aamand* ("river man").

CONSTRUCTION AND ORGANIZATION OF THE SPACE

Once the estate was delineated, the house would be built along with the various enclosures. The organization of the space proceeded together with its hallowing, and it can be conceptually represented by a series of circles centered on the main dwelling, which, as the evidence confirms, had a sacred character. Perhaps this is because the good dead were buried there, who would gradually transform into ancestral spirits and then into place spirits that would keep watch over the family's affairs. The enclosure in front of the house (*tún*) was a hallowed space and a tree stood within it, under or in which the place spirit dwelled.[20] Sometimes its dwelling place was a stone.[21] Around the enclosure stood the *garðr*, a hedge or low wall made of stones, or even a barrier of wooden stakes connected by clumps of dirt and stones as a protection against men and spirits. A wight reminiscent of the Roman Sylvanus orientalis resided there.

The human thus appropriates the land and tames his space in successive waves, reminiscent of the rings made by a rock falling into the water, and the thematics of the circle, evident in enclosure procedures, are predominant in the relationship human beings maintain with their space. But in the early Middle Ages, human habitation was sparse, and while a person was protected on his lands—there he enjoyed his sacred inviolability—as soon as he left them, he was again confronted with the problem of spirits. This is something that is clearly visible in the charms and spells intended to guarantee a peaceful journey. He therefore must conquer a new space.

This can be seen through the organization of space based on naming places: the place names demarcating roads, setting the boundaries of estates, districts, and so forth served as a support to these landmarks. Space lost its anxiety-causing immensity and the "wild" gradually receded. Now, the choice of place names—when they are not simply based on a physical element of the landscape—is not something random: mythical and religious elements factor in their selection.

Circumambulation is one of the oldest forms of establishing ownership of a piece of land, and it had the same standing as a legal act, but it should be recognized that in these olden times law and religion were inseparable. These rites continued to be upheld for a long time, even when their original meaning was lost:

> In Gelida [Catalonia], until the middle of the last century, when one was to begin construction of a house, a furrow was dug in the ground that would serve as its intended perimeter. This furrow was not unbroken: the plow would be lifted where the doors were planned. It was believed that if this was not done, the house would collapse.

Catalonian traditions maintain that the city of Villareal was founded by the great king Jaime himself, who "taking a plow, marked off the borders of the city and its streets with furrows." In this same province, another rite that should be pointed out: "In Cardadeu there was a family whose heir would plow the town square on the Sunday afternoon of Carnival to show his ancient right to ownership of the village"—which is nothing other than a renewal of the rite for taking possession of a piece of land.

The *Vita sancti Goeznovei*, the hagiography of Saint Goeznoveus dating from 1019, tells us this: Count Comoor donated to Goeznoveus as much land for his monastery as he could enclose within the trenches he dug in one day. It took a day and an hour, during which the holy man had to complete his circuit (*assignata est dies qua sanctus debuit terram circuire*). Our man thus started off headed north, dragging a pitchfork on the ground behind him—"and as he dragged this forked staff, the earth, an odd thing, rose on either side to form a large ditch"—and walked for one stade, then he turned east and walked straight ahead until he reached a place called *Caput nemoris*, which today is Penhoat, the "Wooden Head." From there he turned right to head southward, and after walking in that direction for four stades, he turned westward and walked another four stades before turning one last time to the east in order to return to his starting point. As it happens, this procedure is the precise counterpart of the outline of the sacred square among the Romans and the Indo-Europeans, as shown by Georges Dumézil.

Let us sum up the information that our various testimonies have provided to us. The choice of the place for humans to settle is entrusted to supernatural beings, God, or the gods, or in liaison with them (saints, the dead, fairies). Behind the different rites—delimitation by means of fire, a furrow, a strip, or on horseback—the essential feature of the operation emerges: it involves the formation of an enclosed space, a space of culture in every sense of the word, in opposition to the wildness of untamed nature, which is always comparable to primordial chaos and, as Mircea Eliade notes:

> still participate[s] in the undifferentiated, formless modality of pre-Creation. This is why, when possession is taken of a territory—that is, when its exploitation begins—rites are performed that symbolically repeat the act of Creation; the uncultivated zone is first "cosmicized," then inhabited.[22]

Through the rituals of taking ownership of the land, chaos is transformed into cosmos in imitation of the gods.

In rediscovering the land spirits, we cannot fail to notice their modernity. They prompted our ancestors to respect their environment, to be careful, for they knew that they were not alone and had accounts to settle with those that were called—and are still called, here and there—the "Invisible People," or the "Subterranean People." Only a few decades ago we saw in Iceland how the population refused to allow a hydroelectric power station to be built because they believed it would harm the spirit of the waterfall. Has the disappearance of land spirits not provoked catastrophes by giving free rein to the presumptions of modern man? It clearly seems that these spirits were part of the regulating elements of the lives of our ancestors and, whatever they may prove to be, they have bequeathed us with one essential law: man must live in symbiosis with the nature that surrounds him and treat it as a living being. In short, he must continue to venerate and respect the nature spirits in order to prosper.

Notes

[In the notes, several standard sources for older texts are referred to by the following abbreviations: MGH = *Monumenta Germaniae Historica*; *Pat. lat.* = Patrologia Latina; *Pat. graec.* = Patrologia Graeca.]

INTRODUCTION

1. Régis Boyer, "En hommage . . . ," in *Formes et difformités médiévales: En hommage à Claude Lecouteux*, ed. Florence Bayard and Astrid Guillaume (Paris: PUPS, 2010), 13–15, here at 14.

2. Remarks made by Claude Lecouteux for the article by Hélène Delavigne, "Claude Lecouteux: Itinéraire d'un chercheur," in *Formes et difformités médiévales*, 21–33, here at 30.

3. Term discussed by Régis Boyer in "Petite mythologie: qu'est-ce à dire?" in *Formes et difformités médiévales*, 63–74. "This is why there are no grounds for making a strict distinction between 'large' and 'small' mythology. Let us just say that this discipline can be practiced a number of ways, starting from a variety of premises, but there is no way to see how a hierarchy of myths could be established. This is something that Claude Lecouteux clearly saw or felt!" (p. 74).

4. Boyer, "En homage . . . ," 14.

5. Catherine Velay-Vallantin, "Lire la 'méthode Lecouteux' à l'épreuve de Mélusine," in *Formes et Difformités*, 75–80, here at 79.

6. The reader will notice some repetition in several articles. We are fully aware of this, and it is probably inevitable in a collection of scarce articles united by similar themes. However, these repetitions are fairly rare and make it

possible to emphasize points that we believe are essential to the perspective that we want to give this anthology.

7. Astrid Guillaume, "Faire entrer dans tous les dictionnaires 'animal liminaire' et 'liminarité animalière'," *Revue de la Fondation Droit Animal, Éthique et Sciences* 111, special supplement: *Faune sauvage*, (2021). Available online at the Fondation Droit Animal website.

8. Velay-Vallantin, "Lire la 'méthode Lecouteux,'" 78.

CHAPTER 1. THE RAMSUND STONE

This essay was originally published in *Études germaniques* 53 (1997), 559–61.

1. H. R. Ellis Davidson, "Sigurd in the Art of the Viking Age," *Antiquity* 16 (1942): 216–236; Erik Brate and Elias Wessén, *Sodermanlands runinskrifter: granskade och tolkade* (Stockholm: Norstedt, 1924–1936); Klaus Düwel, *Runenkunde* (Stuttgart: Metzler, 1968), 78; Sue Margeson, "The Volsung Legend in Medieval Art," in *Medieval Iconography and Narrative*, ed. F. G. Andersen et al. (Odense: Odense University Press, 1980), 183–211, reproduction of the stone on p. 192; Régis Boyer, *La Saga de Sigurdr ou la parole donnée* (Paris: Cerf, 1989), 102–3.

2. Cf. Peter Dinzelbacher, "Die Jenseitsbrücke im Mittelalter," dissertation, University of Vienna, 1973. For information on another kind of supernatural bridge, see Viljo J. Mansikka, *Über russische Zauberformeln mit Berücksichtigung der Blut- und Verrenkungssegen* (Helsingfors: Finnische Literaturgesellschaft, 1909), 250–59.

3. I am borrowing the elements from the study by Ioanna Andreesco and Mihaela Bacou, *Mourir à l'ombre des Carpathes* (Paris: Payot, 1986), which contains a bibliography of the primary Romanian works.

4. Much information can be found in Claude Carozzi, *Le Voyage de l'âme dans l'au-delà d'après la littérature latine (Ve–XIIIe siècle)* (Rome: L'École française de Rome, 1994); Claude Lecouteux, *Mondes parallèles, l'univers des croyances médiévales* (Paris: Champion, 1994), 66–100; other texts in Peter Dinzelbacher, *Mittelalterliche Visionsliteratur: Eine Anthologie* (Darmstadt: Wissenschaftliche Buchgesellschaft, 1989); Jean Marchand, *L'Autre monde au Moyen Âge: Voyages et visions* (Paris: De Brocard, 1940); Alexandre Micha, *Voyages dans l'au-delà d'après les textes médiévaux, IVe–XIIIe siècles* (Paris: Klincksieck, 1992).

5. Cf. Peter Dinzelbacher, *Vision und Visionsliteratur im Mittelalter* (Stuttgart: Hiersemann, 1981).

6. Cf. Kurt Ranke, *Indogermanische Totenverehrung*, vol. 1 (Helsinki: Suomalainen Tiedeakatemia, 1950).

CHAPTER 2. EYRBYGGJA SAGA

This essay was originally published as "Snorri le Godi" in *Mythologies* (February 2020).

CHAPTER 4. FANTASY AND THE MIDDLE AGES

1. See the entry in Claude Lecouteux, *Encyclopedia of Norse and Germanic Folklore, Mythology, and Magic*, trans. Jon E. Graham; ed. Michael Moynihan (Rochester, VT: Inner Traditions, 2016).

2. For more on the journeys of Thorkillus (Thorkil), see chapter 6 in Claude Lecouteux, *The Pagan Book of the Dead: Ancestral Visions of the Afterlife and Other Worlds*, trans. Jon E. Graham (Rochester, VT: Inner Traditions, 2020).

3. J. K. Rowling, *Harry Potter and the Half-Blood Prince* (London: Bloomsbury, 2005), 536 and 556.

4. See Claude Lecouteux, *The High Magic of Talismans and Amulets*, trans. Jon E. Graham (Rochester, VT: Inner Traditions 2014).

5. Astrid Guillaume, "Pour une sémiotique diachronique des cultures: De Perceval à Avatar," *texto!* (electronic journal of the Institut Ferdinand de Saussure) 18.2 (2013), and "Pour une sémiotique diachronique des cultures: le 'Moyen-Âge' aujourd'hui," in *Textes, Documents, Œuvre: Perspectives sémiotiques*, ed. Driss Ablali, Sémir Badir, and Dominique Ducard (Rennes: Presses Universitaires de Rennes, 2014), 381–406.

CHAPTER 5. A TYPOLOGY OF SEVERAL KINDS OF EVIL DEAD

This essay was originally published in *Cahiers slaves* 3 (2001), 227–44.

1. For more on the phenomenon, see Claude Lecouteux, *The Return of the Dead: Ghosts, Ancestors, and the Transparent Veil of the Pagan Mind*, trans. Jon E. Graham (Rochester, VT: Inner Traditions, 2009). French transla-

tions of numerous Latin texts can be found in Claude Lecouteux and Phillipe Marcq, *Les esprits et les morts, croyances médiévales: Textes traduits du latin, présentés et commentés* (Paris: Champion, 1990). On the type of revenant called the "vampire," see Claude Lecouteux, *The Secret History of Vampires*, trans. Jon E. Graham (Rochester, VT: Inner Traditions, 2010).

2. Walter Map, *De nugis curialium*, ed. Montague Rhodes James (Oxford: Clarendon, 1914). [English: *Master Walter Map's Book* De Nugis Curialium *(Courtiers' Trifles)*, trans. Frederick Tupper and Marbury Bladen Ogle (New York: Macmillan, 1924), 125–26.]

3. Karl Ferdinand von Schertz, *Magia posthuma* (Olomouc: Rosenburg, 1706).

4. Augustin Calmet, *Dissertation sur les revenants en corps, les excommuniés, les oupires ou vampires . . .* (Grenoble: Millon, 1986), 139.

5. *Flóamanna saga*, chap. 22, in Þórhallur Vilmundarson and Bjarni Vilhjálmsson, eds., *Harðar saga* (Reykjavík: Hið Íslenzka Fornritafélag, 1991).

6. *Contes populaires d'Islande*, trans. Régis Boyer (Reykjavik: Iceland Review, 1983), 50–53.

7. Joseph Pitton de Tournefort, *Voyage en Levant* (Amsterdam: Compagnie, 1718), I, 52ff.

8. Józef Klapper, "Die schlesischen Geschichten von den schädigenden Toten," *Mitteilungen der Schlesischen Gesellschaft für Volkskunde* 11 (1909): 58–94, at 88.

9. Cited by Augustin Calmet, *Dissertation sur les apparitions des esprits, et sur les vampires ou les revenans de Hongrie, de Moravie, etc.* (Einsiedeln, 1749; rpt. Grenoble: Millon, 1986).

10. Calmet, *Dissertation sur les apparitions des esprits*.

11. I would like to thank J.-P. Sémon (Paris-Sorbonne) who provided me with this text. He translated it and provided the philological commentary.

12. Cf. Claude Lecouteux, *Phantom Armies of the Night: The Wild Hunt and the Ghostly Processions of the Undead*, trans. Jon E. Graham (Rochester, VT: Inner Traditions, 2011).

13. Saxo Grammaticus, *Gesta Danorum*, ed. Alfred Holder (Strassburg: Trübner, 1858), bk. V, 162–63; *Egils saga einhanda ok Ásmundar berserkjabana*, ed. Guðni Jónsson, in *Fornaldar sögur norðurlanda* (Reykjavik: Íslendingasagnaútgáfan, 1954), III: 323–65, chap. 7, here at 338.

14. *La Saga d'Éric le Rouge*, ed. and trans. Maurice Gravier (Paris: Aubier, 1955), chap. 6, 75–76.

15. Burchard of Worms, *Decretum*, XIX, 5, 179, in H.-J. Schmitz, ed., *Die Bußbücher* (Düsseldorf: N.p., 1898), II: 448.

16. Cf. M. L. Le Bail, "Le mort sur le vif," *Hésiode: Cahiers d'ethnologie méditerranéenne* 2 (1994): 157–177, at 172.

17. Michael Ranfft, *De masticatione mortuorum in tumulis* (1728), trans. D. Sonnier (Grenoble: Millon, 1995), 25–27.

18. Hieronimus Cardanus, *Magia seu mirabilium historiarum de spectris et apparitionibus spiritum* (Eisleben: Grosius, 1597), 56.

19. Cf. Claude Lecouteux, *Au-delà du merveilleux: Des croyances au Moyen Âge* (Paris: PUPS, 1982), 87–117.

20. Cf. Kurt Ranke, "Alp," in *Handwörterbuch des deutschen Aberglaubens*, ed. Hanns Bächtold-Stäubli, 2nd ed. (Berlin and New York: De Gruyter, 1987), vol. 1, col. 281–305, at 293.

21. Von Schertz, *Magia posthuma*.

22. *Schlesisches historisches Labyrinth Oder Kurtzgefaste Sammlung Von hundert Historien Allerhand denckwürdiger Nahmen, Oerter, Personen, Gebräuche, Solennitäten und Begebenheiten in Schlesien.* (Breslau and Leipzig: Hubert, 1737), 351–52.

23. Cf. L. C. F. Garmann, *De miraculis mortuorum* (Dresden and Leipzig, 1660), I, 3: "*De cadaveribus, porcorum mandentium instar, in cryptis feralibus sonantibus, vulgo schmaetzende Tode*"; Philipp Rohr, *Dissertatio historico-philosophica de masticatione mortuorum* (Leipzig: Vogtius, 1679).

24. Calmet, *Dissertation sur les apparitions*, 88.

25. *Malleus maleficarum* (Strassburg, 1486–87; facsimile ed. Hildesheim: Olms, 1992), I, 15. [English translation from *The Hammer of Witches*, trans. Christopher S. Mackay (Cambridge: Cambridge University Press, 2010), 237.]

26. Georgius Aelurius, *Glaciographia oder Glätzische Chronik* (Leipzig: Ritzsch, 1625), 236–37.

27. *Tischrede* nr. 6823, in *Luthers Werke* (Weimar: Böhlaus, 1921), 6: 214.

28. Cited in Klapper, "Die schlesischen Geschichten," 85.

29. Gabrielis Rzaczynski, *Historia naturalis curiosa regni Poloniae* (Sandomir: Collegius Soc. Jesu, 1721), 365.

30. *Monatsschrift von und für Schlesien* 1 (1829), 411.

CHAPTER 6. GRIMOIRES AND THEIR ANCESTORS

1. The manuscript, which consists of 148 folios, is preserved in the Ghent University Library, ms. 1021A. The manuscript in Halle should also be

mentioned: Universitäts- und Landesbibliothek Sachsen-Anhalt ms. 14 B 36, fol. 160v°–170r°, 260v°–265v°; it has a wealth of figures and is a compilation of astrological treatises (*Liber ymaginum, Ymagines super septem dies ebdomade et sigilla planetarum, Tractatus de imaginibus*, Thetel, Thebit, Ptolemy . . .).

2. Compare with the text of the Halle manuscript, ms. 14 B 36, fol. 160v°–170r°; 260 v°–265v°.

3. The text of Trithemius was reproduced by Will-Erich Peuckert, *Pansophie: Ein Versuch zur Geschichte der weissen und schwarzen Magie* (Berlin: Schmidt, 1956), 47–55 (= *Antipalus maleficiorum*, I, 3).

4. Cf. S. L. MacGregor Mathers, ed. and trans., *The Grimoire of Armadel* (York Beach, ME: Weiser: 1995).

5. We know a *Book of Raziel* (*Sepher Raziel*) in Hebrew, attributed to Eleazar of Worms, published in Amsterdam in 1701, for which a manuscript exists in the British Library, ms. Sloane 3826.

6. Tenny L. Davis, trans., *Roger Bacon's Letter Concerning the Marvelous Power of Art and of Nature and Concerning the Nullity of Magic* (Easton, PA: Chemical Publishing, 1923), 25.

7. Jean-Baptiste Thiers, *Traité des superstitions* (Paris: Dezallier, 1679), 247.

8. The best study on this figure is Klaus Arnold, *Johannes Trithemius (1462–1516)* (Würzburg: Schoningh, 1971).

9. Cf. Alfred Morin, *Catalogue descriptif de la Bibliothèque bleue de Troyes* (Geneva: Droz, 1974), 405–407.

10. Victor Joly, *Les Ardennes* (Brussels: Van Buggenhoudt, 1854).

11. Cf. Dieter Harmening, "Okkultkommerz—Vermarktete Reste magischer Traditionen," in *Hexen heute: Magische Traditionen und neue Zutaten*, ed. Dieter Harmening (Würzburg: Könighausen & Neumann, 1991), 103–14, at 105.

12. Anatole Le Braz, *La Légende de la mort* (Marseille: Lafitte, 1982), 370.

13. For more on all this, cf. Harmening, "Okkultkommerz."

14. Twenty-seven vellum folios, in duodecimo, with two "Letters from Heaven," the "letters" (i.e. *caracteres*) of Charlemagne, numerous magical symbols, the seal of Solomon, a conjuration of evil spirits, and so forth.

15. Cf. David Pingree, "The Diffusion of Arabic Magical Texts in Western Europe," in *La diffuzione delle scienze islamiche nel Medio Evo Europeo*, ed. Biancamaria Scarcia Amoretti (Rome: Accademia Nazionale dei Lincei, 1987), 57–102.

16. Cf. Lynn Thorndike, "Traditional Medieval Tracts concerning Engraved Astronomical Images," in *Mélanges Auguste Pelzer* (Louvain: Bibliothèque de l'Université, 1947), 217–274; here 256–61.

17. Balenis is undoubtedly identical to Baleemus, Balaminus, in other words, al-'Amid, author of a book with the identical title and subtitled *The Images of the Seven Planets*. Cf. Thorndike, "Traditional Medieval Tracts," 242–43. We should note that an initial identification was proposed to Balinas, the Pseudo-Apollonius of Tyana.

18. Cf. Thorndike, "Traditional Medieval Tracts," 223–24, 229–38. Another important document is the Biblioteca Medica Laurenziana manuscript Plut. 89 Sup. 38, in which we have by Thebit the *Tractatus de proprietatibus quarundam stellarum et convenentia earundem quibusdam lapidibus et herbis*, folios 1r°–3v°; the text was published in Francis J. Carmody, *The Astronomical Work of Thabit B. Qurra* (Berkeley and Los Angeles: University of California Press, 1960), 179–97. The manuscript also contains the *Tractatus de imaginibus*, folios 3v°–8v°; *Ptolomei Tractatus de imaginationibus*, fol. 9r°–17r°; and *Theyzelius Quedam imaginum secundum planetatas* (!) *extracte de quodam libello*, fol. 282v°–294v°. Cf. also the National Library of Florence manuscript II III 214 (fifteenth century).

19. Johannes Hartlieb, *Das Buch aller verbotenen Künste, des Aberglaubens und der Zauberei*, ed. and trans. by Falk Eisermann and Eckhard Graf (Ahlersted: Param, 1989).

20. Translation of the first book and the beginning of the second, preserved in three seventeenth-century manuscripts.

21. Alfonso d'Agostino, ed., *Alfonso X el Sabio: Astromagia* (Naples: Liguori, 1989).

22. Cf. Alejandro García Avilés, "Two Astromagical Manuscripts of Alfonso X," *Journal of the Warburg and Courtauld Institutes* 59 (1996): 14–23.

23. Cf. Juan A. Paniagua, *Studia Arnaldiana: Trabajos en torno a la obra médica de Arnau de Vilanova*, c. 1240–1311 (Barcelona: Fundación Uriach 1848, 1994); Nicolas Weill-Parot, *Les Images astrologiques au Moyen Âge et à la Renaissance: Spéculations intellectuelles et pratiques magiques* (Paris: Champion, 2002), chap. 8.

24. Edited in Oswald Cockayne, *Leechdoms, Wortcunning, and Starcraft of Early England* (London: Longman, Green, Longman, Roberts, and Green, 1864–1866), vol. 2.

25. Edited in Cockayne, *Leechdoms, Wortcunning, and Starcraft*, vol. 2.

26. Louis Delatte, ed., *Textes latins et vieux français relatifs aux Cyranides* (Paris: Belles Lettres, 1942).

27. Cf. Nr. 28: *Fiskessvartebok, Jaktssvartebok*, in Velle Espeland, *Svartbok frå Gudbrandsdalen* (Oslo: Universitetsforlaget, 1974).

28. Edited in Espeland, *Svartbok frå Gudbrandsdalen*. I am following Espeland's numbering.

29. I am not taking into consideration the books on divination like *L'Avenir dévoilé*; *Éléments de chiromancie*; *Petit Traité de la baguette divinatoire*; *Prescience*; *Le Miroir d'astrologie naturelle ou le passe-temps de la jeunesse* (Troyes: chez la citoyenne Garnier, n.d. [eighteenth century]).

30. Espeland, *Svartbok frå Gudbrandsdalen*, 21–24.

31. Museum of Icelandic Sorcery & Witchcraft, Strandagaldur, Galdrasyning in Ströndum.

CHAPTER 7. BIG BELLS AND LITTLE BELLS

This essay was originally published in *Cloches et Horloges dans les textes médiévaux*, edited by Fabienne Pomel (Rennes: Presses Universitaires de Rennes, 2012), 109–26.

1. Jacob Grimm, *Deutsche Rechtsaltertümer* (Hildesheim: Olms, 1992 [1899]), 2:546.

2. Grimm, *Deutsche Rechtsaltertümer*, 2:470–71.

3. *Reimchronik*, Heidelberg, Cod. Pal. 336, fol. 21–273. This story corresponds to the tale type ATU 207C, "Animals Ring Bell and Demand Justice," which we also find in the *Gesta Romanorum*, cap. 105.

4. Cf. Marcel van den Berg, *De volkssage in de Provincie Antwerpen in de 19de en 20ste eeuw* (Ghent: Koningl. Akad. voor Nederlandse Taal- en Letterkunde, 1993), 3:1909.

5. Hugo von Trimberg, *Der Renner*, v. 3802, ed. Günther Schweikle (Berlin: De Gruyter, 1971), vol. 4.

6. Jacobus de Voragine, *Sermones aurei de praecipuis sanctorum festis*, ed. Rudolphus Clutius (Cracow: Bartl, 1760), 173b–174a.

7. "*Diu venster unde die gloggen die bezaichent alle gaistliche lerær, die paidiu mit den guoten worten unde mit guoten werchen der heiligen christenheit die guote lere suln vor tragen*" (chap. 43, ll. 18–20), in *Altdeutsche Predigten*, ed. Anton E. Schönbach (Graz: Styria, 1891), 3:98.

8. *Eckenlied*, ed. Francis B. Brevart (Tübingen: Niemeyer, 1999), 36, ll. 8–13:

    den heln man horte maenicvalt

    wider us dem walde erclingen,

    reht als ain glogge waer erschalt:

    swa in ain aste geruorte,

    mit clang er im das galt.

9. Edmund Wiessner, ed., *Heinrich Wittenwilers Ring: Nach der Meininger Handschrift* (Leipzig: Reclam, 1931), v. 81–82:

    Lieben gsellen, höret, wie

    Ir der rugg was überschossen:

    Man hiet ein gloggen drüber gossen

10. Pierre-Jean Bérenger, *Œuvres complètes* (Paris: Perrotin, 1847), 1:viii.

11. G. H. Buijssen, ed., *Durandus' Rationale in spätmittelhochdeutscher Übersetzung nach der Hs. CVP 2765*, 4 vols. (Assen: Van Gorcum, 1966–1983).

12. A fine example of this belief being recycled in a romance is found in the *Prosa-Lancelot*, ed. Reinhold Kluge (Berlin: Akademie-Verlag, 1980 [1948]), Pt. 1, p. 537, ll. 19–25: *Da hort der konig ein glocken lútenzu eim closter, dar hub er sich bald und sin gesinde.*

13. *Otia imperialia*, III, 69.

14. Ulrich von Zatzikhoven, *Lanzelet*, trans. René Pérennec (Grenoble: ELLUG, 2004), 205.

15. Jules Baudot, *Les Cloches, étude historique, liturgique et symbolique* (Paris: Bloud, 1913), 26.

16. Jacques Berlioz and Jean-Luc Eichenlaub, eds., *Stephani de Borbone Tractatus de diversis materiis predicabilibus* (Turnhout: Brepols, 2002), I, 7, 1:304.

17. Paul Sébillot, *Le Folklore de France* (Paris: Imago, 1968 [1907]), 4:147.

18. Motif V115.1: Church bell sunk in river (sea). [The Motifs cited in this article are from Stith Thompson, *Motif-Index of Folk-Literature: A Classification of Narrative Elements in Folktales, Ballads, Myths, Fables, Mediaeval Romances, Exempla, Fabliaux, Jest-Books, and Local Legends*, 6 vols. (Bloomington, IN: Indiana University Press, 1955–1958). —*Ed.*]

19. Cf. Leander Petzold, *Historische Sagen* (Munich: Beck, 1976), 1:85. Other examples in Sébillot, *Le Folklore de France*, 4:142–43.

20. Motif E533.1: Ghostly bell sounds from under water; F993: Sunken bell sounds. See also van den Berg, *De volkssage in de provincie Antwerpen*, 2:1015–1020.

21. Charles Joisten, *Êtres fantastiques: patrimoine narratif de l'Isère* (Grenoble: Musée dauphinois, 2005), 163.

22. A goat, for example Theodor Vernaleken, *Alpensagen* (Salzburg and Leipzig: Pustet, 1938), 236; the legend adds that someone carved on the bell: "The goat's foot discovered me."

23. Hans Bächtold-Stäubli, Eduard Hoffmann-Krayer, *Handwörterbuch des deutschen Aberglaubens* (Berlin and New York: De Gruyter, 1987), vol. 3, col. 868–76.

24. Éloïse Mozzani, *Le Livre des superstitions: mythes, croyances, légendes* (Paris: Laffont, 1995), 464–65; Sébillot, *Le Folklore de France*, 4:145.

25. Jacob Grimm, *Deutsche Mythologie* (Darmstadt: Wissenschaftliche Buchgesellschaft, 1965 [1875–1878]), 3:313.

26. Grimm, *Deutsche Mythologie*, 2:908.

27. Grimm, *Deutsche Mythologie*, 1:380, n. 1.

28. Cf. Lowry Charles Wimberly, *Death and Burial Lore in the English and Scottish Popular Ballads* (Lincoln: University of Nebraska Press, 1927), 88–89.

29. Wirnt von Grafenberg, *Wigalois, le chevalier à la roue d'or*, ed. and trans. Claude Lecouteux and Véronique Lévy (Grenoble: Ellug, 2001).

30. Edward R. Haymes, trans., *The Saga of Thidrek of Bern* (New York and London: Garland, 1988) chap. 330.

31. See Ion Taloş, *Petit Dictionnaire de mythologie roumaine* (Grenoble: ELLUG, 2002), s.v. "*balaur*," "fees méchantes."

32. *Lohengrin*, ed. Heinrich Rückert (Quedlinburg and Leipzig: Basse, 1858), v. 372–80 and 492–509.

33. *Ut cloccas non baptizent . . . propter grandinem* (the text is edited in the MGH *Leges*, 2 I 64 c. 34.)

34. Ms. 672, Reims bibliothèque municipale (trésor de la cathédrale).

35. Jules Baudot is not in agreement with Edmond Martène in attributing the text to Alcuin; cf. *Les Cloches* (cited above, n. 15).

36. *Exorcismus ad consecrandum signum basilicae et benedictio eiusdem.*

37. Ed. Marius Férotin, in *Monumenta Ecclesiae liturgica*, vol. V (Paris: Didot, 1904), col. 159–60.

38. 4 vols. (Antwerp: de La Bry, 1736–1738).

39. Cf. Johann Wilhelm Wolf, *Deutsche Hausmärchen* (Göttingen: Dieterich, 1851), 560–61.

40. Sébillot, *Le Folklore de France*, 4:144. For Austria, cf. Vernaleken, *Alpensagen*, 208.

41. *Württembergisches Jahrbuch* 1857/II, 151. The bells quashing storms are, for example, those of Pappelau (Blaubeuren), the Bell of Nine Hours (*Neunuhrglocke*) of Zwiefalten, two others in the Stuttgart Monastery, and those on the Brackberg in Brackenheim.

42. Charles Joisten, *Les Êtres fantastiques dans le folklore de l'Ariège* (Portet-s-Garonne: Loubatières, 2000), 31.

43. Cf. Claude Lecouteux, "Les maîtres du temps: tempestaires, obligateurs, défenseurs," in *Le Temps qu'il fait au Moyen Âge: Phénomènes atmosphériques dans la littérature, la pensée scientifique et religieuse*, ed. Joëlle Ducos and Claude Thomasset (Paris: PUPS, 1998), 151–69, and in the present book.

44. *The Hammer of Witches*, trans. Christopher S. Mackay (Cambridge: Cambridge University Press, 2010), 237.

45. Taloş, *Petit Dictionnaire*, s.v. "grêle."

46. Cf. Claude Lecouteux, *Charmes, conjurations et bénédictions* (Paris: Champion, 1996), 46.

47. J. Habets, "Middeleeuwse klokken en klokinschriften," *Publications de la société historique et d'archéologie dans le duché de Limbourg* 5 (1870), 313.

48. Vernaleken, *Alpensagen*, 211.

49. Adolph Franz, *Die kirchlichen Benediktionen des Mittelalters* (Freiburg im Breisgau: Herder, 1909), 2:572.

50. *Philippi Theophrasti Bombast von Hohenheim Paracelsi genannt, Geheimnüß aller siner Geheimnüsse* (Leipzig: Fleischer, 1750); Pseudo-Paracelsus, *Liber secundus Archidoxis magicae: De sigillis duodecim signorum et secretis illorum* (1570), bk. VI.

51. Kurt Köster, "Alphabet-Inschriften auf Glocken: Mit einem Katalog europäischer ABC-Glocken vom 12. bis zum 18. Jahrhundert," in *Studien zur deutschen Literatur des Mittelalters*, ed. Rudolf Schützeichel (Bonn: Bouvier, 1979), 371–422.

52. Franz Dornseiff, *Das Alphabet in Mystik und Magie* (Leipzig and Berlin: Teubner, 1925), 75 and 123.

53. Cf. Claude Lecouteux, *The Book of Grimoires: The Secret Grammar of Magic*, trans. Jon E. Graham (Rochester, VT: Inner Traditions, 2013), 57–94, and *The High Magic of Talismans and Amulets: Tradition and Craft*, trans. Jon E. Graham (Rochester, VT: Inner Traditions, 2014).

54. Baudot, *Les Cloches*, 26.

55. Tony Hunt, *Popular Medicine in Thirteenth-Century England: Introduction and Texts* (Cambridge: Brewer, 1994), 9, nr. 67.

56. David Pingree, ed. *Picatrix: The Latin Version of the Ghāyat Al-Ḥakīm* (London: Warburg Institute, 1936).

CHAPTER 8. WEYLAND THE SMITH

This essay was originally published in *Mythologie française* 235 (2009), 26–32.

1. Text in Ferdinand Holthausen, ed., *Beowulf nebst den kleineren Denkmälern der Heldensage: Finburg, Waldere, Deor, Widsith, Hildebrand* (Heidelberg: Winter, 1921).

2. On the suggested theories and proposed emendations, cf. George Philip Krapp and Elliot Van Kirk Dobbie, eds., *The Exeter Book* (New York: Columbia University Press, 1936), 318–19.

3. Kemp Malone, ed., *Deor* (London: Methuen, 1966), 6–7.

4. R. E. Kaske, "Weland and the *wurmas* in *Deor,*" *English Studies* 44 (1963): 190–91.

5. Oskar Jänicke, ed., *Biterolf und Dietleib Laurin und Walberan* (Berlin and Zurich: Weidmann, 1963), stanza 652, p. 120.

6. André Schnyder, ed., *Biterolf und Dietleib* (Bern and Stuttgart: Haupt, 1980), v. 11158ff.

7. Francis B. Brévart, ed., *Das Eckenlied: Sämtliche Fassungen*, 3 vols. (Tübingen: Niemeyer, 1999).

8. Cf. W. G. Collingwood, "The Early Crosses of Leeds," *The Publications of the Thoresby Society* 22 (1915), 267–338. The grayed-out parts of the illustration are those that are preserved.

9. Heinrich Beck, "Der Kunstfertige Schmied—ein ikonographisches und narratives Thema des frühen Mittelalters," in *Medieval Iconography and Narrative: A Symposium*, ed. F. G. Andersen, et al. (Odense: Odense University Press, 1980), 15–37.

10. Cf. Servius, *Commentaires sur les Géorgiques de Virgile*, III, 113; Ovid, *Les Métamorphoses*, II, 552ff.; Pausanias, I, 2, 6; Apollodorus, *Bibliothèque*, III, 14, 6.

11. Jean-François Bladé, *Contes populaires de la Gascogne* (Paris: Maisonneuve, 1886).

12. In English literature and folklore, Weyland has left traces. Also named Wayland in Britain, our smith is connected to a megalithic tomb, Waylands Smithy, located near White Horse, Oxfordshire and Uffington Castle, which

is 185 feet long, 43 feet wide; the monument dates to 3700–3400 BCE. Excavations made in 1919 unearthed the remains of seven adults and one child.

13. Ralph W. V. Elliott, *Runes: An Introduction* (Manchester: University Press, 1959), 96–109.

14. Alfred Becker, *Franks Casket: Zu den Bildern und Inschriften des Runenkästchens von Auzon* (Regensburg: Carl, 1973), 154–86.

15. Elliot, *Runes*, 99.

16. Cf. Anton Christian Bang, *Norske Hexeformularer og Magiske Opskrifter* (Kristiania [Oslo]: Dybwad, 1901–1902), nr. 977, 1174d, 1196, 1325; nr. 1574 is titled *Fiskebønna*, "fish charm/conjuration."

CHAPTER 9. THE MAGNETIC MOUNTAIN

This essay was originally published in *La Montagne dans le texte médiéval: Entre mythe et réalité*, edited by Claude Thomasset and Danièle James-Raoul (Paris: PUPS, 2000), 167–86.

1. Thompson, *Motif-Index of Folk-Literature*: Motif F 754: magnetic mountain. The present essay is a summary of my study "Der Magnetberg," *Fabula* 25 (1984), 35–65, which I am completing. The German, Dutch, and Frisian texts can be found in it.

2. Cf. Leonhard Intorp, "Brandans Seefahrt," in *Enzyklopädie des Märchens* (Berlin: De Gruyter, 1979), vol. 2, col. 654–58.

3. For example, Bernhard Sowinsky, *Herzog Ernst: Ein mittelalterliches Abenteuerbuch* (Stuttgart: Reclam, 1970), 386.

4. Among others I am drawing from the works of Gédéon Huet, "La légende de la Montagne d'Aimant dans le roman de *Berinus*," *Romania* 44 (1915–17): 427–53; Arturo Graf, *Miti, leggende e superstizioni del medio evo* (Turin: Loescher, 1893), 2:363–64; Karl Bartsch, ed., *Herzog Ernst* (Vienna: Salzwasser, 1869), CXXXVff.; and Franz Kirnbauer and Karl Leopold Schubert, eds., *Die Sage vom Magnetberg: Leben und Werk* (Vienna: Montan, 1957).

5. Cf. Jean Sauvaget, "Les merveilles de l'Inde," in *Mémorial Jean Sauvaget*, ed. L. Robert (Damas: Institut français de Damas, 1954), vol. I, 190–309, here at 247.

6. Ed. J. J. Salverda de Grave (Paris, 1964–1968), 1:14.

7. *Géographie* 7, 2, 31; text in Moriz Haupt, "Herzog Ernst [C]," *Zeitschrift für deutsches Altertum* 7 (1849): 193–303, here at 298.

8. Bernhard Kübler, ed., "Commonitorium Palladii. Briefwechsel zwischen Alexander dem Großen und Dindimus, dem König der Bramanen. Brief Alexanders des Grossen an Aristotles über die Wunder Indiens," *Romanische Forschungen* 6 (1891): 203–37, here at 211. Cf. also Graf, *Miti, leggende e superstizioni*, 2:379–80, which cites other versions.

9. Cf. Th. Henri Martin, "Observations des anciens sur les attractions magnétiques," *Atti dell' Accademia nazionale di Lincei* 18 (1864–1865): 16–32 and 97–123, here at 19.

10. Martin, "Observations des anciens," 19; Kirnbauer and Schubert, *Die Sage vom Magnetberg*, 8.

11. Kirnbauer and Schubert, *Die Sage vom Magnetberg*, 8.

12. Cited from Valentin Rose, "Aristoteles De lapidibus und Arnoldus Saxo," *Zeitschrift für deutsches Altertum* 18 (1875): 321–455, here at 410. For Ibn al-Djazzar: Ferdinand Wüstenfeld, *Geschichte der arabischen Ärzte und Naturforscher* (Göttingen: Vandenhoeck und Ruprecht, 1840), 60–61 (author nr. 120).

13. German translation by Hermann Ethé, *Zakarija ben Muhammad ben Mahmûd el-Kazwînîs Kosmographie* (Leipzig: Fues, 1868), 244.

14. Cf. Julius Ruska, ed. and trans., *Das Steinbuch des Aristoteles* (Heidelberg: Winter, 1912), 52 and 91.

15. Ruska, ed. and trans., *Das Steinbuch des Aristoteles*, 77–78.

16. Rose, "Aristoteles De lapidibus," 410; Graf, *Miti, leggende e superstizioni*, 380.

17. Bartholomaeus Anglicus, *De proprietatibus rerum*, 16, 23: *Lapis magnes calidus est et sicuus in tertio gradu. Virtutem habet attrahendi ferrum. Montes enim sunt ex huiusmodi lapidibus.* Vincent de Beauvais, *Speculum naturale*, 8, 21; Constantine, *Liber de gradibus*, (Basel, 1536), 378.

18. Cf. Gundolf Keil, "Circa instans," in Kurt Ruh et al., *Die deutsche Literatur des Mittelalters, Verfasserlexikon* 1 (Berlin: De Gruyter, 1978), col. 1282–85. Hans Wölfel, ed., *Das Arzneidrogenbuch "Circa instans" in einer Fassung des XIII. Jahrhunderts aus der Universitätsbibliothek Erlangen* (Berlin: Preilipper, 1939); Paul Dorveaux, ed., *Le Livre des simples médecines* (Paris: Hachette, 1913); for the manuscripts, cf. Paul Meyer, "Manuscrits médicaux français," *Romania* 44 (1915–1917): 161–214.

19. Cf. G. Keil, "Gart der Gesundheit," in Ruh et al., *Die deutsche Literatur des Mittelalters* (see n. 18), vol. 2, col. 1072–92.

20. François Pétis de Lacroix, trans., *Les Mille et un jours: Contes Persans* (Paris: Delagrave, 1848), 217–18, 226–28. [English: "Singular Adventures of Aboulfaouaris, surnamed, The Great Traveller," in François Pétis de La Croix, *The Persian and Turkish Tales, Compleat*, trans. Dr. King (London: Ware, 1744), 2:27–110; Magnetic Mountain at 63–64.]

21. Cf. Philip Blommaert, *Oudvlaemsche Gedichten der XIIe, XIIIe en XIVe eeuwen* (Ghent: Hebbelynck, 1838–1841), 1:100–120, 2:3–28; Carl Schröder, ed., *Sanct Brandan: Ein lateinischer und drei deutsche Texte* (Erlangen: Besold, 1871).

22. For this motif, see Konrad Hofmann, "Über das Lebermeer," *Sitzungsberichte der Königlich-Bayerischen Akademie der Wissenschaften Philosophisch-philologische Klasse* 2 (1865): 1–19; Macolm Letts, "The Liver Sea," *Notes & Queries* 191 (1946): 47–49.

23. Version F was edited by Karl Bartsch (see n. 4); version E by Birgit Gansweidt, *Der Ernestus des Odo von Magdeburg* (Munich: Arbeo-Gesellschaft, 1989), and version C by Moriz Haupt (see n. 7).

24. Cf. Johannes Siebert, "Virgils Fahrt zum Agetstein," *PBB* 74 (1952): 193–225.

25. Karl Bartsch, ed., *Reinfrid von Braunschweig* (Tübingen: Literarischer Verein, 1871), v. 21022–35; v. 21548–71; v. 24256–69.

26. Cf. Claude Lecouteux, "'Herzog Ernst' v. 2164ff., das böhmische Volksbuch von Stillfried und Bruncwig und die morgenländischen Alexandersagen," *Zeitschrift für deutsches Altertum* 108 (1979): 306–322. See also, Julius Feifalik, "Zwei böhmische Volksbücher zur Sage von Reinfried von Braunschweig," *Wiener Sitzungsberichte* 29 (1859): 83–97; 30 (1860): 21–30.

27. Friedrich Heinrich von der Hagen, ed., "Historie-Liedeken van den Hertog van Bronswyk," *Neues Jahrbuch der Berlinischen Gesellschaft für deutsche Sprache und Alterthumskunde* 8 (1848): 359–369.

28. Barend Symons, ed. *Kudrun* (Tübingen: Niemeyer, 1964).

29. Ed. B. A. Brewka, "*Esclarmonde, Clarisse et Florent, Yde et Olive I, Croissant, Yde et Olive II, Huon et les géants*: Sequels to *Huon de Bordeaux*," dissertation, Vanderbilt University, 1977. [The English translations of the verses from the Old French *Esclarmonde* that appear here are based on modern French versions kindly provided by François Suard. —Ed.]

30. Cf. Huet, "La légende de la Montagne d'Aimant," who cites the manuscript Fr. 24372, fol. 42r°–v°, of the Bibliothèque Nationale.

31. Huet, "La légende de la Montagne d'Aimant," based on MS 2985, fol. 632ff., of the Bibliothèque de l'Arsenal.

32. Robert Bossuat, ed., *Berinus, roman en prose du XIVe siècle*, 2 vols. (Paris: Société des Anciens textes Francais, 1931); cf. also Huet, "La légende de la Montagne d'Aimant," 427ff.

33. Cf. Huet, "La légende de la Montagne d'Aimant," 448–49.

CHAPTER 10. THE RAFT OF THE WINDS

1. Elias Lönnrot, comp., *The Kalevala or Poems of the Kaleva District*, trans. Francis Peabody Magoun, Jr. (Cambridge, MA: Harvard University Press, 1963), 6.

2. *The Poetic Edda*, trans. Carolyn Larrington, rev. ed. (Oxford: Oxford University Press, 2014), 54.

3. Cf. Claude Lecouteux, *Les Monstres dans la littérature allemande du Moyen Âge* (Besançon: La Völva, 2016), 196.

4. Adolph Franz, *Die kirchlichen Benediktionen des Mittelalters* (Freiburg im Breigau: Herder, 1909), 2:19–104.

5. *The Poetic Edda*, trans. Larrington, 107, slightly modified [Larrington's "wind-floaters" has been changed to "wind-rafts" to match Lecouteux's title. —*Ed.*]

6. Agobard, *De grandine et tonitruis*, in *Agobardi Lugdunensis Opera omnia*, ed. L. Van Acker (Turnhout: Brepols, 1981), 3–15.

7. Gervase of Tilbury, *Otia Imperialia: Recreation for an Emperor*, ed. and trans. S. E. Banks and J. W. Binns (Oxford: Clarendon, 2002), 81.

8. Gervase, *Otia Imperialia*, trans. Banks and Binns, 83.

9. Cf. Reinhold R. Grimm, *Paradisus coelestis, paradisus terrestris: Zur Auslegungsgeschichte des Paradieses im Abendland bis um 1200* (Munich: Fink, 1977), 106–7.

10. Israel Friedländer, *Die Chadhirlegende und der Alexanderroman: Eine sagengeschichtliche und literarhistorische Untersuchung* (Leipzig: Teubner, 1913), 21–22.

11. Cf. Hermann Ethé, "Alexanderzug zum Lebensquell im Lande der Finsternis," *Sitzungsberichte der Bayerischen Akademie* (1871): 343–405, here at 393.

12. *The Travels of Sir John Mandeville*, trans. C. W. R. D. Moseley (London: Penguin, 1983), 183

13. *The Travels of Sir John Mandeville*, trans. Moseley, 163.

14. Gerald of Wales, *The Journey through Wales and The Descriptions of Wales*, trans. Lewis Thorpe (London: Penguin, 1978), 133–34; cf. Claude Lecouteux and Phillippe Marcq, *Les Esprits et les Morts: Croyances médiévales* (Paris: Champion, 1990), 67–71.

15. Cf. "Gylfaginning" in Finnur Jónsson, ed., *Edda Snorra Sturlusonar* (Copenhagen: Gyldendal, 1931).

16. Ulrich von Zatzikhoven, *Lanzelet*, ed. K. A. Hahn (Berlin: De Gruyter, 1965), v. 6990ff.

17. Chrétien de Troyes, *Erec et Enide*, ed. Mario Roques (Paris: Champion, 1952), v. 5420ff. *Les Quatre Branches du Mabinogi et autres contes gallois*, trans. P. Y. Lambert (Paris: Gallimard, 1993), 282–330, here at 326–29.

18. Cf. Jacob Grimm, *Deutsche Mythologie* (Darmstadt: Wissenschaftliche Buchgesellschaft, 1965 [1875–1878]), vol. 3.

19. Wirnt von Grafenberg, *Wigalois der Ritter mit dem Rade*, ed. J. M.N. Kapteyn (Bonn: Klopp, 1926), v. 6725ff.

20. Cf. Claude Lecouteux, *Les Monstres dans la pensée médiévale occidentale*, Paris: Univers. Paris-Sorbonne, 1994.

21. *The Saga of the Jomsvikings*, ed. and trans. N. F. Blake (London: Nelson and Sons, 1962).

22. Gregory of Tours, *The History of the Franks* trans. Lewis Thorpe (London: Penguin, 1974).

23. Cf. Claude Lecouteux, *Demons and Spirits of the Land: Ancestral Lore and Practices*, trans. Jon E. Graham (Rochester, VT: Inner Traditions, 2015), 92–102 et passim.

24. Text in Elmar Bartsch, *Die Sachbeschwörungen der römischen Liturgie* (Münster: Aschendorff, 1967), 415–16.

25. Cf. Monica Blöcker, "Wetterzauber: Zu einem Glaubenskomplex des frühen Mittelalters," *Francia* 9 (1981): 117–31.

26. Cf. Franz, *Die kirchlichen Benediktionen*, 2:77.

27. Ed. Georg Waitz, MGH SS 15.1 (Berlin: Hahn, 1887), 253–64.

28. Cf. Lecouteux and Marcq, *Les Esprits et les Morts*, 189–90.

29. Facsimile of this loose sheet in Gisela Ecker, *Einblattdrucke von den Anfängen bis 1555: Untersuchungen zu einer Publikationsform literarischer Texte* (Göppingen: Kümmerle, 1981), vol. II, nr. 195.

CHAPTER 11. THE MASTERS OF WEATHER

This essay was originally published in *Le Temps qu'il fait au Moyen Âge: Phénoménes atmosphériques dans la littérature, la pensée scientifique et religieuse*, edited by Joëlle Ducos and Claude Thomasset (Paris: PUPS, 1998), 151–69.

1. Adam of Bremen, *Gesta Hammaburgensis Pontificum* (IV, 26): *Thor, inquiunt, presidet in aere, qui tonitrus et fulmina, ventos ymbresque, serena et fruges gubernat.*

2. In the original French version of this article, "Les maîtres du temps," in *Le Temps qu'il fait au Moyen Âge*, ed. Joëlle Ducos and Claude Thomasset (Paris: PUPS, 1998), an illustration can be seen depicting Erik and his spear.

3. Jacques Paul Migne, ed., *Pat. graeca* 11, col. 621.

4. Jacques Paul Migne, *Pat. lat.* 15, col. 1319.

5. Cf. Claude Lecouteux, *Demons and Spirits of the Land: Ancestral Lore and Practices*, trans. Jon E. Graham (Rochester, VT: Inner Traditions, 2015), 23–28.

6. For more on this figure, see Claude Lecouteux, *Charmes, conjurations et bénédictions* (Paris: Champion, 1996), 83; *Dictionary of Ancient Magic Words and Spells: From Abraxas to Zoar*, trans. Jon E. Graham (Rochester, VT: Inner Traditions, 2015), s.v. "Mermeut."

7. Cf. Monica Blöcker, "Wetterzauber: Zu einem Glaubenskomplex des frühen Mittelalters," *Francia* 9 (1981): 117–31, here at 120.

8. For example in the *Hrólfs saga Gautrekssonar* (Saga of Hrolf, Son of Gautrek), chap. 19, easily found in *Deux Sagas islandaises légendaires*, trans. Régis Boyer (Paris: Belles Lettres, 1996). [English translation: *Hrolf Gautreksson: A Viking Romance*, trans. Hermann Pálsson and Paul Edwards (Edinburgh: Southside, 1972).]

9. *Lex Visigothorum*, VI, 2, 4 and VI, 2, 5; MGH *LL nat. Germ.* I, 259.

10. *Praeloquia*, I, 10; Migne, *Pat. lat.* 136, col. 158.

11. Agobard of Lyon, *De grandine et tonitruis*, cap. 2, in *Agobardi Lugdunensis Opera omnia*, ed. L. van Acker (Turnhout: Brepols, 1981), 3–15. [English translation from Fordham University's Medieval Sourcebook website.]

12. Cf. Hanns Bächtold-Stäubli, ed., *Handwörterbuch des deutschen Aberglaubens* (Berlin: De Gruyter, 1987), vol. 5, col. 1483.

13. Edited in Thomas Wright and James Orchard Halliwell, *Reliquiæ*

antiquæ: Scraps from Ancient Manuscripts, Illustrating Chiefly Early English Literature and the English Language (London: Smith, 1845), 2:103–7.

14. Adolph Franz, *Die kirchlichen Benediktionen des Mittelalters* (Freiburg im Breisgau: Herder, 1909), 2:102.

15. *In his regionibus pene omnes homines, nobiles et ignobiles, urbani et rustici, senes et iuvenes, putant grandines et tonitrua hominum libitu posse fieri.* Agobard (I,145; 158; 161; cf. also I, 146; 153; 159).

16. *De proprietatibus rerum*, XV, 172.

17. Cf. Lecouteux, *Demons and Spirits of the Land*, 33–34.

18. *Ruodlieb*, ed. Benedikt K. Vollmann (Wiesbaden: Reichert, 1985).

19. *Bonum universale de apibus* (Apiarus), II, 57 (Douai, 1627).

20. Cf. Francis Dubost, *Aspects fantastiques de la littérature narrative médiévale (XIIème–XIIIème siècles): L'autre, l'ailleurs, l'autrefois* (Paris: Champion, 1991), 459–62.

21. *The Hammer of Witches*, trans. Christopher S. Mackay (Cambridge: Cambridge University Press, 2010), 384, 382.

22. See Lecouteux, *Charmes, conjurations et bénédictions*, s.v. "cloches."

23. Franz, *Die kirchlichen Benediktionen*, 2:104.

24. *Rationale divinorum officiorum* (Lyon, 1584), I, 4, 4.

25. *The Hammer of Witches*, trans. Mackay, 467.

26. Franz, *Die kirchlichen Benediktionen*, 2:47.

27. Letter of Gregory VII to Haakon of Danmark, MGH *Epp.* 2.2, 497–98.

28. Franz, *Die kirchlichen Benediktionen*, 2:105–23

29. *The Hammer of Witches*, trans. Mackay, 466.

30. Jacob Grimm, *Deutsche Mythologie* (Darmstadt: Wissenschaftliche Buchgesellschaft, 1965), 2:145.

31. *Otia imperialia*, ed. Felix Liebrecht (Hanover: Rümpler, 1856), 34–35.

32. Franz, *Die kirchlichen Benediktionen*, 2:77 and 81.

33. *The Hammer of Witches*, trans. Mackay, 463.

34. Cf. also Marbode of Rennes, *De lapidibus*, ed. John M. Riddle (Wiesbaden: Steiner, 1977), VII (p. 45).

35. Cf. for example, Thomas de Cantimpré, *De natura rerum*, X, 23.

CHAPTER 12. MYTHICAL ASPECTS OF THE MOUNTAIN IN THE MIDDLE AGES

This essay was originally published in *Le Monde alpin et rhodanien* (1982): 43–54.

1. Gottfried von Strassburg, *Tristan und Isold* (ed. Friedrich Ranke [Berlin: Weidmann, 1930]), v. 11695.

2. The tangled forest (*der verworrene tan*) is a place name in the *Lanzelet* by Ulrich von Zatzikhoven (ed. Karl August Hahn [Frankfurt: Bronner, 1845]), v. 4981. For more on the forest, cf. Marianne Stauffer, *Der Wald: Zur Darstellung und Deutung der Natur im Mittelalter* (Zurich: Francke, 1958).

3. The Latin text for the material quoted in the footnote is: *Est aliud sepulchrum in Brittannia in cacumine montis Cruc Mayr, iuxta quod qui se extenderit, si longus aut brevis fuerit, iuxta staturam unius cuiusque sepulchrum aptatur, omnis autem peregrinus, si iuxta sepulchrum illud ter flectaverit, itineris tedio non gravabitur. Est miraculum in Brittannia valde mirandum de lapide quodam qui nocturnis temporibus invenitur in valle Cheym, in die vero supra montem repperitur; quem cum incole regionis in aquis proiciunt vel sub terra abscondunt, mane semper in montis vertice vel nocte in valle repperitur.* The source for the quoted material is *Historia Brittonum* (ed. Edmond Faral, in *La Légende arthurienne* [Paris: Champion, 1969], 3:4–62).

4. I will not discuss well-known legends like that of the crystal mountain (cf. O. Huth, "Der Glasberg des Volksmärchens," *Symbolon* II [1955]: 15–31), the dead in the mountain, or the mountain as *medium mundi*.

5. Cf. Vincent de Beauvais, *Speculum naturale*, VI, 20: *Montes sunt tumores terrarum altissimi* (Mountains are very tall swellings of the lands).

6. Cf. *Das Lied vom Hürnen Seyfrid* (ed. Walther Golther [Halle: Niemeyer, 1911]), st. 18: *er fuert sie in das gbirge / auff eynen stayn so lang, / das er ein vierteyl meyle / den schat auffs birge zwang* ("He led her into the mountains to a peak so high, that it cast its shadow on the mountains a quarter-mile away").

7. Cf. Alexander Haggerty Krappe, *La Genèse des mythes* (Paris: Payot, 1952), 273.

8. Thomas de Cantimpré, *Liber de natura rerum*, ed. Helmut Boese (Berlin: De Gruyter, 1973), XIX, 2, 85–86: *Terra in initio dispositionis sue rotunda fuit et plana, in qua non erant montes et valles* ("In its first arrangement, the earth was circular and flat; there were no mountains or valleys"). Vincent de Beauvais (*Spec. nat.*, VI, 20) cites Pierre le Mangeur and writes: *Sunt autem*

qui putant altitudinem montium ante diluvium non fuisse tantam quanta nunc est ("Some think that before the Deluge the height of mountains was lower than it is today").

9. *Gylfaginning*, chap. 7, in Snorri Sturluson, *Edda: Gylfaginning og prosafortellingene av Skáldskaparmál*, ed. Anne Holtsmark and Jón Helgason (Copenhagen: Munksgaard, 1950).

10. Vincent de Beauvais, *Spec. nat.*, VI, 20: *Quandoque ex causa essentiali montes fiunt, quando scilicet ex vehementi terraemotu elevatur terra et fit mons* ("The fundamental reason for the creation of mountains is a violent seismic event that upends the earth and creates a mountain").

11. Cf. the characteristic list of Vincent de Beauvais, *Spec. nat.*, VI, 21–22; here is what he says about the Alps: *Alpes sunt proprie montes Galliae. . . . Nam Gallorum lingua Alpes montes alti vocantur* ("Strictly speaking, the Alps are the mountains of Gaul. In the language of the Gauls, in fact, the Alps are called the very tall mountains").

12. Thomas de Cantimpré, *De nat. rer.*, XVI, 9, 12–13: *Homines qui illic ascendere voluerunt, opportuit, ut haberent spongias aqua plenas, a quibus humidiorem aerem attraherent naribus et non sufrocarentur* ("The men wishing to climb there have to carry water-soaked sponges, through which they can breathe a moister air in order to avoid suffocating").

13. Thomas de Cantimpré, *De nat. rer.*, XIX, 5, 22–23: *Circa montes vero est subtilis (aer) nimium et penetrabilis. Mediis autem locis, que non sunt nimis alta vel demissa, optimus est* ("In the mountains, the air is subtle and most inconsistent. At an average altitude that is neither too high nor too low, it is very good").

14. Adam of Bremen, *Gesta Hammaburgensis Ecclesiae Pontificum*, IV, 32 (ed. Bernhard Schmeidler, MGH *SS rer. Germ.* 2 (Hanover: Hahn, 1917): *In asperrimis, quae ibi sunt, alpibus audivi mulieres esse barbatas* ("In the Alps [in other words, the tall mountains] that are quite steep for those there, I have heard tell that the women are bearded").

15. Jacques de Vitry, *Historia Orientalis* (Douai, 1597), chap. 92, 217; Thomas de Cantimpré, *De nat. rer.*, III, 5, 26; Gossouin de Metz indicates that these people live near Mount Gieu (*Image du Monde*, ed. O. H. Prior [Lausanne and Paris: Payot, 1913], 134).

16. For example, Thomas de Cantimpré, *De nat. rer.*, XIV, 19. In fact, this idea was widespread in antiquity.

17. Cf., for example, *Das Himmlische Jerusalem*, in Joseph Diemer, ed., *Deutsche*

Gedichte des XI. und XII. Jahrhunderts (Vienna: Braumüller, 1849), 366, ll. 12–17.

18. Cf. Wolfram von Eschenbach, *Parzival* (ed. Albert Leitzmann [Tübingen: Niemeyer, 1961–1965]), 71, 17ff.

19. *De gestis Langobardorum*, II, 8, in MGH *SS rerum Lang.* (Hanover: Hahn, 1878).

20. Cf., for example, Joachim Heinzle, *Mittelhochdeutsche Dietrichepik* (Munich: Artemis, 1978), 34–37. On the presence of dragons in the Alps: Othenio Abel, *Die vorzeitlichen Tierreste in Märchen, Sagen und Aberglauben* (Karlsruhe: Braun, 1923), 150–200.

21. Cf. Claude Lecouteux, "Des Königs Ortnit Schlaf," *Euphorion* 73 (1979): 347–55.

22. Cf. *Eckenlied*, (ed. Martin Wierschin [Tübingen: Niemeyer, 1974]), 52, 2ff.

23. Cf. Ulrich von dem Türlin, *Willehalm* (ed. Samuel Singer [Prague: Verlag des Vereins für Geschichte der Deutschen in Boehmen, 1893]), LXIV, 6. On these monsters, see: Claude Lecouteux, "Drachenkopp," *Euphorion* 73 (1978): 339–43.

24. Cf. Photios, *Bibliothèque*, ed. Migne, *Pat. Graeca* 103, col. 215–16 and 222–23; Claude Lecouteux, "Les Cynocéphales," *Cahiers de civilisation médiévale* 34 (1981): 117–28.

25. Cf. Felix Jacoby, *Die Fragmente der griechischen Historiker* (Berlin and Leiden: Brill, 1926), nr. 119, frag. 5. The same fable is found in Megasthenes (Jacoby, *Fragmente*, nr. 715, frag. 27–28). It was Strabo that gave these individuals the name of Opisthodactyles (*The Geography*, II, 1, 9 and XV, 1, 57).

26. Thomas de Cantimpré, *De nat. rer.*, III, 2.

27. Thomas de Cantimpré, *De nat. rer.*, III, 5, 32.

28. Cf. Geoffroy of Monmouth, *Historia Regum Britanniae*, chap. 128ff. (in Faral, ed., *La Légende arthurienne*, 3:71–303); Giraldus Cambrensis, *Topographia Hibernica*, II, 18 (in *Giraldi Cambrensis opera*, vol. 5, ed. J. F. Dimock [London: Longmans, Green, Reader, and Dyer, 1867]).

29. *Tandareis und Flordibel* (ed. F. Khull [Graz: Styria, 1885]), v. 9986ff.

30. Cf. *Dietrichs erste Ausfahrt* (ed. Franz Stark [Stuttgart: Litterarischer Verein, 1860]), 1–178; *Virginal* (ed. Julius Zupitza, in *Deutsches Heldenbuch* 5 [Berlin: Weidmann, 1870]), 23–66; Lütz Röhrich, "Die Frauenjagdsage," *Laographia* 22 (1965): 408–23.

31. Heinrich von Neustadt, *Apollonius von Tyrland* (ed. Samuel Singer [Berlin: Weidmann, 1906]), v. 4442ff.

32. Wolfram von Eschenbach, *Parzival* (ed. Leitzmann), 496, 9ff.

33. Cf. the prose preface of the *Straßburger Heldenbuch* (ed. Adelbert von Keller [Stuttgart: Litterarischer Verein, 1867]), 1, 28–2, 11.

34. Cf. *Der Jüngere Titurel*, st. 6109 (ed. Werner Wolf, Berlin: Akademie-Verlag, 1955, 1968). In *Der Priester Johannes* (ed. Friedrich Zarncke [Leipzig: Hirzel, 1876], 914), we read: *Tribus dietis longe ab hoc mari* [it concerns the "sandy" sea] *sunt montes quidam, ex quibus descendit fluvius lapidum eodem modo sine aqua, et fluit per terram nostram usque ad mare harenosum. Tribus diebus in septimana fluit et labuntur parvi et magni lapides* ("Three days' journey by foot from this sea there are mountains from which fall a river of stones, seemingly lacking in water, and it crosses our land until it reaches the sandy sea. It flows three times a week and rolls both large and small stones").

35. *Der jüngere Titurel* (ed. Wolf), st. 6118ff.

36. *Herzog Ernst* (ed. Karl Bartsch, Vienna: Braumüller, 1869), v. 4450ff.

37. *Reinfried von Braunschweig* (ed. Karl Bartsch [Stuttgart: Litterarischer Verein, 1871]), v. 18340ff.

38. Cf. Claude Lecouteux, "Zur anderen Welt," in Wolf-Dieter Lange, ed., *Diesseits- und Jenseitsreisen im Mittelalter* (Bonn and Berlin: Bouvier, 1992), 79–89.

39. Theodor Gaster, *Les plus anciens contes de l'humanité* (Paris: Payot, 1953), 39ff.

40. Cf. Mircea Eliade, *Le Chamanisme*, rev. ed. (Paris: Payot, 1968), 221.

41. *Skáldskaparmál*, chap. 1, in Snorri Sturluson, *Edda*.

42. Text in J. M. Heer, *Ein karolingischer Missions-Katechismus* [Freiburg: Herder, 1911], 81.

43. On the mountain as abode of God, cf. Gerhard Kittel, ed., *Theologisches Wörterbuch zum Neuen Testament* (Stuttgart: Kohlhammer, 1932), 5:475–86ff. In Middle High German, we frequently encounter the same notion expressed by the turn of phrase *der saelden berc* or *der berc der seligkeit*.

44. Cf. *Abor und das Meerweib*, ed. Heinrich Meyer-Benfey, in *Mittelhochdeutsche Übungsstücke* (Göttingen: Niemeyer, 1920), 180–83.

45. *Friedrich von Schwaben* (ed. M. H. Jellinek [Berlin: Weidmann, 1904]), v. 4312ff.

46. Ulrich von Zatzikhoven, *Lanzelet* (ed. Hahn), v. 204ff.

47. *Seifrid de Ardemont*, st. 260–519 (in *Merlin und Seifrid de Ardemont von Albrecht von Scharfenberg*, ed. Friedrich Panzer [Stuttgart: Bibliothek des litterarischen Vereins in Stuttgart, 1902]).

48. Cf. *Otia imperialia* (ed. G. W. Leibnitz, in *Scriptores rerum Brunsvicensium* I, Hanover: Förster, 1707), III, 42 and 66.

49. Cf. Claude Lecouteux, *La Légende de Siegfried d'après le Seyfried à la Peau de Corne et la Þiðrekssaga* (Paris: Porte Glaive, 1994), st. 25 and 28.

50. Cf. the study by J. M. Clifton-Everest, *The Tragedy of Knighthood: Origins of the Tannhäuser-Legend* (Oxford: Medium Aevum, 1979).

51. François Grégoire, *L'Au-delà* (Paris: PUF, 1965), 35.

52. *Edda: Die Lieder des Codex Regius*, ed. Gustav Neckel (Heidelberg: Winter, 1914), st. 15, p. 1:128. [English: *The Poetic Edda*, trans. Carolyn Larrington, rev. ed. (Oxford: Oxford University Press, 2014), 112.]

53. Cf. E. Freymond, "Artus' Kampf mit dem Katzenungetüm: Eine Episode der Vulgata," in *Festgabe Gustav Gröber* (Halle: Niemeyer, 1899), 311–96. André names the monster C(h)apalu; the triads of the *Livre rouge* tell us that this is the cat of Paluc (cf. Henri d'Arbois de Jubainville and Joseph Loth, *Cours de littérature celtique* [Paris: Thorin, 1869], 5:249).

54. Cf. *Historia Brittonum*, chap. 40–42; Geoffroy of Monmouth, *Historia Regum Britanniae*, chap. 106 (both texts in Faral, ed., *La Légende arthurienne*, vol. 3).

55. Cf. Engelbert Kirschbaum et al., eds., *Lexikon der christlichen Ikonographie* (Freiburg: Herder, 1968), s.v. "Siebenschläfer (Sieben Kinder)"; bibliography.

56. Cf. Jacques de Guyse, *Annales Historiae illustrium Principum Haunoniae* chap. 6: *Hic Albericus aram Minervae supra montem, qui nunc a christiani Mons sancti Aldeberti et tunc Mons Alberici dicebatur, reparavit. Item aliam in alio monte propinquo, qui dicitur gallice La Houppe d'Albertmont. Item in silva Visconiae fundavit aram, et castrum suo proprio nomine denominatum* [to be read as *designatum*] *ordinavit iuxta Marcisium* ("Alberich restored an altar to Minerva on the mountain that bore the Christian name of Saint Aldebert, and was formerly called Mount Alberich. He did the same on another nearby mountain, called La Houppe d'Albertmont in French. In addition, he created an altar in the forest of Visconia, and ordered the construction of a castle bearing his own name, next to Marcisium"). This passage was also borrowed by Hugues de Toul (twelfth century). On the relationship between Alberich/Auberon and the mountains, cf. Claude Lecouteux, "Zwerge und Verwandte," *Euphorion* 75 (1981): 366–78.

57. On this point, cf. Jacob Grimm, *Deutsche Mythologie* (Darmstadt: Wissenschaftliche Buchgesellschaft, 1965), 2:794ff.; Lütz Röhrich, *Sage* (Stuttgart: Metzler, 1971), 55–56.

58. Cf. Claude Lecouteux, "'Herzog Ernst' v. 2164ff.: Das böhmische Volksbuch von Stillfried und Bruncwig und die morgenländischen Alexandersagen," *Zeitschrift für deutsches Altertum* 108 (1979): 311ff.: more information on the mountains in the legend of Alexander, according to Eastern traditions.

59. On this point in the legend of Sigurðr/Sigfrid, cf. Régis Boyer and Éveline Lot-Falck, *Les Religions de l'Europe du Nord* (Paris: Fayard, 1974), 260ff.

60. Jean d'Arras, *Mélusine*, ed. Louis Stouff (Dijon: Bernigaud et Privat, 1932), 11ff.

61. Jean d'Arras, *Mélusine*, ed. Stouff, 13.

62. The first occurrence of this legend in the *Dialogues* of Gregory the Great (IV, 30: *De morte Theodorici regis Ariani* [Migne, *Pat. lat.* 77, col. 368ff.]). The same thing was told of the Merovingian Dagobert I (*Gesta Dagoberti*, in MGH *SS rer. Merov.* 2: 421–22); of Magnus of Danemark, cast into the Hekla, an Icelandic volcano (Alberic of Trois-Fontaines, *Chronica*, anno 1130, in MGH *SS 23*, 829); and of Frederick II (Thomas of Eccleston, *Tractatus de adventu fratrum minorum in Angliam*, ed. A. G. Little [Manchester: Manchester University Press, 1951], 96). Cf. also the *exempla* of Caesarius of Heisterbach, *Dialogus miraculorum*, XII, 7; 12 and 13. In the tale known as the "Reuner Relations," a cleric given to necromancy promises his companion to appear thirty days after his death on a mountain he designates: *sus zaiget er im vil balde / gen ainem vinsteren walde / ainen berk wild vnd hoch.* ("Then he indicated to him immediately [with his hand] a wild, tall mountain, facing a dark forest"), v. 523ff. (in *Die Vorauer Novelle und Die Reuner Relationen*, facsimile ed. by H. Gröchenig (Göppingen: Kümmerle, 1981), 44; there he revealed to him the torments he was suffering in hell.

63. Volcanoes deserve a detailed study. In the Middle Ages they were regarded as the mouths of hell. Godfrey of Viterbo (born around 1120) writes: *mons ibi flammarum, quas evomit Aethna vocatur: hoc ibi Tartareum dicitur esse caput* ("The mountain that spits flames here is named Etna: it is said to be the head of Tartarus"); cited by Arturo Graf, *Miti, Leggende e Supperstizioni del Medio Evo* (Turin: Loescher, 1892–1893), 2:316. The same opinion can be found in the novella by Hans Folz, *Der Pfarrer im Ätna* (ca. 1480–1481). The other mouths of hell are Stromboli and Hekla (Iceland), about which Alberic of Trois-Fontaines says: *mons quidam regionis* [i.e., Hysselandiae] *sub quo et in quo homines loci maximum arbitrantur esse infernum* ("A mountain of the country Iceland under which people believe there is a large hell"); *Chronica*

(cited in previous note), 829. But Etna is not only that: its sides also shelter the sleeping King Arthur (cf. Gervase of Tilbury, *Otia imperialia*, II, 12, and Graf, *Miti, Leggende e Supperstizioni*, 302–25). The fairy Morgana owns an enchanted castle on the Montgibel, another name for Etna (cf. *Floriant et Florete: A Metrical Romance of the Fourteenth Century*, ed. H. F. Williams [Ann Arbor: University of Michigan Press, 1947], v. 8242–50); she is the fairy of Montgibel according to *Le Chevalier du Papegaut* (ed. Ferdinand Heuckenkamp [Halle: Niemeyer, 1896], 11). Gregory of Tours (538–594) associates Etna to a fountain near Grenoble; in his eyes, they are foreshadowings of hell: *et ignem figurant, ut est Ethna, fons Gratianopolitanus* ("And they feature fire, as is the case for Etna and the fountain of Grenoble"), *De cursu stellarum* 10, MGH *SS rer. Merov.* 1, 860. This was a "burning fountain," now gone, which was located in the commune of Guâ.

64. It is probably for this reason that Purgatory was often seen to be located in Mount Etna. Odilo of Cluny (died in 1048) is said to have established the All Souls' Day in 998, after having heard the moans of the souls in Purgatory located here in a mountain close to Pouzzoles (near Naples), cf. Pierre Damien, *Vita Odilonis*, in Migne, *Pat. lat.* 144, col. 936ff.; Helinand of Froidmont, *Chronica*, anno 998, in Migne, *Pat. lat.* 212, col. 920; Sigebert of Gembloux, MGH *SS* 5, 353. Gervase of Tilbury (*Otia imperialia*, III, 17), gives the same location. Thomas de Cantimpré (*De bon. univ.*, II, 51) places it in a valley surrounded by mountains: *invenit locum planum, pulchrum valde atque gramineum inter montes in quo quasi hominem magnum et elegantem forma, facie tenus prostratum videns, duas clavas ferreas ad utrumque iacentis horrentibus oculis intueretur* ("He found a flat and grassy, and quite beautiful place between the mountains, where he saw something that was almost a man, large in size and handsome in appearance, prostrate, his face against the ground, and he saw to his horror that the prone figure carried two iron clubs"); the hero of the story heard: *ordinatione divina tibi talis appareo, ut in me misero poenitentiae sumas exemplum. Mortuus sum, licet tibi corporalis appaream* ("It is by divine command that I appear this way so that in my misfortune you can learn from the example of penitence. I am dead, although you see me in physical appearance").

65. Jean d'Arras, *Mélusine*, ed. Stouff, 13.

66. Gaster, *Les plus anciens contes*, 39ff. *Sankt Brandan* (ed. C. Schröder [Erlangen: Besold, 1871]), v. 674ff. In one of the Latin versions of the *Peregrinatio S. Brandani*, Judas is expiating his sin in an infernal mountain

and tells Brandan: *ardeo sicut massa plumbi . . . in medio montis quem vidistis. Ubi est Leviathan cum suis satellitibus* ("I burn like a lead mass . . . in the heart of the mountain you saw. There where reside the Leviathan and his acolytes").

67. The fifteenth-century German translation called *Tondolus der Ritter* (ed. Nigel F. Palmer [Munich: Fink, 1980]) makes the soul of Tnugdale (Tondale, etc.) pursue the following itinerary: 1. cross through the darkness; 2. come to a valley full of fire (165ff.); 3. then to a mountain (191ff.); 4. then to another valley (217ff.); 5. then to a mountain (228ff.); 6. and another; 7. encounter with a monster (248ff.); 8. reaches the edge of a lake of fire; 9. another mountain (434ff.); 10. encounter with an animal emerging from a frozen lake; 11. another mountain (637ff.); 12. the valley of Vulcan (660ff.). A study of the vocabulary is instructive because it makes it possible to see what was thought of mountains; we find the following adjectives: "grand" (*gross*), "high" (*hoh*), "disproportionate"/"frightening" (*vngehur*), "inaccessible" (*schwer*), "rugged" (*ruh*), and "difficult" (*hart*).

68. Eliade, *Le Chamanisme*, 185.

69. Eliade, *Le Chamanisme*, 197.

70. Cf. Friedrich Pfister, *Kleine Schriften zum Alexanderroman* (Meisenheim am Glan: Hain, 1976), 149.

71. Cf. Krappe, *La Genèse des mythes*, 216.

72. Heinrich von Neustadt, *Apollonius von Tyrland* (ed. Singer), v. 8840ff.

73. Bede, *In Genesim*, I, 1436–50. Remy (died ca. 908), in Migne, ed., *Pat. lat.* 131, col. 60.

74. *Cosmographiam Aethici Istrici ab Hieronymo et graeco in latinum frenarum redactam* (ed. Heinrich Wuttke [Leipzig: Dykianus, 1853]), chap. 23 and 105.

75. Migne, ed., *Pat. lat.* 115, col. 129–30.

76. Cf. Pfister, *Kleine Schriften zum Alexanderroman*, 359–65 (text). French translation in Claude Lecouteux, *Mondes parallèles* (Paris: Champion, 1994), 25–33.

77. Isidore of Seville wrote early on (*Etymologiae*, XIV, 3ff.): *Paradisus est locus in orientis partibus constitutes. . . . Septus est enim undiquo romphea flamma, id est muro igneo accinctus* ("Paradise is a site located in the East. . . . It is surrounded on all sides by a flame, in other words girded by a wall of fire"). Honorius (in Migne, ed., *Pat. lat.* 72, col. 65ff.) also discusses the rivers of paradise, but he is the sole person to indicate that the source of the Tigris is the *mons Barchoatrus*.

78. Cf. *Der jüngere Titurel* (ed. Wolf), st. 337. In the German texts, the Grail

temple has all the features of the Celestial Jerusalem; it is a true earthly paradise where the true servants of God have found refuge.

79. *Der jüngere Titurel* (ed. Werner Wolf [Bern: Francke, 1952]), st. 6108.

80. Cf. the legend of the impure people, the *reclusi*, who imprisoned Alexander the Great behind the gates of the Caucasus (Friedrich Pfister, "Gog und Magog," in Hanns Bächthold-Stäubli, ed., *Handwörterbuch des deutschen Aberglaubens*, vol. 3 [Berlin: De Gruyter, 1930–1931], col. 910–18).

CHAPTER 13. THE SEA AND ITS ISLES DURING THE MIDDLE AGES

1. *The King's Mirror (Speculum regale-Konungs skuggsjá)*, trans. Laurence Marcellus Larson (New York: American-Scandinavian Foundation, 1917), 135–36.

2. Gervase of Tilbury, *Le Livre des merveilles* (Pt. 3), trans. Annie Duchesne (Paris: Belles Lettres, 1992), 75–76.

3. Gervase of Tilbury, *Otia imperialia: Recreation for an Emperor*, trans. S. E. Banks and J. W. Binns (Oxford: Oxford University Press, 2002), 335.

4. Gervase of Tilbury, *Otia imperialia*, trans. Banks and Binns, 329. The entire chapter (II, 12) is dedicated to the islands of the Mediterranean.

5. On the Magnetic Mountain, see chapter 9 in the present volume.

6. Cf. *Orendel: Ein deutsches Spielmannsgedicht*, ed. A. E. Berger (Bonn: Weber, 1888).

7. Arnold de Lubeck, *Geeta Gregorii peccatoris*, ed. Johannes Schilling (Göttingen: Vandenhoek und Ruprecht, 1986).

8. *Jourdain de Blayes*, (ed. P. F. Dembowski [Paris: Champion, 1991]), v. 2157.

9. Cf. Wilhelm Frahm, *Das Meer und die Seefahrt in der altfranzösischen Literatur* (Göttingen: Haensch, 1914), 19.

10. For further information, see Rudolf Simek, *Erde und Kosmos im Mittelalter* (Munich: Beck, 1992); Hartmut Kugler and Eckhard Michael, eds. *Ein Weltbild vor Columbus: Die Ebstorfer Weltkarte* (Weinheim: VCH, 1991); Anna-Dorothee von den Brincken, *Finis terrae: Die Enden der Erde und der vierten Kontinent auf mittelalterlichen Weltkarten* (Hanover: Hahnsche Buchhandlung, 1992).

11. Cf. Claude Lecouteux, "Kleine Beiträge zum Herzog Ernst," *Zeitschrift für deutsches Altertum* 110 (1981): 210–221, here at 217ff.

12. Adam of Bremen, *History of the Archbishops of Hamburg-Bremen*, trans. Francis J. Tschan (New York: Columbia University Press, 2002), 220–21.

13. *Nec satis procul ab hoc de quo praemisimus litore, contra occidentalem partem, qua fine oceanum pelagus patet, profundissima aquarum illa vorago est, quam usitato nomine maris umbilicum vocamus. Quae bis in die fluctus absorbere et rursum evomere dicitur.*

14. Strabo, *Geographica*, ed. August Meineke (Leipzig: Teubner, 1866), 2: IV, 1.

15. Cf. Claude Lecouteux, "Herzog Ernst V. 2164ff.," *Zeitschrift für deutsches Altertum* 108 (1979): 306–22, here at 315–16.

16. Cf. Ch. Weule, "La surface terrestre," in Hans Kraemer, ed., *L'Univers et l'Humanité: Histoire des Differents Systems Appliques a L'Etude de la Nature. Utilsation des Forces Naturelles au Service des Peuples* (Paris: Bong, 1904–1905), 3:438–39.

17. Cf. Hans von Mžik, "Parageographische Elemente in den Berichten der arabischen Geographen über Südostasien," in *Beiträge zur historischen Geographie, Kulturgeographie, Ethnographie und Kartographie, vornehmlich des Orients* (Leipzig and Vienna: Deutike, 1929), 74–190.

18. On this development, cf. Kuno Meyer, *The Voyage of Bran Son of Ferbal to the Land of the Living*, ed. and trans., 2 vols. (London: Nutt, 1895–1897).

19. Carl Wahlund, *Die altfranzösische Prosaübersetzung von Brendans Meerfahrt nach der Pariser Hdschr. Nat.-Bibl. fr. 1553* (Uppsala: Alquvist & Wiksell, 1900), 171.

20. An excellent French translation with the facing-page Latin text can be found in Phillipe Walter, *Le devin maudit: Merlin, Lailoken, Suibhne. Textes et études* (Grenoble: ELLUG, 1999), 56–171.

21. Walter, *Le devin maudit*, 177–79.

22. Cf. Jean Marchand, *L'Autre Monde au Moyen Âge* (Paris: de Boccard, 1940).

23. Marchand, *L'Autre Monde*, 172–73.

24. Cf. Jeanne-Marie Boivin, "Merveilles d'Irlande dans la *Topographia Hibernica* de Giraud de Barri: contribution à l'étude du merveilleux encyclopédique vers 1200," *Revue des Langues romanes* 101 (1997): 23–53.

25. Marco Polo, *La Description du monde*, ed. Louis Hambis (Paris: Klincksieck, 1955), 292.

26. Stuttgart, Württembergische Landesbibliothek ms. HB X 22, fol. 198v°–199v°.

27. On all this, cf. Claude Lecouteux, "'Herzog Ernst' v. 2164ff.: Das böhmische Volksbuch von Stillfried und Bruncwig und die morgenländischen Alexandersagen," *Zeitschrift für deutsches Altertum* 108 (1979): 306–22, here at 309.

28. *Huon de Bordeaux* in *Les Anciens Poètes de la France*, ed. F. Guessard and C. Grandmaison (Paris: Vieweg, 1860), 5:210.

29. *The Medieval French* Roman d'Alexandre, ed. Edward C. Armstrong (Princeton: Princeton University Press, 1937), vol. 1, v. 7601–7614.

30. These can be found in Eusèbe Renaudot, *Anciennes Relations des Indes et de la Chine de deux voyageurs mahométans* (Paris: Coignard, 1718); *Les Merveilles d'Inde* (*Kitab agaib al-Hind*), trans. Jean Sauvaget, in *Mémorial Jean Sauvaget* (Damascus: Institut Français de Damas, 1954–1961), 2:189–309; *Relation de la Chine et de l'Inde rédigée en 851* (*Aḫbār aṣ-Ṣīn wa l-Hind*), trans. Jean Sauvaget (Paris: Belles Lettres, 1948); M. Reinaud, *Relation des voyages faits par les Arabes et les Persans dans le IXe siècle de l'ère chrétienne*, 2 vols. (Paris: Imprimerie Royale, 1845); Pierre Bergeron, *Voyages faits principalement en Asie dans les XII, XIII, XIV, et XV siècles*, 2 vols. (The Hague: Neaulme, 1735).

31. Cf., for example, Claude Thomasset, "Naufrage et sauvetage dans la littérature médiévale," in *Le Naufrage*, ed. Christian Buchet and Claude Thomasset (Paris: Champion, 1999), 163–78.

32. Marco Polo, *La Description du monde*, 248.

33. Marco Polo, *La Description*, 163.

34. As in the passage I cited from *The Voyage of Saint Brendan*.

CHAPTER 14. THE BACKDROP OF THE ADVENTURE SITES IN MEDIEVAL ROMANCES

1. *Persibein aus dem Buch der Abenteuer Ulrich Füetrer*, ed. Renate Munz (Tübingen: Niemeyer, 1964).

2. *Poytislier aus dem Buch der Abenteuer von Ulrich Fuetrer*, ed. Friederike Weber (Tübingen: Niemeyer, 1960). On Ulrich Füetrer, cf. the article by Kurt Nyholm in *Die deutsche Literatur des Mittelalters, Verfasserlexikon*, ed. Kurt Ruh et al. (Berlin: De Gruyter, 1979), vol. II/4, col. 999ff. I would also like to point out D. H. Green, *Der Weg zum Abenteuer im höfischen Roman des deutschen Mittelalters* (Göttingen: Vandenhoeck & Ruprecht, 1974), which touches on the essentially literary aspects of the subject under discussion here.

3. *Handwörterbuch des deutschen Aberglaubens*, ed. Hanns Bächtold-Stäubli, 2nd edition, 10 vols. (Berlin: De Gruyter, 1987); cf., for example, s.v. *Wald, Kreuzweg, Brunnen, Unstütte*. Cited as *HDA*.

4. *Atlas der deutschen Volkskunde,* new series under the editorship of Matthias Zender (Marburg: Elwert, 1958–1964).

5. Paul Sébillot, *Le Folklore de la France,* 4 vols. (Paris: Imago, 1968).

6. Anatole Le Braz, *La légende de la mort en Basse-Bretagne* (Paris: Champion, 1902).

7. Jón Árnason, *Íslenzkar þjóðsögur og Aevintýri,* 2 vols. (Leipzig: Hinrichs, 1862–1864).

8. *Heldenbuch,* facsimile edition by Joachim Heinzle (Göppingen: Kümmerle, 1981). Cf. Claude Lecouteux, *The Hidden History of Elves & Dwarves: Avatars of Invisible Realms,* trans. Jon E. Graham (Rochester, VT: Inner Traditions, 2018).

9. On this point point, see Dieter Harmening, *Superstitio: Überlieferungs- und theoriegeschichtliche Untersuchungen zur kirchlich-theologischen Aberglaubensliteratur des Mittelalters* (Berlin: Schmidt, 1979), in which the most important texts have been collected.

10. Cf. Ernst Förstemann, *Altdeutsches Namenbuch* II: *Ortsnamen* (Munich/ Hildesheim: Fink/Oms, 1967 [1872]).

11. Cf. Claude Lecouteux, "Zwerge und Verwandte," *Euphorion* 75 (1981): 366–78.

12. L. Knappert, "La vie de saint Gall et le paganisme germanique," *Revue de l'Histoire des religions* 29 (1894): 259–95.

13. Cf. Hermann Reichert, *Lexikon der altgermanischen Namen* I (Vienna: Österreichischen Akademie der Wissenschaften, 1987), 545b, s.v. *Quadriburgi.*

14. Martin of Braga, *De correctione rusticorum,* ed. C. P. Caspari (Christiana [Oslo]: Malling, 1883), §7ff.

15. Pirmin of Reichenau, *Dicta de singulis libris canonicis,* cap. 22 (text edited in Gall Jecker, *Die Heimat des Hl. Pirmin, des Apostels der Alamannen* [Münster: Aschendorff, 1927]).

16. Erika Lindig, *Hausgeister: Die Vorstellung übernatürlicher Schützer und Helfer in der deutschen Sagenüberlieferung* (Frankfurt: Lang, 1987), 74–75.

17. Cf. Edgar Polomé, "L'étymologie du terme germanique *ansuz* 'Dieu souver- ain,'" *Études germaniques* 8 (1953): 36–44.

18. Cf. W. P. Ker, "The Craven Angels," *Modern Language Review* 6 (1911): 85–87; M. Dando, "The Neutral Angels," *Archiv für das Studium der neueren Sprachen & Literatur* 217 (1980): 259–76.

19. Cf. August Lütjens, *Der Zwerg in der deutschen Heldendichtung des*

Mittelalters (Breslau: Marcus, 1911) 110, n. 10. [English translation by Michael Moynihan.]

20. On this encounter, see E. Freymond, "Artus' Kampf mit dem Katzenungetüm: Eine Episode der Vulgata," in *Festgabe Gustav Gröber* (Halle: Niemeyer, 1899), 311–96.

21. Text from Claude Lecouteux, *Kleine Texte zur Alexandersage* (Göppingen: Kümmerle, 1984), 59.

22. Jacques Le Goff, "Culture ecclésiastique et culture folklorique au Moyen Âge: Saint Marcel de Paris et le Dragon," in *Pour un autre Moyen Âge: Temps, travail et culture en Occident* (Paris: Gallimard, 1977), 236–279, here at 257: "Wouldn't Marcel's victory over the dragon be the taming of the *genius loci*, the reorganization of a natural site between the *deserta* of the forest (*silva*), the lair of the chthonic serpent, and the marshes of the confluence of the Seine and Bièvre (*mare*) rivers where the water dragon is invited to disappear?"

23. Cf. Lutz Röhrich, "Le Monde surnaturel dans les légendes alpines," in *Mélanges Charles Joisten* in *Le Monde alpin et rhodanien* (1982), 28: The animals hunted by man—the chamois—are the domestic animals of the spirit that protects them." Comparison of this legend, collected by Joseph Müller in Uri canton of Switzerland, and the texts of the Middle Ages seems fully justified to me as the Alps form a closed world that has preserved beliefs of great antiquity as has been shown by the works of Lutz Röhrich, and those of Christian Abry and Charles Joisten (via the Centre alpin et rhodanien d'ethnologie in Grenoble).

24. Cf. Georges Zink, ed., *Le Wunderer: Fac-similé de l'édition de 1503* (Paris: Aubier, 1949), 71ff., with a legend from the Berry region that reveals the antiquity of the facts.

25. Knappert, "La vie de saint Gall et le paganisme germanique," 288–89.

26. *Corpus Inscriptionum Latinarum*, XIII, 8830.

27. Cf. Paul Hermann, *Erläuterungen zu den ersten neun Büchern der Dänischen Geschichte des Saxo Grammaticus* (Leipzig: Engelmann, 1901–1922), 1:385; 2:585–86.

28. *Elucidation*, prologue to the Perceval romance of Christian de Troyes; in *Der Percevalroman (Li Contes del Graal)*, ed. Alfons Hilka (Halle: Niemeyer, 1932), 417–429, v. 34–96.

29. Two books by Philippe Walter—*La Mémoire du Temps: Fêtes et calendriers de Chrétien de Troyes à La Mort Artu* (Paris: Champion, 1989) and

Canicule: Essai de mythologie sur Yvain de Chrétien de Troyes (Paris: SEDES, 1988)—have demonstrated all the benefits that result from including with the analysis of the texts everything that comes from the folk culture of which the writers are tributaries. The romance writers are a link in a long enduring chain and serve, *volens nolens,* as a relay. Philippe Walter was thereby able to shed light on an additional stratum of the giant, which rounds off my analysis that was presented in the *Cahiers de civilisation médiévale* 30 (1987): 219–25.

CHAPTER 15. THE TAMING OF THE LAND

1. *Atlas der deutschen Volkskunde,* new series, ed. Matthias Zender (Marburg: Elwert, 1958–1964).

2. *Handwörterbuch des deutschen Aberglaubens,* ed. Hanns Bächtold-Stäubli, 2nd edition, 10 vols. (Berlin: De Gruyter, 1987). Cited as *HDA.*

3. Marianne Stauffer, *Der Wald: Zur Darstellung und Deutung der Natur im Mittelalter* (Bern: Francke, 1959).

4. It seems relevant to me to point out a passage of *De vita sua sive monodiae,* by Guibert of Nogent (ca. 1055–1125), in which individuals appearing in a vision are the size of dwarfs (*statura cubitali in morem eorum quos vulgos nanas vocitant*); ed. and trans. by E. R. Labande (Paris: Belles Lettres, 1981), 128.

5. Snorri Sturluson, *Heimskringla* (ed. Bjarni Adalbjarnarson [Reykjavik: Hið Íslenzka Fornritafélag, 1941]), 1:271 (chap. 33).

6. "Guta Saga," French trans. J. M. Maillefer, *Études germaniques* 40 (1985): 131–40.

7. These rites were meticulously studied by Dag Strömbäck, "Att helga land: Studier i Landnáma och det äldsta rituella besittningstagandet," in *Festskrift tillägnad Axel Hägerström den 6 September 1928* (Uppsala: Almqvist & Wiksell, 1928), 198–220. On more recent methods for banishing spirits, cf. Erika Lindig, *Hausgeister: Die Vorstellung übernatürlicher Schützer und Helfer in der deutschen Sagenüberlieferung* (Frankfurt: Lang, 1987), 143–46. One may also consult Jacob Grimm, *Deutsche Rechtsaltertümer* (Göttingen: Dieterich, 1854), 86–92, 184ff. and 194ff.; Claude Lecouteux, *Geschichte der Gespenster und Wiedergänger im Mittelalter* (Cologne: Böhlau, 1987), 177–79.

8. Cf. *HDA,* vol. 9, col. 496–547; H. F. Feilberg, "Der Kobold in nordischer Überlieferung," *Zeitschrift des Vereins für Volkskunde* 8 (1898), 1–20, 130–46, 264–77, esp. 6, 130, 139, 141, and 269; Lindig, *Hausgeister,* 132ff.

9. Cf., for example, *Landnámabók*, ed. Jacob Benediktsson, 2 vols. (Reykjavik: Hið Íslenzka Fornritafélag, 1968).

10. *Ares Isländerbuch* [*Íslendingabók*], ed. Walter Golther (Halle: Niemeyer, 1892), 31.

11. *Egils saga Skallagrímssonar* (ed. Sigurður Nordal [Reyjavik: Íslenzk fornrít, 1933]), chap. 57.

12. Cf. *Kulturhistorisk Lexikon för Nordisk Medeltid* (Malmö: Allhems, 1956–1978), s.v. *tún*.

13. As in *Kristni saga*, ed. Guðni Jónsson, in *Íslendinga Sögur* I (Reykjavik: Íslendingasagnaútgáfan, 1953), 243–80 (chap. 2). It is worth consulting Reidar Christensen, "Gårdvette og markavette," *Maal og Minne* (1943): 137–60.

14. *Egils saga* (ed. Nordal), chap. 56.

CHAPTER 16. BORDERLANDS OF
THE OTHERWORLD

1. Charles Higounet, *Les Allemands en Europe centrale et orientale au Moyen Âge* (Paris: Aubier, 1989), 163, 165, 171, 182, 198, 201, 206, 217.

2. Cf., for example, M. L. Chênerie, "Le motif de la fontaine dans les romans arthuriens en vers des XIIe et XIIIe siècles," in *Mélanges de langue et littérature françaises du Moyen Age et de la Renaissance offerts à Monsieur Charles Foulon* (Rennes: Université de Haute-Bretagne, 1980), 1:99–104.

3. Claude Thomasset, "Du pont de l'épée au pouvoir royal," in *La figure du roi: Actes du Colloque du Centre d'Études Médiévales et Dialectales de Lille 3. Université Charles-de-Gaulle Lille 3 24–26 septembre 1998* (Villeneuve d'Ascq: Centre d'Études Médiévales et Dialectales de Lille 3, 2001), 2:171–83.

4. Jacob Grimm, *Deutsche Rechtsaltertümer* (Hildesheim: Olms, 1992 [1899]), 2:435.

5. Claude Lecouteux, "Zur anderen Welt," in W. D. Lange, *Diesseits- und Jenseitsreisen im Mittelalter / Voyages dans l'ici-bas et dans l'au-delà au Moyen Âge* (Bonn: Bouvier, 1992), 79–89; Claude Lecouteux, *Eine Welt im Abseits: Zur niederen Mythologie und Glaubenswelt des Mittelalters* (Dettelbach: Röll, 2000), 157–67.

6. Cf. Claude Lecouteux, *Demons and Spirits of the Land: Ancestral Lore and Practices*, trans. Jon E. Graham (Rochester, VT: Inner Traditions, 2015), 68–126.

7. Claude Lecouteux, "Hagazussa—Striga—Hexe," *Hessische Blätter für Volkskunde und Kulturforschung* 18 (1985): 57–70.

8. Grimm, *Deutsche Rechtsaltertümer*, 2:319–21, 329.

9. Cf. Claude Lecouteux, "Siegfried, Kuperan et le dragon," *Études germaniques* 49 (1994): 257–66.

10. Francis Dubost, *Aspects fantastiques de la littérature narrative médiévale (XIIème–XIIIème siècles): L'autre, l'ailleurs, l'autrefois*, 2 vols. (Paris: Champion, 1991).

11. Cf. Adolph Franz, *Die kirchlichen Benediktionen des Mittelalters* (Freiburg im Breisgau: Herder, 1909), 2:77 and 81.

12. Jordanes, *Getica*, ed. Theodor Mommsen, MGH *Auct. ant. 5,1*, 127–28. Cf. also Ammianus Marcellinus, *Rerum gestarum libri*, ed. Wolfgang Seyfarht (Leipzig: Teubner, 1978), XXXI, 2, 1–2.

13. Cf. Ion Taloş, *Meşterul Manole: Contribuţie la studiul unei teme de folclor European* (Bucharest: Minerva, 1973); with French summary at 393–412.

14. Claude Lecouteux, "Romanisch-germanische Kulturberührungen am Beispiel des Mahls der Feen," *Mediævistik* 1 (1988): 87–99.

15. *Kormák's saga*, ed. Einar Sveinsson (Reykjavik: Hið Íslenzka fornritfélag, 1939), chap. 22.

16. *Kristni saga*, ed. Guðni Jónsson, in *Islendinga sögur* 1 (Reykjavik: Íslendíngasagnaútgáfan, 1953), 243–80.

17. *Landnámabók*, ed. Jacob Benediktsson, 2 vols. (Reykjavik: Hið Íslenzka fornritfélag, 1968), *Sturlubók* 348.

18. Cf. Claude Lecouteux, *The Hidden History of Elves & Dwarves: Avatars of Invisible Realms*, trans. Jon E. Graham (Rochester, VT: Inner Traditions, 2018), 76–126; and on the same subject: "Zwerge und Verwandte," *Euphorion* 75 (1981): 366–78.

19. Cf. Lauri Honko, *Krankheitsprojektile: Über eine urtümliche Kranheitserklärung* (Helsinki: Suomalainen Tiedeakatemia, 1967).

20. Claude Lecouteux, *Charmes, conjurations et bénédictions: Lexique et formules* (Paris: Champion, 1996), 122, text nr. 2.

21. A French translation of the text can be found in Claude Lecouteux and Philippe Marcq, *Les Esprits et les Morts, croyances médiévales* (Paris: Champion, 1990), 149–51.

22. M. R. James, "Twelve Medieval Ghost-Stories," *English Historical Review* 37 (1922): 413–23.

23. Ion Taloş, *Petit Dictionnaire de mythologie roumaine*, French trans. Anneliese

Lecouteux and Claude Lecouteux (Grenoble: UGA, 2002). Cf. also P. H. Stahl, "L'organisation magique du territoire villageois roumain," *L'Homme* 13.3 (1973): 150–62.

24. It concerns the first hemistich of a spell found in a manuscript in the Madrid National Library (ms. S 164) that says:

> *Vox mea cunctorum sit terror demoniorum*
>
> *Sorbendo brodia gaudet Aragonia tota.*

Cf. Wilhelm von Hartel and Zacharias Garcia, *Bibliotheca patrum latinorum Hispaniensis* (Hildesheim: Olms, 1972 [1866–1915]), 443.

25. Von Hartel and Garcia, *Bibliotheca patrum latinorum Hispaniensis,* 18.

26. Kurt Köster, "Alphabet-Inschriften auf Glocken, mit einem Katalog europäischer ABC-Glocken vom 12. bis zum 18. Jahrhundert," in Rudolf Schützeichel, *Studien zur deutschen Literatur des Mittelalters* (Bonn: Bouvier, 1979), 371–422, with iconographical dossier.

27. Cf. Claude Lecouteux, *Au-delà du merveilleux: Des croyances au Moyen Âge* (Paris: PUPS, 1982), 89ff. and 161ff.

28. Claude Lecouteux, *The Return of the Dead: Ghosts, Ancestors, and the Transparent Veil of the Pagan Mind* (Rochester, VT: Inner Traditions, 2009), 65–68.

29. Cf. James, "Twelve Medieval Ghost-Stories."

30. Cf. *Amadas et Ydoine, roman du XIIIe siècle,* ed. John R. Reinhard (Paris: Champion, 1974), v. 5584ff.

31. Lecouteux and Marcq, *Les Esprits et les Morts,* 131–32, in which we find one of these narratives.

32. Bernward Deneke, "Legende und Volkssage: Untersuchungen zur Erzählung vom Geistergottesdienst," dissertation, Johann Wolfgang Goethe-Universität, 1958.

33. A good example can be found in Lecouteux and Marcq, *Les Esprits et les Morts,* 179ff.

34. Grimm, *Deutsche Rechtsaltertümer,* 2:428.

35. Felix Karlinger, *Zauberschlaf und Entrückung: Zur Problematik des Motivs der Jenseitszeiten der Volkserzählung,* (Vienna: Österreichisches Museum für Volkskunde, 1986): numerous examples of traveling into the otherworld by going down into a grave.

36. Cf. Émile Jobbé-Duval, *Les Morts malfaisants* (Paris: Recueil Sirey, 1924), 93ff.

37. Hanns Bächtold-Stäubli, *Handwörterbuch des deutschen Aberglaubens,* vol. 8, col. 1465.

38. On the cemetery and its boundaries, cf. P.-A. Sigal, *L'Homme et le miracle dans la France médiévale (XIe-XIIe siècle)* (Paris: Cerf, 1985), 62.

39. *L'atre perilleux: roman de la Table ronde*, ed. Brian Woledge (Paris: Champion, 1936).

40. Claude Lecouteux, "Eine orientalische Sage in Heinrichs von Neustadt Apollonius von Tyrland," *Fabula* 24 (1983): 195–214.

41. E. Weber, "La ville de cuivre, une ville d'al-Andalus," *Sharq Al-Andalus* 6 (1989): 43–81.

42. Claude Lecouteux, *Encyclopedia of Norse and Germanic Folklore, Mythology, and Magic*, trans. Jon E. Graham; ed. Michael Moynihan (Rochester, VT: Inner Traditions, 2015) s.v. *Geirvimull, Gjöll, Slíðr*.

43. French translation of the text by Saxo in Claude Lecouteux, *Mondes parallèles: L'univers des croyances au Moyen Âge* (Paris: Champion, 2007), 85–100.

44. Henric van Veldeken, *Eneide*, ed. Gabriele Schieb and Theodor Frings (Berlin: Akadamie, 1964–1970), v. 2881.

45. Donatien Laurent, "Le juste milieu: Réflexion sur un rituel de circumambulation millénaire: la troménie de Locronané," in *Tradition et Histoire dans la culture Populaire: Rencontres autour de l'œuvre de J. M. Guilcher* (Grenoble: Centre de recherche bretonne et celtique, 1990), 255–92.

CHAPTER 17. THE SPIRITS OF NATURE AND OF HUMANS IN THE MIDDLE AGES

1. See Hermann Reichert, *Lexikon der altgermanischen Namen* I (Vienna: Österreichischen Akademie der Wissenschaften, 1987), 545b, s.v. *Quadriburgi*.

2. Snorri Sturluson, *Heimskringla* (ed. Bjarni Adalbjarnarson [Reykjavik: Hið Íslenzka Fornritafélag, 1941]), 1:271 (chap. 33).

3. "Guta Saga," French trans. J. M. Maillefer, *Études germaniques* 40 (1985): 131–40.

4. *Ares Isländerbuch* [*Íslendingabók*], ed. Walter Golther (Halle: Niemeyer, 1892).

5. Cf. Ernst Förstemann, *Altdeutsches Namenbuch* II: *Ortsnamen* (Munich/Hildesheim: Fink/Oms, 1967 [1872].

6. Cf. Claude Lecouteux, "Zwerge und Verwandte," *Euphorion* 75 (1981): 366–78.

7. These rites were meticulously studied by Dag Strömbäck, "Att helga land: Studier i Landnáma och det äldsta rituella besittningstagandet," in *Festskrift tillägnad Axel Hägerström den 6 September 1928* (Uppsala: Almqvist & Wiksell, 1928), 198–220. On more recent methods for banishing spirits, cf. Erika Lindig, *Hausgeister: Die Vorstellung übernatürlicher Schützer und Helfer in der deutschen Sagenüherlieferung* (Frankfurt: Lang, 1987), 143–46. One may also consult Jacob Grimm, *Deutsche Rechtsaltertümer* (Göttingen: Dieterich, 1854), 86–92, 184ff. and 194ff.; Claude Lecouteux, *Geschichte der Gespenster und Wiedergänger im Mittelalter* (Cologne: Böhlau, 1987), 177–79.

8. Cf. Hanns Bächtold-Stäubli, *Handwörterbuch des deutschen Aberglaubens*, vol. 9, col. 496–547; H. F. Feilberg, "Der Kobold in nordischer Überlieferung," *Zeitschrift des Vereins für Volkskunde* 8 (1898): 1–20, 130–46, 264–77, esp. 6, 130, 139, 141, and 269; Lindig, *Hausgeister*, 132ff.

9. Cf., for example, *Sturlubók*, 29, in *Íslendingabók—Landnámabók*, ed. Jacob Benediktsson, 2 vols. (Reykjavik: Hið Íslenzka fornritfélag, 1968).

10. Martin of Braga, *De correctione rusticorum*, ed. C. P. Caspari (Christiana [Oslo]: Malling, 1883), §§7–8.

11. Gerald of Wales, *Itinerarium Cambriae* (I, 12).

12. Cf. Ovid, *Metamorphoses*, I, 190ff.

13. Gervase of Tilbury, *Otia imperialia*, I, 18.

14. Lindig, *Hausgeister*, 74–75.

15. On this encounter, see E. Freymond, "Artus' Kampf mit dem Katzenungetüm: Eine Episode der Vulgata," in *Festgabe Gustav Gröber*, (Halle: Niemeyer, 1899), 311–96.

16. Text from Claude Lecouteux, *Kleine Texte zur Alexandersage* (Göppingen: Kümmerle, 1984), 59.

17. Jacques Le Goff, "Culture ecclésiastique et culture folklorique au Moyen Âge: Saint Marcel de Paris et le Dragon," in *Pour un autre Moyen Âge: Temps, travail et culture en Occident* (Paris: Gallimard, 1977), 236–279, here at 257: "Wouldn't Marcel's victory over the dragon be the taming of the *genius loci*, the reorganization of a natural site between the *deserta* of the forest (*silva*), the lair of the chthonic serpent, and the marshes of the confluence of the Seine and Bièvre (*mare*) rivers where the water dragon is invited to disappear?"

18. Cf. L. Knappert, "La vie de saint Gall et le paganisme germanique," *Revue de l'Histoire des religions* 29 (1894): 259–95.

19. *Kristni saga*, ed. Guðni Jónsson, in *Íslendinga Sögur* I (Reykjavik: Íslendingasagnaútgáfan, 1953), chap. 2. [English: *Íslendingabók, Kristni Saga—The Book of the Icelanders, The Story of the Conversion*, trans. Siân Grønlie (London: Viking Society for Northern Research, 2006), 35–36.]

20. Cf. *Kulturhistorisk Lexikon för Nordisk Medeltid* (Malmö: Allhems, 1956–1978), s.v. *tún*.

21. As in *Kristni saga*, ed. Jónsson, 243–80 (chap. 2). It is interesting to consult Reidar Christensen, "Gårdvette og markavette," *Maal og Minne* (1943): 137–60.

22. Mircea Eliade, *Cosmos and History: The Myth of the Eternal Return*, trans. Willard R. Trask (New York: Harper & Brothers, 1959), 9–10.

Index

Note that page numbers in *italics* refer to illustrations.